J. B. PRIESTLEY
Portrait of an Author

Mark Gerson

J. B. Priestley

J. B. PRIESTLEY
Portrait of an Author

by
SUSAN COOPER

1817

HARPER & ROW, PUBLISHERS
New York, Evanston, San Francisco, London

PUBLISHER'S NOTE

The page numbers in the footnotes of this volume refer to the British editions of Mr. Priestley's works. In many cases the page numbers of the American editions are very close to the British editions and in some instances are identical.

*B
Priestley*

For Nicholas

CONTENTS

PROLOGUE

In J. B. Priestley's book of 'reminiscences and reflections', *Margin Released*, there is a photograph of eleven shirt-sleeved lads aged about fifteen. A sturdy, determined bunch they look, and well they might, for the caption announces that this is Jack Priestley's tug-of-war team, Bradford *circa* 1908. One's eye instantly picks out young Priestley: a belligerent-looking fellow sitting symmetrical and straight-backed, legs neatly crossed, arms firmly folded. His cap is set squarely on his head, dislodge it who dare; his jaw is up and his mouth grim, as he glares the camera straight in the lens. Ah yes, there he is, the child foretelling the man; there already we have the confidence and the no-nonsense directness, the dogmatic stance of social-realist novelist, Labour Party supporter, prophet of Northern common-sense. Every aspect of the persona is there.

So says the casual reader to himself, and indeed this stalwart Edwardian youth may have become all these things; he may in fact have become anything from a mill-owner to a Trades Union peer, but there is one thing he did not become and that is J. B. Priestley. For when the eye glances down to the names in the caption it finds that it was quite wrong. This obvious-looking boy is not the one after all. The real young Jack is sitting at the far edge of the group, shoulders slightly hunched, arms propped casually on one upbent knee; he looks a little as though he were not sure whether he were really there. The face is melancholy, in a curiously adult way, and the eyes gaze not at the camera but through it. From his semi-slouched attitude, his expression of distant concentration, and possibly the fact that he is the only boy in the group not wearing a cap, this one looks as though he has in his heart no connection whatsoever with 1908, Bradford or the tug-of-war team, but is off somewhere in another world, another time.

Nobody changes very much. Sixty years of circumstance can accomplish a lot, but the personality is there from the beginning —even though no one, including its owner, may be able to distinguish very much of it through the first vague protoplasmic outlines. J. B. Priestley is now seventy-five years old. He is probably the most widely-known of all living English writers: the only one whose name can produce beams of recognition among readers from Liverpool to Los Angeles, Sydney to Smolensk, and so on through the alphabet and around the world. He has put his ideas, his people, his reflections into so far more than eighty books, more than thirty plays, and goodness knows how many essays and articles. Yet somehow in all these years and pages the man inside the writer has managed, during an age of ever brighter and more searching spotlights, to avoid stepping into the centre of the stage. Young Jack Priestley never left his place at the edge of the picture, gazing separate and reflective into his own world and time.

Albany, W.1, is a very English address. It lies at the heart of London, yet the tourists march brisk and unwitting past it, on their way from Piccadilly Circus to the Royal Academy summer show. Behind the unobtrusive entrance, the small courtyard beyond, and a splendid liveried giant who must once have been the prince of all Regimental Sergeant-Majors, there stretches a complex of dwellings like a cross between a university quadrangle and an Inn of Court: a long straight roofed-over path, bright with tubs of flowers and small trees, broken at intervals by entrances to the staircases from which the flats—somehow in the context an unsuitable word—lead off. Once, all this was a house with spacious gardens, built for Lord Melbourne, but in 1804 the gardens were built over and the Albany converted into 'chambers for bachelors'. Its more notable tenants included Lord Byron, Canning, and Lord Lytton; today, the stipulation 'for bachelors' has gone the way of all such limits (even the Athenaeum, after all, will let us in at the side door), and the tenants include Dame Edith Evans and Mrs. Fleur Cowles. They also include, from time to time, Mr. and Mrs. J. B. Priestley. The Albany has been Priestley's London foothold for more than twenty years: an environment rather different from the Walham Green flat he, shared with the poet Edward Davison, one of his oldest friends, when he first arrived after World War One.

One expects, at that first sight inside the front door, to find a large fat man bearing all the signs of a lifetime of over-indulgence; after all he has been referring to himself in print in such terms for years and years. At the very least one expects, from the Grumbler's Apology in *Delight*, 'a sagging face, a weighty underlip, what I am told is "a saurian eye", and a rumbling but resonant voice from which it is difficult to escape.'[1] But the person who opens the door has none of these. 'Come in, come in,' he says, in a kind of welcoming mumble with a slight, indefinable Northern accent. He is about medium height; he is certainly stocky, and solid, with a generous chin, but he does not make his clothes look unhappy in the way that fat men cannot help but do. Indeed his clothes seem very happy; they have a faintly baggy, affectionate look, nicely illumined on this particular day by a bright blue tie. No doubt this is the solution to the puzzle of the self-image: it is the men who are merely overweight who describe themselves as fat, just as it is the men whose hair is merely receding who call themselves bald; those who have reached the ultimate fate try to forget it, knowing it is only too obvious to all. 'Let me take your coat,' says the pseudo-fat man, and receives it with square, workmanlike hands. The same hands, before long, light the pipe which is an undeniable part of the image; still, a pipe is a pipe, the most hyper-imaginative of observers could find no cleft between expectation and reality there. It is the face which puffs at the pipe which has more to say: a convex face, with the eyebrows bristling

[1] *Delight*, p. 1 (Heinemann 1949).

up to outer peaks and the hair bushing in grey wings above the ears and curving longish over the neck. The whole lower half of the face droops downwards when in thought, and is drawn upwards by mirth; and the eyes are the most telling part of all. Nearly all the lines that this face has are there, round the eyes, when they crease in laughter or narrow into contemplative thought. It is the kind of face that began looking this way when it was about forty and has gone on looking much the same, with only minor batterings from the years, ever since. Who was it who said that until forty we have the faces we are given, and after forty the faces we have made for ourselves?

The Priestleys do no writing in Albany; Kissing Tree House, near Stratford-on-Avon, is their real home. They visit London only sporadically, to see friends, publishers (which is not to say that the two terms are not interchangeable) and plays, and for all the other reasons that inevitably draw a busy Englishman, from time to time, to his capital. Priestley is fond of London, and has lived there for several separate periods of his life, including the Blitz. But he has never felt rooted there; possibly he has no real roots anywhere except in the Yorkshire Dales, and he pulled those up, as far as living was concerned, fifty years ago.

The most succinct way of describing J. B. Priestley at 75 is not the most respectful. He is a cosy man with prickles. Like the animal which this phrase inevitably suggests, he is quite liable, when faced with some offensive person or situation, to curl up into an unrecognizable shape with the prickles sticking out in all directions. Or so it might seem, particularly to journalists from the United States of America, some of whose predecessors never took very kindly to Priestley, and wrote stories about him which were not only needling and belligerent but were often spiced with wholly invented anti-American quotes. Most people who imagine themselves confronted by this spiky and alarming object, however, are under an illusion; they very shortly find, if they stand their ground, that the prickles are not really there. Still, the illusion is not unreasonable. It is based on the intimidating solemnity of that face, when a total stranger first finds it sombrely surveying him in what looks like grave disappointment, but is really no more than attentive thought; on, perhaps, the steady deliberation of the voice, simultaneously strong and gentle, with its almost-West-Riding rhythms; on, most likely of all, Priestley's habit of voicing his convictions *with* conviction, which to this same nervous stranger can sound like a huge challenging derisiveness. Priestley has suffered all his life, both as man and as writer, from a devastating cleft between the apparent image and the actual personality; no doubt this is his own fault, but that doesn't alter the fact that the divide is there. 'The most lasting reputation I have,' he wrote mournfully in *Margin Released*, 'is for an almost ferocious aggressiveness, when in fact I am amiable, indulgent, affectionate, shy and rather timid at heart.'

So he is, too. His friends would forgive him anything, but seldom need to. He is a warm-hearted, generous man, with a sharp eye for what might be called guff but a huge delight—none too common—in the talents of others. He is without malice; tolerant of almost every human failing except pretentiousness and deceit; capable of startlingly prejudiced opinions but equally capable of amiably describing them as such. He likes praise, but can smell a hint of flattery half a mile away and set smartly off in the opposite direction. He is one of the most uncompromising men I have ever met, but he likes to be liked. Don't we all?

Priestley is a most curious mixture of extrovert and introvert: a mixture whose composition seems to have changed with the years. Though he has the arrogance of the artist, and the professional's pride in his own mastery of technique, he has no overblown opinion of himself. As a writer, he has himself tagged: 'I have no genius,' he says, peering critically into his pipe, 'but I have . . . one . . . hell . . . of . . . a . . . lot . . . of . . . (puff) . . . talent.' That's the judgement, and that's as far as he takes it. He has lived for much too long with success to be now intoxicated by it; if his head were ever turned at any point—a most unlikely fate for a Yorkshireman—it turned itself back again long since. And as he is fond of pointing out, 'success' is a meaningless word anyway— 'You can't define it, as if it were a lorryload of milk chocolate.'

For himself, he tends to value the condition of success only for the kinds of freedom it has brought him: freedom to write what he likes, when he likes, and to know that it will be published; freedom to travel; freedom to meet only those people he feels like meeting; freedom, even after the gobbles of the Inland Revenue, to live graciously, in an enchanting Georgian manor house with the most English of English meadows outside the windows and numbers of exceedingly beautiful objects scattered about the shelves and walls.

But that's all. He has none of that deep, worshipful respect for success that is the making of many businessmen and the unmaking of many artists. He once described himself as the kind of man who is ready to grumble about a lack of publicity, but who dislikes it when he gets it. Though he is a natural performer, with an uncommon 'feel' for an audience, equally good at extemporizing on radio or television, on platforms or in drawing-rooms, he would never have made a star. He might very well have made an actor, and indeed once briefly appeared in one of his own plays in the West End. But if his talents had been so balanced as to make him an actor instead of a writer, he would have been his publicity man's despair: turning down alluring Hollywood offers to stay on the London stage; running off at some crucial point in his career to join an obscure provincial rep; refusing all 'guest spots' on television quiz games and variety shows. (He has as a matter of fact behaved in somewhat similar ways as a writer: refusing, for instance, the kind of instant popular deification offered by BBC programmes like the Brains Trust, *Face to Face*, *This is Your Life*, and a variety of others since. During the 'thirties he did spend some time in Hollywood as a scriptwriter, but baffled all his colleagues by demanding that his name be left off the credits of the films on which he had worked, and by then refusing all further offers of work and making for home. He was taking away the money, he told them solemnly, before it could turn into dead leaves.)

The fact is that no man can survive star status, in this age of terrifying over-exposure, unless he is fortified either by total cynicism or by an indomitable sense of self-importance: an ability to go about in a shatter-proof cloud of complacence, waving a hand here, signing an autograph there, and privately loving it all. For this, Priestley is quite the wrong kind of man. He had that kind of experience in 1940, when his weekly 'Post-script' talks after the nine o'clock news gave such a lift to public morale that people would stop him in the street, crowd round in pubs just to touch him, send him bushels of fan-mail—and he genuinely hated it all. His pleasure in broadcasting was that of communicating more directly with the unseen millions—or per-haps the unseen individual—than it is possible for even the most widely-read author to feel he is doing as he pounds his typewriter. But the pleasure could survive only so long as the millions, or the individual, remained unseen, with broadcaster and listener linked in a relationship between equals, uncorrupted by celebrity. The Postscripts were essentially a matter of one ordinary Englishman talking to other ordinary Englishmen—which was of course, by the usual irony of such affairs, the reason why their success was so extraordinary. Priestley tells only one story about his period as a national hero; it is typical, and perhaps even symbolic of his ideal relationship with the unseen millions to whom he has always talked, with words both heard and read. 'I was walking home across Trafalgar Square after a broadcast one night in 1941,' he says, squinting reminiscently into a blue wreath of smoke. 'Very dark night, black as your hat. We had the black-out then, of course, but that night was even darker than usual. And as I was groping my way along, very slowly'—he shoves his pipe in his mouth so that it is out of the way, and does a little groping act into the air as he reclines in the big Albany armchair, and he is so much an actor that suddenly you are back there with him in the black-out, trying not to stub your toe on a stone lion—'I suddenly realized there was someone in front of me. Couldn't see his face, of course, he was just a blank dark shape—though I had a vague impression of uniform, he might have been a sailor. Naturally he couldn't see me either. He asked me the way to Waterloo. So I told him which way to go: talking *at* him, two strangers who couldn't see one another, standing there in the darkness in Trafalgar Square; and when I'd finished, he said quite casually: "Thank you, Mr. Priestley." And disappeared.'

And that's as much, or as little, as Priestley has ever asked of fame.

Still, it would be disingenuous to claim that he gives the impression of being just an ordinary chap. I remember once seeing the Priestleys off from an airport, and watching J. B. as he rumbled gently at the ticket counter. Over the slightly baggy suit he wore a splendid cape-like overcoat and his favourite kind of broad-brimmed hat; he was carrying a stick, and a disreputable old rucksack swung from his shoulder. He was not aware of the occasional inquisitive glances directed at his back, not least because he dislikes flying, and tends always to say not, 'We shall arrive on Friday' but 'We *hope* to arrive'. But I reflected, as I watched, that this was certainly no Jess Oakroyd, able to merge indistinguishably into the crowd surging out of the ground after watching t'United play; the man under that hat had more in common with Uncle Nick in *Lost Empires*: a figure mysterious and unpredictable, as real and fallible as the rest of us but likely at any moment to swing round and produce some dark marvel from up his sleeve.

On the whole, that isn't a bad way of describing what Priestley has been doing, on and off, these last seventy-five years.

I

THE SUNLIT PLAIN

People have some funny ideas about writing. They tend in particular to visualize the writer's source of inspiration as a hard clear
shaft of light, which shines down out of Heaven from time to
time and illuminates the world so that then, being 'in the mood',
he can at once sit down confidently and write. Only the writer
knows, to his cost, that nothing so definite exists. The closest he
can come to an image of inspiration is to suggest that he has,
somewhere in the darkness behind his conscious mind, a kind of
room, which is something between Plato's cave and Maeterlinck's
Hall of Night. Into this room, at random intervals and only for a
few instants at a time, a door swings open, giving an imperfect
but totally overwhelming glimpse of great swirling forms and
harmonies and mysteries which can never be forgotten but never
clearly seen. And it is out of these glimpses that the ideas come, to
be trapped in words only by long hard slog.

But after each glimpse too, each writer is left with a hint of
something else, some image or emotion, differing for each man
according to what sort of man he is but every time, for him, the
same. This is the haunting; this is the phrase of music which
never goes away. And though this is not the thing which will
make a man a writer rather than a painter—or vice versa—it is the
thing which will determine, without his really being aware of it,
the matter and manner of his writing. One man may be haunted
by a character, a second by a theme, a third by a place; others by
savagery, or a hope of fame, or a memory, or a dream of power.
And where one man may be fully aware of his haunting, to the
point at which it becomes an obsession, another may die without
ever having known what it was that went murmuring on always
at the back of his mind.

Priestley, I think, is haunted by a world. It is not a lost world, of the kind which keeps many writers trapped in visions of the past, since it never really existed. It is more a kind of ideal: a longing for the way things could be. You could call it, perhaps, a sense of the unfulfilled capabilities of man. It infuses many of his novels, most of his reflective and autobiographical books, and all his more polemical essays; it shows clearly in his plays, most of which are composed of fantasy in one form or another; and it is woven closely into his recurrent fascination with the nature of Time. And it has a great deal to do with the kind of man he is—though to work out which of those two is cause and which effect is not so simple as it might seem. For although this shadowy hovering world, never seen or described clearly, has no identifiable pattern in reality, it has a close connection with the years from 1910 to 1914: the last years of Priestley's own childhood, which happened also to be the last years before the world began on a really large scale to go mad.

By this present point in our century, of course, those years before World War One have acquired a sort of distant golden glow, not only for those who remember them but equally for those who grew up during a larger and later war. They have an almost mythical significance, like the last years of Alfred's Wessex or Arthur's Camelot; the inconvenient dirty details have all vanished into the mist, and we see only the enviable image of a gay, unworried Europe and a prosperous, tranquil—well, fairly tranquil—Britain and British Empire. These were the last years of confidence, of grace, of endless summer afternoons and unclouded blue skies, and they seem luminous with an extra enchantment for us now because we know that they were doomed.

Priestley is not one for nostalgia, and he has seldom written deliberately about his childhood or those vanished years before 1914. When they do occur in detail in his work, they are not enshrouded in wistful longings, but seen with a clear eye and examined for a clear purpose: as in the first autobiographical section, 'The Swan Arcadian' of *Margin Released*, and the painfully ironic flashbacks of the novel *Bright Day*. There are certain aspects of those early years which he has explicitly mourned from time to time, generally things which have more to do with family life in Bradford than with the pre-war world scene. But this mourning is not nostalgia. This is a conscious recognition of early influences, and allegiance to their values; it plays only a small part in the haunting. The thing which has done most to create Priestley's shadow-world, his 'something else', is not a longing to be living again back in 1910; he has none. It is contrast: the hideous force of the bloody crash which divided the years before 1914 from those which came afterwards. Though you find little nostalgia in his work, you do find over and over again the echoes of that crash: references to a generation decimated, chances lost, talents wasted, possibilities destroyed; the sense of a tragic and sudden ravine opened up between things that might have been and things that are.

> Nobody, nothing, will shift me from the belief, which I shall take to the grave, that the generation to which I belong, destroyed between 1914 and 1918, was a great generation, marvellous in its promise. This is not self-praise, because those of us who are left know that we are the runts[1]

No sensitive man living at that time could have failed to be blasted by such a sense of loss, least of all one who had seen one close friend killed in battle, and lost many more when an entire 'Pals' battalion recruited from Bradford was wiped out on the Somme.

So from his earliest years, both as man and as writer, he carried burned into him a sense of the differences between the possible and the real: a sense probably more vivid and bitter than is possible for any of us born since then. Given the awareness of this kind of gulf, there are only two alternative attitudes for a writer: a bleak disillusionment which may dry out into satirical disgust, or a flickering optimism which may either be side-tracked into fantasy or caught up in the dream of an ideal. Priestley does not fall with any tidiness into either category, but he is nearer the

[1] *Margin Released*, p. 136 (Heinemann, 1962).

second than the first. Because he loved the world that might have been, he can never throw off—however great his occasional disgust with the present—a conviction that this same world might yet be.

John Boynton Priestley was born at number 5, Mannheim Road, Bradford, in the West Riding of the county of Yorkshire, in the year 1894: grandson of a mill-worker, son of a lively-minded, humanely socialist schoolmaster. His mother died soon after he was born, but he had the kind of stepmother who managed properly to fill her place. He spent his childhood at number 5, Saltburn Place, a home that contained—for use, not for show—bookshelves and a piano, which in most societies are symbols of a deal of other things; it had warmth and gregariousness and tolerance and enthusiasm, and if young Jack had to learn to cope with a few discrepancies like his father's brief wild eruptions of temper, and deep Baptist distrust of frivolous institutions like theatres, he had also a safe harbour in which to dream his adolescent dreams of becoming an author. Not a writer, since he was that already, scribbling away endlessly in his attic bedroom—nor a Writer, in the sense that many young would-be authors visualize, more in love with the name than the drudgery—but a real wordsmith: a professional. His background was such that there was nothing to prevent him from aiming at one of the two most popular approaches to this condition: that of the journalist, and that of the don.

But although he had what schools are fond of calling 'a university brain', he had no natural academic inclinations to go with it; he was in fact rather bored with school by the time he was sixteen. So he left. Newspapers held no glamour for him either, though there were three dailies flourishing in Bradford at the time—one of the minor remarkable aspects of what was then a most remarkable town. And when his father suddenly side-stepped a lifelong habit of denigrating 'wool men', and informed his son that he must find a job within the solid prosperous walls of the wool trade, young Jack agreed amiably enough. He had no particular immediate ambitions of his own. Certainly he wanted to write, but really he was floating on the surface of a rather vague future; he felt that if life happened to take on a certain pattern he might equally well find himself turning out to be an actor, or even a musician—even though he was not quite a Pachmann at the piano, could one say that if translated to a podium he might not turn out to be another Nikisch? It took only a year or two of the devoted scribbling to convince him that writing, after all, was the thing, but even then his dreams held no images of the grand life, of the kind which seem to have tantalized Arnold Bennett from the moment he first picked up a pen. Priestley's imagined ideal was to earn about twenty-five shillings a week, rent a cottage on the edge of the moors, and write. And if the old world had survived, no doubt he might have been doing precisely that by the time he was twenty-one.

But by the time he was nineteen, and had spent a couple of years as the most junior of clerks with Messrs Helm and Company, Swan Arcade, Bradford, it was the year 1914. He spent his twenty-first birthday, and a good bit of the five years on either side of it, in the muddy front-line trenches of France, and when he came out of the Army the world which he had left was not there to greet and envelop him. It had gone for good.

From our great busy distance of half a century, it is obvious that many of the golden virtues of these pre-1914 years would have vanished in any case. They were the same kind of fragile qualities which are inevitably crushed by technological and social advance. Radio and television were not born, and the cinema and the gramophone still in their very early childhood; canned entertainment would arrive later, and so would the mass media and the great cultural divide they caused. ('When I was young,' says Priestley, looking glumly back, 'the major writers weren't writing for an élite, but for everybody. Nobody thought anything about the height or depth of brows.') Other barriers had not yet been erected either; one could travel to Europe for a pittance, and without a passport—Priestley the clerklet, earning perhaps fifteen shillings a week, had been to Holland, Belgium, Sweden, Denmark and Germany by the time he was nineteen.

The truth is, I was fortunate during those years in my environment. My native city of Bradford is frequently mentioned, mostly by people who know nothing about it, as a kind of symbol of 'muck and brass', a stronghold of North-country narrow provincialism. But when I lived there, as a youth, it was considered the most progressive city in the Kingdom. It was a Labour outpost. The first elementary school in the country where meals were provided was the one of which my father was headmaster. We had a Labour weekly to which, during this period, I contributed a regular page. Moreover, a number of Liberal German-Jewish families had settled there, as in Manchester, to give our West Riding dough a leaven of culture. Our Subscription Concerts followed the same plan as those at Leipzig. We also had our Permanent Orchestra and two great Choral Societies. We had three local daily newspapers as well as several weeklies. We had two theatres and two music halls. We had a flourishing Arts Club and a Playgoers' Society. Our Central Lending and Reference Libraries were excellent. Bradford men were making their names in the arts and sciences. And though the town was ugly enough, the inviolable moors, where we walked and talked most week-ends, began only a tuppenny tram-ride away. For a few pence more, taking a train, you could reach the Dales, the most beautiful countryside in England.

So there we were, walking towards out vast sevenpenny teas, arguing over our pipes of fourpenny Navy Cut, listening to Nikisch and Busoni, Casals and Kreisler, for ninepence, seeing Little Tich and Grock for fourpence, reading H. M. Tomlinson in the local paper and Chesterton's Saturday essay in the *Daily News*, buying our shilling classics or Nelson's old sevenpenny series. . . .[1]

The world was not only cheaper but larger then, regions and towns were smaller and more tightly-knit; instant communications, instant entertainment, instant reputations were as far off as instant coffee and instant tea. It was inevitable that a man's home, and the community around it, should seem warmer and livelier than they generally do today. These are the gloomy commonplaces of our century.

[1] 'On Education' in *Essays of Five Decades*, p. 213 (Heinemann, 1969).

All the same, there was more to it than that. The warmth and liveliness of that world into which Priestley was born had to do with other things than the mere absence of mechanical distractions. When a century turns, everyone willy-nilly is filled with a great uprush of confidence in the things that can be; there is an unspoken feeling that the world has been born again. (If we manage to reach the year 2000 in one piece, no doubt we shall feel it too.) Perhaps this was the core of that pre-war glow; the world had not yet had time to break its New Year Resolutions. Being mercifully unable to see what was waiting for them, people believed in the future, with a different kind of subconscious optimism than is possible today. Or perhaps they thought little about the future at all, and enjoyed their own present more as a result. Even when he had become convinced that he would spend his life as a writer, for instance, Priestley never set about planning a career. He knew from the beginning that he was the kind of man —and perhaps a member of the kind of generation—who would take things as they came. 'Even when I did go to London it wasn't for its own sake, but just to earn my living by writing. I had no long-term plans, never have. Certainly I hadn't in those early days. How far can things that are going to happen affect things that are happening? Possibly to me and to others the future was a blank because unknown to us the war was coming. In some way, men do seem to know the length of time that's available to them. Like Thomas Wolfe. He knew.'

Those years between 1910 and 1914 were the years between Priestley's sixteenth and twentieth birthdays, and they had more effect on his personality and work than any period before or after them. This is not a particularly formative time of life for everyone; many people, indeed, look back on their late adolescence as a kind of awful confused limbo, about which they can remember very few externals, but only great see-sawings of emotion, ranging from gut-wrenching love to black clouds of rebellious rage. Not Priestley. The emotions were there all right, but not to the uncontrollable extent that they pulled him down into a long dark tunnel of introspection. His senses were too busy for that, and behind them his brain, observing and judging and applauding and condemning, and gulping into his memory the kind of potent incidents and ideas which seem mere shadows but which can in fact affect a man's whole life and mind. The effect which they had on his can be judged, at the simplest level, by counting up the number of scenes and people in his writings which belong to Bruddersford, that Priestley-image of Bradford. It is always appearing, dancing in and out like a sort of perennial rite of spring—even though this was a place in which, after the age of twenty, he never really lived again. And another line of contrast is there as well to border it, for the fruitful Bradford years were followed by four and a half years of war about which he has written only once, in the second part of *Margin Released*, and then by three years at Cambridge, about which he has never written at all.

Anyone who thinks that this implies that Priestley is a regional writer could hardly be further from the truth. It was not any timeless undying magic of a particular place which breathed its effect on him; it was another magic, restricted to a particular brief period of time. 'I belong at heart to the pre-1914 North Country,' he wrote. 'Part of me is still in Bradford, can never leave it, though when I return there now I wander about half-lost, a melancholy stranger.'[1] Thomas Wolfe knew that too: you can't go home again. The true regional novelist is a man so totally bewitched by his region that he has grave difficulty in ever living anywhere else; and Priestley has without any trouble at all lived for fifty years in the soft South, a long long way from the mills and the moors. Bruddersford/Bradford is not his ideal world, nor ever was; it just so happened that during the most impressionable period of his life, the Bradford he knew was fortunate enough to contain a good number of the elements of that world. And because there was enchantment in the life it offered, the hideous transformation scene that took place when the enchantment vanished in a cloud of black smoke, and came out grimed and different on the other side, was enough to leave a young man of the time very vulnerable to visions of a lost Atlantis—especially a

[1] *Margin Released*, pp. 31-2.

young man who was to become gradually more and more involved, as he grew older, in theories of a continuum of Time in which nothing is really past, but everything which has ever been is still there. The years from 1910 to 1914, and the qualities of the place in which he spent them, did much to leave Priestley haunted by a kind of shadow-world—not dead, but sleeping—for all the years to come.

He asked, in the deliberate simplicity of one of his wartime broadcasts:

'Do you ever look back on your life, and see it as a road that wanders through wildly varying landscapes? I do. And now, as I look back, before August 1914 the road seems to be in a sunlit plain, coming out of the mists of early childhood. Then, for the next four or five years, the road goes through black and terrible mountains, and is sometimes almost obliterated by avalanches. It comes out into 1919 and enters a confused landscape, with swamps and dark forests and sudden pleasant uplands. These were the years of the false peace, of the defeat of goodwill... Then came the 'thirties, and that road descended into a stony wilderness of world depression and despair; and very soon in that desert, fantastically shaped rocks and cruel jagged ridges began to show themselves, and soon there were more and more of them, closer and closer to the road, until at last it climbed and narrowed to a track between iron-edged boulders and sometimes clinging to the edge of precipices. . . .'[1]

And thirty years later, the track is clinging to the giddiest precipice of all, and the sunlit plain is a very long way away. But Priestley is a Time-haunted man, and when he uses this image of a road of life—a fairly commonplace one, used by any number of writers from Walter Savage Landor to Robert Frost—it acquires a rather different significance from the simple matter of looking back over one's shoulder at the past. To illustrate this through what may seem a rather eccentric parenthesis: consider for a

[1] BBC 'Postscript' broadcast, 4 August 1940.

moment that brief broadcast sketch in comparison with the road-image in one of the few modern fantasies which is longer than anything Priestley himself has ever written: J. R. R. Tolkien's *The Lord of the Rings*. Pictorially, Priestley's sketch is like a tiny prescient miniature of the long questing journey of Tolkien's hobbit-heroes. From their sunlit Shire they tread a long and some-times dark and terrible path, up to the very edge of Doom; but all the while the image of their own sunnier world is with them, though seeming a long way off—and the images of other bright shadow-worlds too, like the far-off Grey Havens across the Wes-tern Seas. Tolkien's travellers come back in the end to their Shire, secure now in contentment after the destruction of the Dark Lord: a return which is not part of Priestley's road-image, since he is writing of the real world, in which all sunlit plains seem ever further off. But the shadow-world of his haunting, the one of which pre-1914 England is only a part, is made out of the same stuff as the other which hovers throughout Tolkien's fantasy. It is not altogether coincidental that both authors belong to the same generation. Tolkien intends no allegorical overtones in *The Lord of the Rings*, but in his life too there was once a sunlit plain which was engulfed and devastated by war: 'By 1918,' he wrote once, 'all but one of my close friends were dead.' The words might be Priestley's; in different ways, the same sense of loss and longing runs through the work of both men.

But Tolkien has at the same time something else, which Priest-ley has not: a strong sense of evil. If there are lost worlds in *The Lord of the Rings*, they are lost because the forces of evil have swallowed them up. By the traditions of magic, they are still accessible to rescue, and the major part of the trilogy deals with the bringing of that rescue: the recurrent battle between good and evil, light and dark. Priestley's work, on the other hand, is never concerned with any such battle. He is no moralist. He seldom judges. More relevant, his imagination is not haunted by the Devil; possibly because he is not a Celt, possibly because he is not a Christian. His lost world, in the form of the haunting, hovering shadow which drifts continually in and out of his work, has been lost not to the powers of darkness but to Time, and thus it cannot be rediscovered, cannot be won back in battle: can never be seen or visited again, except in dreams—unless it is brought back by Time itself. To envisage this takes a certain amount of concentration. Suppose—not easy—if nothing which has ever been can ever stop being, then everything which has ever happened is still happening. If there is, in effect, a fifth dimension from which one can observe not only the present moment but also everything which runs before it and behind—then things which seem lost have never really been lost at all. It is partly because Priestley subscribes to this part of J. W. Dunne's Time theories that his shadow-world, though not shown as redeemable by any defeat of evil, does not seem dead and gone, but emerges as a vision combining might-yet-be with might-have-been. If he is haunted by anything, it is not by the intensity of the darkness enveloping the mountains, but by the unending brilliance of the sun lighting the plain.

This feeling has put itself subconsciously into Priestley's novels and consciously into some of his plays, and though it has seldom been fully explicit its nature has remained constant. It exists, for instance, both in *Bright Day* and, twenty years later, in *Lost Empires*. As narrators of these two books, the screenwriter Gregory Dawson and the artist Richard Herncastle are both looking back from a distance of some decades at a period of youth which seems to them in retrospect to have possessed a peculiar luminous quality shared by no other period, however happy or prosperous. It is not simply the glow of youth, which tends to be made brighter yearly by its contrast with the gloomy present matter of growing old; it seems in fact to have very little to do with nostalgia of any kind. Both Dawson and Herncastle, who as individuals have little in common with their creator, seem to be not so much reminiscing of a golden past as reporting on a separate world which, somewhere, still exists. Even in *Bright Day*, which takes the reader through a series of flashbacks and never lets him forget for long the bleak outcome of early promise—even there, the music of the Alington family, and all the joyous warmth it conveyed, seems to be echoing not out of a house which has long been deserted but out of some neighbouring room, into which one might at any moment have the chance to step. Perhaps the sound of it is the reason why *Bright Day* is Priestley's favourite among his own novels.

The character and actions of the writer Gregory Dawson may have little connection with those of the writer J. B. Priestley, but there is not much doubt about the derivation of his vanished world. If any reader were in doubt about the geographical location of Bruddersford, he would only have to set side by side these two descriptions of a very young man in a very small room.

> The writing itself was done at home, where I had transformed the front attic, my bedroom for years, into a sitting-room of sorts. A small gas-fire had been installed up there, but, apart from that, everything that had to be done I had to do myself. We were not poor and lived comfortably, but there was no money to spare, certainly not for any fancies of mine. On the colour-washed walls I pinned reproductions of pictures I liked. I cut and trimmed and then stained some orange boxes, which really looked like bookcases, at least in artificial light. Many of the books in them I had been able to buy only by spending tuppence instead of the eightpence I was allowed for lunch. . . . Most of the books I was able to buy were chosen from those lists of the World's Best that deceive innocent youth, so that I was never able to finish reading some of them then and have never read them since. Others, wiser purchases, mostly of standard poets, still have a place on my shelves and a larger place in my affections. Between the bed and the gas-fire, a fierce little thing that could not begin to warm the room without grilling your shins, there was just enough space for two smallish old armchairs, so that when I was not scribbling and scribbling away I could entertain a friend— male of course, no girls allowed up there. . . .

> The house was unpretentious and very snug. I was given the large back bedroom, not only to sleep in but to use as my own place. In two little bookcases I arranged and re-arranged, with the solemnity of some royal librarian, my *Everyman* volumes and

World's Classics and the slender rest. I peppered the walls with my photographs and uncertain but hopeful reproductions of Master-pieces of Art. A noisy little gas-fire was installed. From the attic I brought down an old desk that had belonged to my grand-father and also two lopsided leather armchairs; so that now it was a sitting-room too, and I could entertain a friend there, once I had succeeded in finding one. The room was lit by two angry little gas-mantles, white and trembling with fury. I recalled the view outside my two windows; first a rather melancholy prospect of back gardens and sooty privet and clothes-lines, and of some stacks of builders' timber in a ruined field; and then to one side there was a constant sight of the vast square chimney of Higdens' giant mill, the largest chimney and the largest mill of their kind, it was said, in the world then; and on the other side, above the clustered roofs, there was an occasional hazy glimpse of the moor-land skyline. I was delighted of course to have this room, and I doubt if any room I have occupied since—although I have ranged at some expense from Amalfi to Santa Barbara, California —has ever brought me such a satisfying sense of possession as that one did. . . .

One of these passages comes from *Bright Day*, published in 1946; the other from the autobiographical *Margin Released*, six-teen years later. There are no prizes for guessing which is which, but it is, I hope, fairly obvious that they are both descriptions of the same room.[1] There are other parallels between the surround-ings and circumstances of the young Dawson and the young Priestley, but even if this were the only one it would be enough to identify the magical youthful world at which Dawson is looking back with the equally magical world that Priestley lost sight of in 1913. When Priestley is writing fiction, he never behaves re-motely like a reporter: the whole works—it is a deliberate prin-ciple—must come out of his imagination. There are hardly any deliberate portraits or caricatures in his novels identifiable with single individuals he has known. He does not go in search of a place in order to write about it as a background; indeed he is

[1] The first extract is from *Margin Released*, pp. 26-7, the second from *Bright Day*, pp. 16-17 (1968 Heinemann edition).

more likely to do the reverse—two of his novels which were particularly warmly praised for their 'reporting' of the landscape of London, for instance, were written respectively in Devon and Arizona. Similarly, he wrote *The Good Companions* with no experience of the life of a travelling concert-party; *Angel Pavement* without ever having worked in an office in the City; *Wonder Hero* without having observed popular newspapers' circulation campaigns; *The Image Men* without ever having been involved closely with either sociology departments or public relations men. Fiction is fiction, journalism is journalism, autobiography is autobiography, says Priestley, and after writing quantities of all three he has no difficulty in keeping them apart. Only in *Bright Day* do the boundaries blur, and once you have the first evidence of that blurring you know that it is safe to identify Dawson's peculiarly strong feeling for a certain place and a certain time with Priestley's own. The country of this book is the country of his heart. But the story is another matter.

Gregory Dawson is a scriptwriter; faced with a sudden deadline for the full shooting script of an impending film, he removes himself to a hotel in Cornwall with his typewriter. The time is the present day—that is to say, the year 1946, when Priestley wrote the book. Dawson keeps apart from the other guests in the hotel in order to be free to work, but there is one couple, stiffish and sixtyish, a Lord and Lady Harndean, whose appearance niggles at his mind because he has that familiar vague feeling of having seen them somewhere—*where?*—before. It is music which snaps him backwards in time (and the magical effect of music is all through the book, whose own spell is itself music-magical, deeply evocative of any sense of loss that may lie buried in the reader himself). The trio which plays away in the hotel lounge, determined to show him that they have more to offer than the usual diet of Cole Porter or Eric Coates when they try, one afternoon plays something else.

> It was the slow movement from Schubert's *B Flat Major Trio*, as I knew at once when the 'cello began the exquisite quiet tone, slowly and gravely rocking in its immeasurable tenderness. A

few moments later, when the 'cello went wandering to murmur
its regret, and the violin with its piercing sweetness curved and
rocked in the same little tune, I was far away, deep in a lost world
and a lost time. I was back again—young Gregory Dawson,
eighteen, shy but sprawling—in the Alingtons' drawing-room
in Bruddersford, before the First World War, years and years
ago, half a good life-time away. The thin ribbon of sound pulled
back curtain after curtain. People and places that I had thought
had dwindled and faded to the dimmest shades of memory, to
smudged scrawls in an old diary, came flashing back, burningly
alive, as the music went winding through my heart like a slow
procession of fire-raisers. . . .[1]

The time-shifts along which the book travels after this, like a
piece of floating driftwood washed to and fro by each successive
wave, but moving all the time gradually forward until finally it is
washed up on to the shore, are put together with such strange
intuitive skill that they deserve better than the flat word of the
craft: 'flashback'. Yet each time Dawson goes back in his mind to
that world of 1913, it is with a kind of flash of memory; while his
own 1946 life goes on, he is compelled, once the process has begun,
to set himself deliberately on his own and open the door in his
mind out of which there shines the brilliant light of the past.
Somehow the remembering is crucial for his future. So he relives
the story of his eighteen-year-old happiness in Bruddersford: the
young clerk in the wool trade who will one day be a writer, living
meanwhile in the glow cast by the family of John Alington, the
humane, miscast manager of the firm for which he works. There
are two boys in that family, the ebullient undergraduate Oliver
and the quiet schoolboy David, and three girls, all attractive in
very different ways, Joan, Eva and Bridget; and perhaps Gregory
is a little in love with all three. More than anything he is in love
with the family and its whole ambience of laughter and music
and nonsense, lively talk and liberal socialist views. Chamber
music, charades, private languages, private jokes, warm hos-
pitable entertainment, bursts of enormous idiotic hilarity: all the

[1] *Bright Day*, pp. 7–8.

favourite Priestleyan elements of family life are there. Young Dawson has fallen under the spell even before he has first entered the Alington house; when he is at a Hallé concert, looking across the gallery towards the whole golden Alington group, only two of whom he has so far met.

> Yes, it was the group most formidably arrayed, with a hundred orchestral players below tuning up, and Brahms, Wagner and Richard Strauss waiting in the wings, so to speak, of heighten the magic. Joan saw and recognized me, smiled and waved, and then obviously mentioned me to her father, who also smiled and waved; and several of the others looked my way. I experienced that feeling—common in childhood, rarer in youth and almost unknown later in life, at least among men—of cosy enchantment, that sense of having snugly to hand, under the same protecting roof, almost all this earth's most precious persons and things; which is the secret of a child's Christmas.[1]

And afterwards, when he goes back with them to the house full of music and warmth for the first time: 'It seemed to me the most wonderful thing that could ever happen that I should simply be there. The evening ought to go on and on, I felt, for ever.' The magic of the world was not confined altogether to his feeling for the Alington family; it was a magic of a whole social order, and naturally enough it could be seen and felt at its peak in the most magical and ancient landmarks in the year; Christmas in fact, in 1912. All the people that he knew, especially those of his uncle's and aunt's generation, glowed with it then.

> They existed in their own atmosphere, and it was an atmophere of friendliness, affection, easy hospitality and comfortable old jokes. No doubt they had troubles unknown to me then as a youth. Their world didn't seem as secure, rich, and warm to them as it has since appeared to me. Nevertheless, when all allowance has been made for my youth and ignorance, I am certain these people lived in a world, in an atmosphere, that I have never discovered again since 1914, when the guns began to roar and the corpses piled up. The gaiety, at Christmas Eve or any

[1] *Bright Day*, p. 49.

other time, has always seemed forced and feverish since then. My
Uncle Miles and his friends weren't trying to forget anything.
The haunting hadn't begun. The cruelty was still unrevealed; the
huge heartbreak wasn't there. No irony in the bells and the carols.
You could still have a Merry Christmas.[1]

All the same, the Alingtons were the fulcrum of his world.
Reluctantly he went off to a party that Boxing Day, certain that
since he was not at the Alington house, no celebration anywhere
could have much to recommend it: and lo, the three Alington
girls were there, smiling at him. 'I was one of the magic circle.
And this, I realized at once, was a wonderful party.'[2]

But each time the magic takes hold, Priestley twitches it away
again; often with a reminder of the uneasy Dawson of 1946, who
has realized once he has begun his obsessional remembering that
it has to be finished, in order to answer some deep buried significance it has had in his mind and life all these years. 'So they
played the César Franck sonata, and I could see and hear them
still, two World Wars away, as I closed my eyes to the Cornish
sunlight and shut out of my mind the whole fretting and half-
ruined planet of this later year. I could still hear Bridget's brave if
rather uncertain tone . . .'[3] The nudges are gratuitous, a deliberate
stressing of the gulf that Time has dug between the narrated
world and that of the narrator. At the Boxing Day party given
by Joe Ackworth of the wool office, Joan Alington kisses Gregory;
and again there is the swift switch in and out of Time.

> It was a light kiss but very firm and sweet. And sitting there, a
> middle-aged man, on that Cornish cliff edge, thirty-odd years
> afterwards, I remembered it as if it had happened only a few
> minutes before. So much had gone, and yet the memory of that
> sudden quick pressure of a girl's lips remained. And then a weight
> of sadness fell on that fragrant hollow in the cliff, and I felt as if
> I had been dead for years and years and had not known it until
> then. With an effort I wrenched myself out of this blue-and-gold

[1] *Bright Day*, p. 86.
[2] *Ibid.*, p. 89.
[3] *Ibid.*, p. 98.

afternoon, which no longer had any more life in it for me than a vast painted curtain, and returned to the hall in Joe Ackworth's house.[1]

There are other nudges at the mind more ominous than these: reminders of the holocaust that was lying in wait for this golden crew. Most of them are bitter flickers of hindsight from the middle-aged narrating Dawson of 1946: reminders that Jock Barniston, the most remarkable of all the members of the Alington circle, will be killed on the Somme in 1916 and awarded a posthumous V.C.; Oliver Alington blown to bits near Givenchy in 1915; Ben Kerry, whom Eva Alington loved, also killed on the Somme. Within the remembered time, young Gregory's 1913, there is only one equivalent piece of foresight, but that a very marked one: when Jock Barniston's sister, a strange prescient woman whom most uncomplicated Yorkshire lads would have dismissed as plain barmy, looks in the cards for Gregory. 'Always the same,' she says, 'always the same. Every time I look for anybody. Change and an ending . . . everything changing . . . ending and beginning again . . . with rivers of blood flowing towards us . . . great rivers of blood . . .' And one extra thing for Gregory: 'something of him will be caught, fastened, left behind while he goes on. . . .'[2]

And after she has done, Priestley uses just once the simple symbol that he used years later for a similar purpose in a play about Time: Gregory bursts out: 'I hate that beastly clock in the corner. . . . I feel it's just ticking us away.'[3]

And of course it is. The magic circle of the Alingtons is in fact broken before the war descends to break the whole golden 1913 world: by the symbolic cracking into violence of one of its members (though it is a very long time before Dawson discovers which) and by the invasion of two others, a couple called Nixey, who arrive in the Alington house at the moment when a trio is playing that Schubert trio. The 1946 Dawson sits on his Cornish

[1] *Ibid.*, p. 91.
[2] *Ibid.*, p. 184.
[3] *Ibid.*, pp. 185–6.

cliff remembering the instant when the two strangers, shapes of things to come, were standing in the doorway, among the splinters of the Schubert:

> And at this very moment when I was busy holding the image of Eleanor Nixey, as she appeared that first night, in my mind's eye, I was disturbed by the sound of somebody approaching along the cliff path that came near where I was sitting. I turned round and saw an elderly lady, fairly erect but moving slowly and using a stick. It was Lady Harndean: it was Eleanor Nixey with thirty-odd more years on her back. And as she came nearer, looked at me with those same eyes, recognized me and smiled, I experienced a sensation so profoundly disturbing that it seemed as if my spine contracted and shivered. What I perceived then, in a blinding flash of revelation, was that the real Eleanor Nixey was neither the handsome young woman I had been remembering nor the elderly woman I saw before me, both of whom were nothing but distorted fleeting reflections in time, that the real Eleanor Nixey was somewhere behind all these appearances and fragmentary distortions, existing outside change and time, and that what was true of her was of course true of us all. It is easy enough to say this, but at that moment I *felt* it too, felt it in all my being, and was left shaken by it, half terrified, half in ecstasy.[1]

After this point, the telescoping of past into present becomes a repeated pattern; but although one or two ghosts are perhaps put to rest, there is no resolving of the gigantic block which Dawson realizes has been lying in his life for years. He has a 1946 world that appals him, in its contrast with the one that is gone, and all this deliberate searching and remembering seems to do nothing but open the old wound left by its disappearance.

> ... as I lay there in bed, with the medinal already thickening and dulling the dark, there came, like the ache of a badly-healed wound, that sense of loss and desolation and bereavement which I had felt downstairs. I fell asleep, but it was an uneasy sleep crowded with dreams, in which a self that was neither the lad in

[1] *Ibid.*, pp. 127–8.

Bruddersford nor the middle-aged man of the Royal Ocean Hotel, but an ageless secret self, flitted through bewildering telescoped scenes that ran the chalk trenches of Picardy into Piccadilly Circus, and jammed Brigg Terrace and Canal Street into Hollywood and Beverly Hills; and everywhere that wandering secret self cried, 'Lost, lost, lost!', searched and searched, and could never find what had to be found. . . .[1]

Jock Barniston had warned him, back in the golden Alington days, against investing the family with the kind of magic that should be attached only to things not human; against turning them into a kind of composite *anima* figure. 'You can go a long way—and give us something good—if you travel easily and lightly, seeing people as they are, just as people and not as symbolic figures, and not leaving parts of yourself behind, frozen in some enchantment.'[2] And if Priestley intended any kind of message in *Bright Day*, which is doubtful, perhaps it is that. Dawson did in a sense leave a vital part of himself frozen in that vanished world, having treated people as symbols and not as living beings, and it is only through finally looking at the people of 1913 as people, and meeting again the only one of them that he had almost forgotten, that he comes to terms with himself, his work and the whole of life. It was as if, he says, he had spent years secretly building a great black wall around himself, and had only realized when he first began his journey back into memory that the wall was all-excluding and complete. This last encounter in the book, with a woman who was a child in the old world, brings a revelation that by shattering the myth of the Alingtons finally reveals Gregory Dawson's world of youth as the shadow-world of Priestley's haunting, which is not necessarily lost but can somehow, somewhere, be built again. The hope of it forms a crack in Dawson's black wall:

'And for the last two hours the crack's been widening and widening, with more and more light streaming through, and

[1] *Ibid.*, pp. 234–5.
[2] *Ibid.*, pp. 113–14.

I know now there's a world on the other side. It's not as secure and cosy as the one I'd been remembering—it's a bit hungry and tattered and bomb-dazed—but if I could live and work in it properly I might soon find it the same rich warm world.'[1]

Priestley, as always, puts his finger on the one way of turning the present into the past which could not be called retrogressive. The time-haunted Gregory Dawson can make a future for himself only if he takes the past with him, for it is pointless to mourn Time, and impossible to make it stand still.

★   ★   ★

The basis of the whole vision behind *Bright Day* is hope; a feeling that things whose light has glowed so brightly through the past cannot possibly fade, but must go on to illumine the future. It was the same kind of fundamental optimism—always rather a strain on its indomitable owner, so that it tends to go hand-in-hand with a recurrent surface melancholy—which made Priestley so extremely effective as a broadcaster during World War Two. The qualities which his seed-world, the world of his youth at the turn of the century, had given to his own personality combined themselves at that particular moment with the complementary qualities of his subconscious vision, his shadow-world; his heart, if you like, combined itself with his mind. And as a result, the things which he had to say, together with the way in which he said them, emerged as a composite series of bits of work which may not have had much to do with literature but which had an extraordinary impact upon their time.

It was a very brief time: it lasted from June to October in 1940, and again for a shorter period in 1941. During the ominous days after Munich, the BBC had commissioned Priestley to write a serial story for radio; he produced the light-hearted novel *Let the People Sing* (a powerful title under the circumstances, and one which was whisked into popular usage, generally attributed

[1] *Ibid.,* p. 366.

thereafter not to its author but to that other prolific fellow, Anon.). On the day set for him to read the first instalment over the air, war was declared: 'So that I groped my way to Broadcasting House through an appalling blackness, my very first taste of it, and almost felt I was back in the First War when in Broadcasting House I found myself among sandbags, bayonets, nurses in uniform.'[1] The long months of 'phoney war' passed, and then erupted, with the Blitz blasting London and Hitler's armies filling Europe. At the peak of national emergency Priestley offered the BBC a sample—about the Little Ships of Dunkirk—of a very different kind of talk, and soon he was broadcasting a fifteen-minute 'Postscript' after the Nine O'Clock News every Sunday night. These were the spoken essays whose impact was so great. The Nine O'Clock News deserves its capital letters; in millions of wartime British households it was a major landmark of the day, the time when every adult within reach of a radio set would turn the knob to find out the pattern of that day of war, and sit listening for the nine long solemn strokes of Big Ben with hope and foreboding chasing one another round his mind. Once a week, most of those millions remained listening as Priestley's slow, warm North-country voice followed the News.

He gave them exactly what they most needed: a personal, compassionate amalgam of narrative chat, down-to-earth encouragement and flashes of unabashed rhetoric; and he did it not with the kind of out-and-out jingoism you might have found a Kipling using in similar circumstances, but with stirring hints and glimpses of his ever-hovering, past-future shadow-world. One broadcast, for instance, on the 14th July 1940, had him describing a visit to Margate: a strange and silent Margate, with all its bandstands and theatres and beaches lying empty under the high summer sun. Empty, that is, of everything but tank-traps and bomb-craters and a great deal of barbed wire.

> 'I remembered so vividly a day I'd spent here ten years ago, when the whole coast was crammed and noisy with folk and it

[1] From the preface to *All England Listened*, a collection of J. B. Priestley's wartime broadcasts published in the U.S.A. in 1967.

was all a jolly, sweaty pandemonium. Had that been a dream?—
or was this strange silent afternoon a dream? It seemed impossibe
that they should both be real. Yet here we were, alone, hearing
our own footfalls on the lifeless promenade. The evil magician
had muttered the enchanted phrase—and a wind had come from
Hell and blown away all the trippers and paddlers and pierrots
and hawkers—all that perspiring, bustling, rowdy, riotous
holiday-making.

'And as I stood there, half bemused in the blazing ironic sun-
shine, I asked myself what I would do if another and better
magician should arrive and tell me that he had only to wave
his wand to send time hurtling back, so that once again these
sands would be thick with honest folk, the boarding-houses
bursting again with buckets and spades and the smell of cabbage; the bandstands and stages as lively as ever. Would I agree?
Would I say: "Yes, let time go back. Let this melancholy
silent afternoon be only a dream of an impossible Margate.
Say the word, and let Margate—and Westgate, and Herne Bay
and Broadstairs and Ramsgate and a hundred other resorts—be
as they were a year ago."

'And I said, No, I want no such miracle. Let this be real, so
far as all this muddled groping of ours with the deep purposes
of life can be considered real—and let time tick on. But if you
would help us, then, if you are a great and wise magician, move
our minds and hearts towards steadfast courage and faith and
hope, because we're ready to accept all this: the silent town that
once was gay; the vanished crowds now toiling far from these
vacant sands: this hour of trial and testing—if we know that we
can march forward—not merely to recover what has been lost,
but to something better than we've known before.

'That's what I would have said to that magician. And now I
say to all of you who are listening, for in your common will
there is an even mightier magician: The Margate I saw was
saddening and hateful; but its new silence and desolation should
be thought of as a bridge leading us to a better Margate in a
better England, in a nobler world. We're not fighting to restore
the past; it was the past that brought us to this heavy hour;
but we *are* fighting to rid ourselves and the world of the evil

encumbrance of these Nazis so that we can plan and create a noble future for all our species.'

Irony, irony. The evil encumbrance is long gone, but where is the noble future? That broadcast, at any rate, was typical of the tone Priestley used in his celebrated *Postscripts*. It is not exactly the kind of prose by which he would wish to be remembered: these are words written—and written generally in a hurry—to be spoken aloud by their writer, so that any perilous bits like the hovering bathos of 'a better Margate' could be carried off by the manner of the voice. The thing which is pure Priestley is the implication of an almost Arthurian destiny, for country and people; an illumination of the present by both past and future. It is a challenge and the answer to a challenge, and the vision it offers is one not of a misty Avalon but of a better Camelot. And if the vision has not materialized yet, we could at any rate see it plain then, in the black depths of war, as a motive for hauling ourselves out of the depths.

As for Priestley, he sees it still. 'Though growing old, gouty and grumpy,' he wrote in the preface to an American collection of the broadcasts published in 1967, 'weary of power-mania and propaganda and all their imbecilities, I have not yet abandoned the hope I felt and tried to celebrate in wartime.'

The *Postscripts* themselves were not simply morale-supporting propaganda; Priestley always meant what he said. As things turned out, it was this perilously simple fact which led before long to their disappearance. In the autumn of 1940 he asked to be taken off the air, feeling that the public was probably ready for a new voice and approach; but the protests with which the BBC was then showered proved him wrong, and some months later he began his weekly talks again. When they next ended, it was not at his own request. His shadow-world had begun to seem a liability to Authority; his usefulness, and indeed his intention, had been entirely apolitical, but in speaking of a new, future England he was treading too near the edge of politics. It was one thing to boost the morale of the public and the forces, and the whole embattled nation, with rhetoric evocative of *Henry V*; but it was quite another thing to start promising the nation a certain kind of life after the war—or worse still, demanding such a life on their behalf. The more edge Priestley put into his talks, the more clearly he painted Britain's shadow-Utopia, the more uneasy his masters became about him—a remarkable emotion, considering that we were all in the middle of a cataclysmic war from which it still seemed possible that we might never emerge. When the crunch finally came, it was the culmination of a series of episodes like Priestley's refusal to write—at the suggestion of the Minister of Information—a talk praising the heroic work of merchant seamen, unless he were allowed at the same time to promise them a postwar improvement in the slum conditions under which most of their families lived on shore.

So although he went on broadcasting three or four times a week to listeners overseas, his *Postscripts* to the English audience ceased. The BBC blamed the Ministry of Information for taking him off; the Ministry of Information blamed the BBC. In fact, according to Priestley, the man ultimately responsible for having the talks stopped was Winston Churchill. It was a curious compliment if so: rather as if a commander-in-chief were to remove an officer from his post in the midst of battle, on a charge of fraternizing with the men.

For a man haunted from early youth by the might-have-been, and intent all through his life and work on transmuting it into the might-yet-be, there was a worldly lesson offered by this wartime episode. It was a lesson others had tried to teach Priestley before. If you are possessed by a vision of a better world, it ran, make sure that you preach its virtues in a vacuum, extolling it only as a theoretical ideal; do not, unless you wish to become a politician, insinuate that with certain changes in the *status quo* this better world could be a practical possibility, an aim as well as an inspiration. Have a dream if you will, but do not let it intrude; you will suffer for it if you do. You may not be classed as a revolutionary, or even as a dotty prophet, but if you insist on talking—even in a mutter—about the positive necessity of your dream one day coming true, you will certainly be classed as unsound:

an unreliable, dissatisfied fellow, not to be trusted to say the right thing at the right time. Have a dream if you will, but keep quiet about it except in the harmless realm of fiction.

But Priestley never did learn to keep quiet about it. He never even tried.

II

PROFESSIONAL

It is a favourite game of biographers, and for that matter of autobiographers, to cast a wise eye back over the decades and to discover a Turning-Point. If, at that moment, Geoffrey Hutchinson had gone into his father's brickworks instead of taking the teaching post in Fiji . . . Had Ellen Robinson not remained in her job, but married the stockbroker's son . . .

Still, each of us does have a turning-point somewhere. Probably we have several dozen, but always there is one that in retrospect looms high over the rest. Priestley had one; it came when he was twenty-eight.

He emerged from the Army in 1919; Lieutenant John Priestley, twenty-four years old, made adult by four and a half years during which he had written little, read hugely, observed most of the range of human behaviour, and developed a black-comedy vision of life which he was never to lose. The Army had one other thing to give him: an educational grant with which—being now in a somewhat different frame of mind from the impatient school-leaver of sixteen—he went up to Trinity Hall, Cambridge, to read English.

Cambridge did not succeed in casting over him that net of bewitchment—sticky as Nessus' shirt, though less discommoding —in which she and Oxford generally manage permanently to entrap the young; he was too old, he had seen too much, left too many illusions flattened in the Flanders mud. This is not to say that Cambridge gave him nothing. Quite the reverse; in the space of the next two years he took his degree (after switching from English to modern history and political science), married a girl from his own West Riding, and published his first book—'a little book of undergraduate odds and ends' called *Brief Diversions*, which produced a number of laudatory reviews but very little else. But he was not natural material for the academic world: already he was too far committed to the creative impulse to develop any real urge to teach. He did dicker with the idea, for a while; since his Army grant was available for three years, he stayed at Cambridge for a third year after taking his degree, 'engaged in post-graduate research on how to make ends meet'. This kind of research had already become familiar, for the grant, though welcome, was not large, and he had squeezed an extra income from coaching and occasional lecturing; now, after looking askance at several posts available in remote foreign universities, he applied for a job as a Cambridge Extension lecturer, and was offered one in North Devon. If he had taken it he would inevitably have been enough influenced by teaching to become a markedly different kind of writer; even ten years or so of immersion in the world of academic English, with its barbed-wire fringe of traditional standards and judgements, would have been bound to exert its own kind of magnetism on the path even of a natural rebel. But he didn't take the job. He didn't take any job. Though he knew he would shortly have a child as well as a wife to support, and though his savings amounted to no more than fifty pounds, he took the popular and perilous step of going to London to earn his keep as a freelance writer.

For a potential 'serious writer', this Whittingtonian plunge was in fact less perilous forty years ago than it is today. With very few exceptions, the young literary hopeful of the 'sixties and 'seventies can extract a living from writing only by committing himself to the kind of full-time professional journalism from which hardly any novelists or playwrights of real stature have yet emerged. But in the 'twenties, as Priestley has pointed out, the world of the periodicals still offered a healthy and lucrative market for critical essays, reviews, general articles, short stories and even verse. It was still possible, by hard solitary work, to earn a very respectable living from these without becoming, in one's own view or anyone else's, a journalist. The mass media had not yet properly arrived, to cause intellectuals to dig their defensive ravine between 'popular writing' and 'literature'. In the 'twenties, this gulf between scholarship and the Press did not yet yawn; it was still bridged by magazines like the *Saturday Review* and the *London Mercury*. Priestley's decision to become a full-time freelance writer rather than to stay within a university ambience was not in itself so tremendous; it is not as if he had been choosing between becoming a deep-sea diver or a bank clerk. After all, if a man is a real writer he is going to write, whatever his nominal profession. After all, dons do write, and write well. There were fewer writer-dons in the 'twenties, certainly, but then there were far fewer dons. It was a turning-point all the same, that deliberate early decision not to become involved in teaching; for it serves peculiarly well as a symbol of the kind of writer which he was destined to become.

Of all Priestley's qualities as a writer, probably the most crucial is his detachment. He is not classifiable—not at any rate among his contemporaries. He has never belonged to, been associated with or paid homage to any school, movement or trend; never been willing to acknowledge the existence of tidal movements in the taste of the reading public; never shown any sign of being swayed by critical opinions of his own work. He has walked while others ran, run while others walked. For anyone viewing him as the prototype Yorkshireman, it would be easy to put this down to simple bloody-mindedness. Too easy: the detachment goes deeper than that, and was there even at the start. It too has something to do with the great safety-curtain that came clanging down in Priestley's life and cut off the old world from the new. He was a writer before he went to Cambridge, experimenting as very young men do with every form from the essay to the epic poem, and he was still very much the same kind of writer when he came out. He had not acquired, in the meantime, any sort of pre-digested Eng. Lit. view of life and literature; had not sat hungrily at the feet of any early equivalent of Dr. Leavis in order to absorb judgements on whom to admire, what qualities to emulate, which writers were acceptable and which 'unsound' or 'second-rate'. It was another aspect of his failure to become enamoured of university life as a career. The pressures of dogmatism must have been there, as they are in any university school of English Literature; Priestley may have been more mature than the average undergraduate, and certainly more self-confident, but he was still young, and in terms of intellectual judgements if not of behaviour the young are a very malleable lot.

Somehow, Priestley contrived from the beginning to avoid getting caught in this kind of web. As at school he had never developed the 'examination mentality', so now he failed to acquire any kind of competitive spirit. At Cambridge, he luxuriated in the unrepeatable chance of hugely wide reading, but it is doubtful whether he ever lost any sleep over his chances of taking a good or bad degree. As with degrees, so with writing. Unlike most young writers, he seems not to have started off with the secret feeling that he was launching himself as a new share-issue on the literary stock market, whose rise or fall would be seen always primarily in relation to the other rising or falling shares. He felt only, I think, that he was entering his natural profession; once he had published *Brief Diversions*, that first book, he simply went on writing, with no very clear idea of where he was going or even where he wanted to go. Down in that deepest corner of the mind's store of ambitions, which we keep resolutely concealed even from ourselves but which our actions make very apparent in the end, he wanted to be a self-respecting writer more than he wanted to be well-known, rich, or stamped with the critical 'first-class' brand. Given a certain amount of real talent, a really determined author can achieve any one of those three latter ambitions—even the third, during his own lifetime if not after it. But no kind of planning of a career can help him to the first; nothing in the world can help it, except to write and write. And to do that—or indeed to be possessed by so deceptively simple-seeming an ambition in the first place—requires an extraordinary rock-like self-confidence; certainty of talent, faith in the nature of one's own standards, and reverence for the worth of profession, art or craft. This kind of confidence may not always be very apparent to its owner, particularly in bleak moments or years (when the novel has bounced back from the twelfth publisher, perhaps, or been published in a deathly critical hush), but if it is there, in the long run nothing whatsoever can take it away. Priestley had it, as of course he still does. From the beginning he was a professional, trained by a long apprenticeship served in solitude. When he turned his back on everything but writing, and went to London, it was not because London was the right place to go in order to be noticed by the right people, but because London was—and is—where the professional writer's markets were.

He plunged into a number of the markets simultaneously right from the start, writing a rapid flow of essays, reviews and critical articles for the *London Mercury*, *The Bookman*, the *Spectator*, the *Saturday Review*, *Outlook*, the *Daily Chronicle* and others. He had already written for some of them; his first collection of such essays, *Papers from Lilliput*, was published almost as soon as he arrived in London, in 1922. Others he was introduced to by J. C. Squire, editor of the *London Mercury* and a power in the literary side of journalism; though Priestley may not have been in deliberate pursuit of the right people, he was not such a fool as to turn down their professional help when it was offered. Squire also helped him to a job as publisher's reader for The Bodley Head—the kind of hard but congenial work which has paid the rent for many a struggling young writer with more talent than capital. By now, Priestley had more to pay than the rent. Financially, he was beset with hospital bills; personally, and far worse, he had to watch while the structure of his personal life fell apart.

Within three years of his arrival in London, his young wife and his father had both died, after long illnesses, from cancer, and he was left—at 29—a widower with two small children. He had already published five books; three volumes of essays and two 'books on the edge of criticism proper'—*Figures of Modern Literature* and the enchanting *English Comic Characters*. In the next two years he published seven more. There were two more books of essays; two books—on Meredith and Peacock—commissioned by Macmillan for their *English Men of Letters* series;

another 'edge of criticism' work on *The English Novel* and his
first two novels: *Adam in Moonshine* and *Benighted*. Seven books
in two years. Though it was not the pattern anyone would hope
for as a confirmation of his capacity as a writer, nothing could
have marked young Priestley more clearly as a professional than
this great pile of work ground out of a period of intense personal
misery. Under such circumstances, the pseudo-writer backs away
from the effort of writing, and seeks some other work which can
provide not only an income but a quicker, more effective anaes-
thetic. It is the born writer, the real craftsman, who soldiers on.
Forty years later, when Priestley set out a statement of this kind
of tenet as advice to young writers in *Margin Released*, it was this
same bleak period of his life which he chose as illustration.

> It is worth recalling how I began that book on Meredith, if only
> for the benefit of any very young writers in the audience. I
> was living then at Chinnor Hill, on the far edge of the Chilterns,
> but spending much time in London, going to and from Guy's
> Hospital. I got back to Chinnor Hill, late one afternoon, so
> deep in despair I did not know what to do with myself. I was
> nearly out of my mind with misery. Had I been close to a town
> I might have visited friends, gone to a pub or a cinema, wan-
> dered about the streets, but Chinnor Hill was miles from any-
> where. Finally, just to pass the time while I was at the bottom
> of this pit, I decided to write something—anything—a few
> pages to be torn up after I felt less wretched. On my desk was a
> rough list of chapters for the Meredith book. I chose one of the
> chapters, not the first, and slowly, painfully, set to work on it.
> In an hour I was writing freely and well. It is in fact one of the
> best chapters in the book. And I wrote myself out of my misery,
> followed a trail of thought and words into daylight.
>
> Notice—and now I address the aspirants in the audience—the
> subject was far removed from my own life; I didn't lighten my
> woes by describing them; both the release from anguish and the
> good work done came from the necessary concentration, the
> effort, the *act* of writing. Perhaps, as I have already suggested,
> it would be better not to be a writer, but if you must be one—
> then, I say, *write*. You feel dull, you have a headache, nobody

loves you—*write*. It all seems hopeless, that famous 'inspiration' will not come—*write*. If you are a great genius, you will make your own rules; but if you are not—and the odds are heavily against it—go to your desk, no matter how high or low your mood, face the icy challenge of the paper—*write*. Sooner or later the goddess will recognize in this a devotional act, worthy of benison and grace. But if what I am trying to say seems non-sense, do not attempt to write for a living. Try elsewhere, making sure the position carries a pension.[1]

The goddess recognized Priestley's devotion all right, and sooner rather than later. She endowed him—and it was a perilous gift, like all such—with the capacity for producing an irrepressible flow of ideas; a flow which was to continue almost unbroken for the next fifty years and which shows no sign of slackening now that he is seventy-five. But it was the professionalism which pro-duced the work. 'When we are young,' Priestley wrote once, 'we think genius or talent is everything; later we discover how much depends on character.'[2] Most writers and would-be writers have ideas enough, even if they lack Priestley's extraordinarily lively imagination, but the ideas are not much good without the per-sistence to carry them through. It is possible that in those early years necessity created in him the habit of persistent application; or more likely, harnessed a persistence that was already there—put there by North-Country heredity, or the middle-class English morality of identifying the good life with hard work—and turned it into a kind of perpetual motion machine. Up to the end of the 'twenties, Priestley constantly needed money, not least because he had shortly a second wife and a stepdaughter as well as his own two daughters to support. Being temperamentally incapable of borrowing, he spent his time producing as many pieces of free-lance income as he could. And before long he was ingrained for life with the habit of hard concentrated work: that curious reli-ance on mental activity which rapidly brings a feeling of unease when one is not working, as if the imagination were poised on

[1] *Margin Released*, pp. 153–4.
[2] *Ibid.*, p. 147.

a kind of treadmill, comfortable only as long as it does not stop.

He was living by then in Church Hanborough, near Oxford. A barn in the garden was made into his study, and he worked there after dinner every night—a second shift, after a day's work writing essays, criticism, reviews. From this pattern he produced, among other things, *Benighted* (published in the United States, and later filmed, as *The Old Dark House*). Few people, I suppose, read *Benighted* today; it has been long eclipsed by Priestley's better-known novels. But it is an intriguing piece of work; a kind of philosophical thriller, foreshadowing not so much his later novels as his later preoccupations. The fantasist is stirring; the Time-haunted man already seeing shapes in the dark.

The characters in *Benighted* see more than their share of shapes in the dark too. Philip and Margaret Waverton, partners in an uneasy marriage, are driving at night through wild Wales with a friend, one Roger Penderel, when a gigantic storm catches them between landslide and flood and sends them scuttling for shelter to the only house within miles. It is a strange, silent house, very sinister there in the roaring Welsh night. It is a house fit for the welter of sardonic horror films which *Benighted* led by a couple of decades, and so is the gentleman who opens the great front door at which Penderel pounds.

> There was somebody at the other side of the door at last. He had a feeling that somebody was there, although he couldn't really hear anything. This door, he was positive, would take some opening; you couldn't imagine it flying open; it looked as if somehow it would have to be unscrewed. Yes, something was happening to it. It was creaking. It was moving. Now for it!—a neat little speech.
>
> The door opened an inch or two, and Penderel saw an eye. There was no talking to an eye and so he waited. The eye withdrew and then the door was slowly pulled back. A huge lump of a man stood there, blankly staring at him; a shapeless man with a full beard and matted hair over a low forehead. For a minute Penderel himself was all eyes and no tongue, staring

blankly back. Then he recovered himself and rapidly plunged
into speech. . . .[1]

The hulking monster at the door has no speech, but only a
blood-chilling gurgling sound. This is not Frankenstein, however,
but Morgan, the servant of the house. As if he weren't enough,
he is shortly joined by a skeletal, creaking man in black, called
Horace Femm, and his sister, a suspicious, waddling old woman
with beady black eyes. The self-parodying melodrama is piled up
with happy relish:

> 'You see how it is,' said Mr. Femm, in his ordinary tones. 'My
> sister, Rebecca here, is somewhat deaf. Morgan, as I have
> already pointed out, is dumb. My brother, Sir Roderick Femm,
> the master of this house, is confined to his bed upstairs, very old,
> very weak, and may not live long. Though not, I beg to assure
> you, without hospitable instincts, I myself am as rusty as an old
> file. This house is partly a barn and partly a ruin and could not
> accommodate you even for a night. I advise you, for your own
> sakes, to look elsewhere. There is, I believe, an inn about twelve
> miles from here. . . .'[2]

Darkness, thunder, lightning, floods, a half-ruined house and a
right bunch of weirdies, all of them given to sinister hissings and
sudden terrors of something unknown: by the end of the second
chapter it is clear that *Benighted* contains the whole Gothic bag of
tricks and that Priestley is out to have great fun with them all.
The road being blocked by fallen chunks of mountainside, the
benighted travellers cannot go seeking shelter anywhere but in
this unnerving house, and clearly they are going to have a night of
it. One turns the page cheerfully, waiting for the lights to go out
and the vampire bats to come swishing down. Splendid stuff.
Pile it on.

But Priestley was already craftier than he seemed. Once the
amiable acceptance of caricature is induced, a curious switch
occurs in the book's hold over its reader; suddenly, before chapter

[1] *Benighted*, p. 19 (Heinemann 1951 edition).
[2] *Ibid.*, p. 25.

three is more than a couple of pages old, the horror begins to
work in its own right. Suddenly this joky house is monstrous, and
its Charles Addams inhabitants appalling; suddenly the tension is
a taut-drawn wire. It doesn't go on unbroken; there are ups and
downs. Two more gasping travellers arrive, a hearty businessman
and his young mistress, and we jump into a state of farce when
Waverton greets the businessman, here in the middle of nowhere, with: 'Surely you're Sir William Porterhouse? I thought
so. I'm Waverton, of Treffield and Waverton, architects. You
once called to see us about something.'[1] The farce becomes an
excess of novelist's licence when a timely game of 'Truth' produces several convenient biographies. But whenever Priestley
switches on the terror of this mad establishment again, it works.
So does the burgeoning relationship between Penderel and Sir
William's young woman, Gladys; so does the gradual, almost
accidental strengthening, in the course of the night, of the Wavertons' marriage. Even the shrieking climax of the book works,
when dumb looming Morgan gets drunk and lets loose the Curse
of the Femms, mad brother Saul who has been kept classically
locked up at the top of the old dark house, and who is met—wild
screams, slavering chin, manic laughter and all—by Penderel in a
desperate fight from which neither emerges alive. *Benighted* is an
odd book; sometimes sloppy, sometimes brilliant, but effective
on several different levels. In one sense it is the book of a man
playing like a delighted boy with a newly-discovered skill;
Priestley was finding himself as a novelist, flexing the muscles
that were proving so astonishingly good at creating mood, inventing incident, describing place, and weaving the lot of them
into a well-shaped whole. But he was not simply having fun.
After all he was thirty-three years old now, a well-known critic
and essayist, and had been writing professionally for more than
five years; he knew pretty well the spells that could be cast with
words. Certainly he enjoyed what Americans would call the
'moonlighting' involved in the novel; the second shift at the
typewriter each day, late at night, in the lonely study-barn out in

[1] *Ibid.,* p. 72.

the garden. It was hard work, but it brought delight. Both his earliest novels, though, were also deliberate experiments: 'experiments that failed', he called them four years later, when he had been roared up into popular fame by *The Good Companions* and *Angel Pavement*, and his publishers hastened to bring out a new edition of the two earlier books which would now, in the reflection of their younger brothers' glory, sell more copies than they ever had before. 'Let me first explain,' wrote Priestley in a preface to this edition, 'what I was trying to do in those two stories . . . :'

> Before turning novelist myself, I had spent a good deal of my time reading and criticizing contemporary fiction, and I had come to the conclusion that what was needed was some form that would enable us to retain objective narrative while we dealt with subjective themes. The intelligent modern novelist cannot help being concerned with ideas and states of mind. We live in a self-conscious, introspective, Hamlet-ish age, and it is natural that fiction should reflect this spirit. It is not so much our hero's outward fortunes that engage us as the drama of his succeeding states of mind, the vague and changing pageant of his ideas. This is what I mean by 'subjective themes'. In my interest in such themes, I believe I am prepared to keep company with the most advanced 'modernists' among our writers of fiction. Where I differ from most of them is in my conviction that the novel demands some sort of objective narrative. I still believe that a novelist should tell a story, and if possible a fairly shapely one, no matter how strong his subjective interests may be. Indeed, I consider this problem—that of combining a reasonably clear-cut narrative, in which may be found definite characters and scenes, with these subjective interests, this flickering drama of the mind or soul—easily the most difficult problem a modern novelist is called upon to solve. You can dodge it, of course, by simplifying or eliminating your subjective stuff, and thus bringing out a plain tale. You can also dodge it by giving subjectivity its head and wrecking the form of the novel, writing things that are only novels because their authors and publishers choose to call them novels. If you do this,

narrative, character-drawing, drama, all vanish, leaving what seems to me a very unsatisfying shadowy sort of fiction.

This was the problem I saw in front of me then, like a lion in the path, when I first began to think of turning novelist. I thought I saw a possible solution in some form of dramatic symbolism, in narrative that would move, so to speak, in two worlds at once. . . .[1]

So out of that came *Adam in Moonshine*, a frothy fantastic tale of a young man caught up in wild Chestertonian adventure on the Yorkshire moors, among people who fade out of his life when the adventure is done and perhaps never really existed at all, being no more than personifications of 'the vague and changing pageant of his ideas'. And next came *Benighted*, in which, said Priestley in his new preface, the travellers are real enough but the inmates of the old dark house are 'only various forms of post-war pessimism pretending to be people'. If you look at *Benighted* with this observation in mind, it is not too difficult to decide which form of post-war pessimism is symbolized by, say, dumb hulking Morgan or mad Saul Femm. But it hardly seems relevant to the book; indeed even Priestley's preface, with its talk of objective narrative and subjective themes, reads now like an apologia for fantasy— not the more obvious science-fiction brand of fantasy, but what C. S. Lewis once called the 'mythopoeic art' which links such wildly diverse writers as Kafka and George Macdonald, Chesterton and Poe.

All kinds of fantasy are more familiar to us now than they were in the 'thirties. Science fiction is common both on the lower foothills of literature and in real life, and it seems sometimes as though the myth-makers will turn out to be the only writers capable of expressing the moods and ideas of the second half of this century —witness Tolkien's popularity among the young. The image of the real man plunged into a confusing world full of people and things and events whose reality is doubtful, and which at any rate he cannot understand: this is the central theme of the writers of

[1] From the preface to the Heinemann 1931 edition of *Adam in Moonshine* and *Benighted*.

this particular brand of fantasy, and it is a fair description too of the plight of twentieth-century man. In a mild way, it is the theme that Priestley was trying to handle in *Adam in Moonshine* and *Benighted*. As has so often happened, he was part of the quiet vanguard of a movement which only became apparent to the average reader very much later—by which time Priestley, generally, would have moved on to some other new preoccupation or idea. In these two early books, he did lay the foundation for a kind of myth-making to which he returned years later by other routes. And though *Benighted* is not one of his major novels, it does contain a few striking moments in which the two-world structure brings out a sudden flash of truth. Penderel, for instance, has two such moments: the first in a quickly-shuttered revelation of the dark subconscious that is more familiar in Kipling's later short stories, or in some of Priestley's own essays. He is very much a young man of the 'thirties, amusing but aimless, bright but bitter, with all his illusions blasted into small lifeless pieces by the First World War. Early in the book, when he and the Wavertons have brought their belongings into the old dark house and are settling in for the night, Penderel sits down and relaxes by the fire with a cigarette, reflecting dreamily on his companions, thinking about nothing of much moment at all.

> The next moment Penderel could have groaned aloud. Suddenly that old feeling had returned. It came, as usual, without warning. A grey tide, engulfing all colour and shape of things that had been or were to be, rushed across his mind, sweeping the life out of everything and leaving him all hollow inside. Once again he sat benumbed in a shadowy show. Yet as ever—and this was the cruel stroke—there was something left, left to see that all the lights were being quenched, left to cry out with a tiny crazed voice in the grey wastes. This was what mattered, this was the worst, and black nights and storms and floods and crumbling hills were not to be compared with this treachery from within. It wasn't panic or despair, he told himself, that made so many fellows commit suicide; it was this recurring mood, draining the colour out of life and stuffing one's mouth

with ashes. One crashing bullet and there wasn't even anything left to remember what had come and gone, to cry in the mind's dark hollow; life could then cheat as it liked, for it did not matter; you had won the last poor trick.[1]

Penderel, or more likely Priestley, pushes the mood out of his mind as swiftly as it has come, and is shortly being offered a drink by the skeletal Mr. Femm. It is not until the very end of the book that the mood's Janus-head shows its other face, in a flash that similarly catches the imagination. Penderel is facing mad Saul, who is free and dangerously raving; standing alone on the black staircase, he can see the maniac's vague form before him in the dark.

'Go back and don't be a fool.' Sheer necessity compelled him to speak again, for only the sound of his own voice kept him from running away. 'You're not coming past here. Get back at once.' It was woefully grotesque and futile perhaps, yet it raised his spirits a little.

Now there came an answering gabble from that vague shape, a gabble that seemed to end in a kind of chuckle. There was a movement, followed by a quick pattering down the landing. He was going away.

In his astonishment and relief, Penderel sank back against the banisters. Was it all over, then? Had he really gone? Did it only need a command or two, however shaky, just simple courage, no matter if it was raised perilously on tiptoe, to turn aside—flicking it away—what had seemed doom itself? There came now a moment of triumph, and his spirits went soaring. It seemed as if the corner were turned at last, and he had a flashing vision of life stretched widely and gloriously before him, the shining happy valley, lost for years and apparently gone for ever, a dream bitterly cast off, until this strange night brought glimpse after glimpse of it through thinning mist, and now finally swung it into full view. Now he knew what it was to be alive. He could have cried aloud with happiness.[2]

[1] *Benighted*, pp. 32–3.
[2] *Ibid.*, pp. 237–8.

But Penderel knows what it is to be alive only in the moment or two remaining before he dies. Mad Saul has not gone; he comes back; and after a brief stumbling fight both he and Penderel are shortly lying dead at the foot of the stairs.

There is a lot of Priestley himself in these two flashing moods of Penderel's. There is probably a lot of him in *Benighted* as a whole, for that matter, lurking behind the 'dramatic symbolism' —one virtue of symbolism being the freedom which it gives the writer to let his subconscious rise to the surface, safely protected by a mask. War and death were still recent memories for Priestley, and perhaps he was disposing of some personal ghosts— ghosts of thoughts and feelings as much as of people. At all events this book has a certain dark philosophical flavour, quite apart from its eye-rolling horrors, which he has never sought to recapture in the same way in a novel since. *The Good Companions*, which came next, was a totally different kind of book. So indeed all the novels after it have been: all set in a single objective world and travelling only through time within that world, rather than conjuring another to travel beside it. Later on he played with the fringes of fantasy: in his only book of short stories, *The Other Place*, published in 1951, and in one or two novels, like *The Magicians*, in 1954, and *Saturn Over the Water*, in 1961. *The Thirty-First of June*, also 1961, was deliberate fantasy of another kind, a happily whacky fairy-tale like a younger cousin of *The Sword in the Stone*. But until *Lost Empires*, in 1965, Priestley had never, as it were, written any novel on paper of the same colour as that he had used for *Benighted*. Only Uncle Nick, the illusionist, that dark and complicated central figure of *Lost Empires*, carries with him the symbolic magic of the old dark house; and this time the book is written by a man almost forty years older and wiser, with no farcical trappings or personified chimeras. Its objectivity is given it, paradoxically, by the use of a first-person narrator; and this time, it is a major novel. During the forty-year gap Priestley had played with ideas about Time and levels of being in some of his plays; but these came from a shadowy side of his mind that he never really forced himself to explore until he began work on the long essay *Man and Time*. And as soon as he had finished *Man and Time*, he began to write *Lost Empires*.

It would of course have been quite pointless to say to him, after *Adam in Moonshine* and *Benighted* appeared: 'It's good, this approach to the novel. I look forward to the way you'll develop it in the next book.' Friends who say this kind of thing to Priestley receive in response either a vague smile or a non-committal grunt, and learn rapidly that there is little point in saying anything of the kind at all. He has never worked to any long-term deliberate plan; he listens only to the voices from his imagination, and refuses to impose any pattern on those. The voice which is loudest has priority, whether or not outside observers may think his listening to it wise. There are of course many precedents among many authors for not thinking it wise, which is why the stubborn deafness of authors who will listen only to their muse is always found particularly maddening by critics. ('In Leonardo's time,' Peter Ustinov once said in a television interview, 'the critics must all have been saying to him: "For goodness' sake stop wasting your time drawing those ridiculous flying machines—more Mona Lisas, boy, that's what you ought to be turning out." ') But there it is. And Priestley, working his two shifts in the garden-study, was already hearing changes in the relative loudness of the voices of his creative ideas. During this period in which he had produced his first two novels, he had reached his peak as an essayist, and was working and writing as well in that form as any man alive and a large percentage of those dead: his three best collections, *Open House*, *Apes and Angels*, and *The Balconinny*, appeared respectively in 1927, 1928 and 1929. But he found the essays too easy now; their challenge had dwindled, and a very loud voice indeed was suggesting another instead.

★ ★ ★

It was one of those ideas: a very large and unpromising idea. He wanted to write a very long—or rather, very broad—novel: a tale of wandering, picaresque, with a few central characters and a host of encounters, in the long-neglected pattern of *Don Quixote*, *Tom Jones*, *Pickwick Papers*. It was a typical Priestley idea, and it filled his publishers with alarm. 'Suppose we were describing English literature in 1928,' wrote Cyril Connolly in *Enemies of Promise* ten years later. 'We would mention Lawrence, Huxley, Moore, Joyce, Yeats, Virginia Woolf, and Lytton Strachey. If clever we would add Eliot, Wyndham Lewis, Firbank, Norman Douglas, and, if solid, Maugham, Bennett, Shaw, Wells, Galsworthy, Kipling.' Not one of these was writing in the kind of pattern which Priestley now proposed to attempt. It was rather as if a poet of the 1970s were to contemplate something along the lines of *The Canterbury Tales*. The roots of the idea, like Priestley's own, were not in the present but in the deeper mainstream of English literature; it was typical that at this early stage he should turn back to a neglected traditional form, just as it was typical, later, that he should spend his time fiddling with new forms at an age when most writers are settling down into the literary rut whose dimensions they have worn into a comfortable fit.

This large new novel required some practical foundation-laying. It could not be written, as the first two had been, on the side, as a series of postscripts to days spent writing essays, critical books and assorted journalism. This time, the mind could not be divided. A really broad canvas is difficult enough to paint under any circumstances; under those, it would have blurred into chaos as soon as it was begun. Priestley needed time, and although he was making a comfortable enough living for his growing family by now, the buying of a big enough parcel of time was well beyond his means. Instead he was given it, or at any rate helped to it, by an older writer.

Hugh Walpole is seldom mentioned and seldom read today; though he had some immense popular successes in the 'twenties and 'thirties, he never really managed to make a lasting name as a novelist. 'As each novel appears,' he wrote, in what might have been his own epitaph, 'I realize once more that the essential thing has escaped me.' But whatever the sum of his own literary achievement may have been, in the course of an indomitably sunny lifetime Walpole managed to give genuinely disinterested help, often at crucial moments, to almost every worthwhile young writer of the generation after his own—from T. S. Eliot and Graham Greene to Dylan Thomas and Thomas Wolfe. Priestley had met him in 1925, after writing to ask him to contribute to a series of books which he was editing for Jarrolds. 'I find Priestley very agreeable,' wrote Walpole then in his faithful and voluminous diary. 'He is cocksure and determined but has a great sense of humour about himself.' And then again, a few days later: 'Priestley is certainly a very clever man. Like all of us he is not perhaps as aware of his own lacks as he is of others, but he is young yet and is fighting a battle. He will certainly go very far.'

Two years later, knowing of Priestley's need for time to write his ambitious novel, Walpole suggested to him that the two of them should collaborate on a book—knowing quite well that although this would accomplish nothing unusual for himself, his name on the title-page would assure the book a far larger advance than Priestley could then have commanded alone. The book, *Farthing Hall*, emerged as a novel written in the form of letters between two friends: a middle-aged scholar (Priestley) and a bright young man (Walpole—who, as Priestley has since observed, was by temperament probably more suited to the side of romantic youth, even though at forty-three he was about ten years the senior). Though it was mainly written by letter, in fact as well as form, it was begun during a visit by Priestley to Walpole's house in Cumberland.

> *September 21st 1927* [wrote Walpole in his diary]: Now the Priestley book is obsessing me ... It is delightful having Jack here—a friendship that does me all the good in the world because I respect so immensely his intelligence.
> *September 22nd.* The book with Priestley moves. I have as I expected a burning desire to get on with it and do it all, but I mustn't be impatient. That would be silly.

September 23rd. I certainly find Priestley an enchanting companion. I've never had a writing man for a friend before who has been so close a companion. Henry James was too old, Conrad too mysterious, Swinnerton too untrustworthy, Bennett too egoistic—all *good* friends, but none of them with this humour and sweetness that Priestley has. A most lovable man.

September 26th. Jack and I now moving at breakneck speed.[1]

The capacity for writing at breakneck speed was one thing this dissimilar pair had in common (though neither Priestley nor anybody else has ever quite matched what Henry James called Hugh Walpole's 'copious flow'—by the time the collaborated novel was finished Walpole had four other books also ready for publication, either in proof or manuscript). The handsome advance cheque for *Farthing Hall* duly bought Priestley his breathing-space, and at once he began work on the quarter-million-word novel for which, despite plaintive commercial objections from his publishers and agent, he was never able to find any other title than *The Good Companions.*

The title proved no drawback. 'J. B. Priestley,' people say now, still. 'Oh yes, of course. *The Good Companions.*' They may never even have read the book, but they say it just the same: sometimes with enthusiastic reverence, sometimes with a patronizing smile. The case of *The Good Companions* would make an interesting challenge to pose to a young—or youngish—writer today. Suppose that at the age of thirty-five you have the opportunity to write a large cheerful book which you have been wanting to write for some time; which exerts considerable strain on your energies and imagination; which, when finished, matches up pretty well to your own professional standards; of which indeed you are rather fond; but for which everyone in authority prophesies doom. You complete this book; you feel fairly well satisfied that you have accomplished the task you set yourself, and you are content to let it be, and to get on with the next piece of work in hand—which, for all authors, is always far more enthralling

[1] This extract from Walpole's diary is taken from Rupert Hart-Davis' biography *Hugh Walpole,* p. 282 (Macmillan, 1951).

than the one before. But suppose then that this large cheerful book, when put into type, suddenly inflates and explodes into a gigantic popular success. It earns you more money than you have ever earned from one piece of work before; it brings you—albeit only in association with itself—a worldwide reputation; it sells quantities of copies far beyond the level which might have been expected as a result of its generally favourable reviews. It transforms you, in the public eye, from a steady workmanlike author into a Name. And you will never again be left in peace to do whatever happens at any given moment to be your own thing. You are now labelled: not so much by your book's simple existence as by the mass media, which in this age of instant communication cannot function without identifying every man they mention with some more or less memorable act, attribute or piece of work. You are labelled, for a long, long time, even though you may already have turned to a totally different style of writing, field of ideas, type of work.

Given this chance, and given these consequences, would you then still write that book?

Any real writer, no doubt about it, would say yes; yes, I would write the book I wanted to write, whatever its effect on my reputation. (He might well add, writers being what they are, that however misleading the success might be, the money it brought would be lovely.) Priestley claims now, looking back, that he wouldn't, but the Priestley of 1929 would not have heeded him; being a man most obstinately devoted to his own ideas, he turned an equally deaf ear both to those who warned him not to attempt a book like *The Good Companions*, and to those who later begged him to write others of the same kind. All the same, he has probably suffered more than any living writer from the after-effects of an early instant popularity.

The Good Companions has damaged Priestley most not because of any intrinsic quality it may or may not possess, but because it has stood throughout his career so far as a symbol of all his work. The labellers have never settled on anything more convenient to take its place. Typically, when the epithet 'Jolly Jack' was first used to describe Priestley in *The New Statesman* after the war—in an ironical sense, as comment on what appeared to the coiner to be a decidedly pessimistic view of the world—it was only its face value which caught on: to most people who happened afterwards to hear the phrase, it seemed a natural description for the author of that jolly book, *The Good Companions*. In that amorphous entity, the public mind, this one novel still stands above all the other books, plays and essays as a symbol of all Priestley's work; yet nobody could find a less suitable symbol if he tried.

He wrote it as a kind of holiday. For a young man, he had spent an uncommon amount of time in the company of violence and personal tragedy: first during World War One, when most of his friends had been killed and he had almost been killed himself; then during the period when his wife was dying of cancer. He had also been working for years like a frenzied ant, not always at books he enjoyed. In writing *The Good Companions*, he escaped into a kind of fairy-tale: the Odyssey of three other fugitives, who break out of their respective worlds to travel into and through another which, though real enough, is so different from their own that it might as well be fantasy. From the writing point of view, 'escape' is a word with the wrong overtones for a broad narrative of this kind, which makes great demands not only on the writer's stamina and imagination but on his powers of concentration, his sheer attentiveness. It was more a matter of total immersion, in a world of far more gaiety than those with which Priestley had so far been familiar. Twenty years later he took the same kind of plunge again, diving out of a black decade into the brighter world of a massive work of fiction—when he wrote, after World War Two and the austere years which followed it, *Festival at Farbridge*: a comedy instead of a romance, but another broad narrative, even longer than the first.

The large narrative novel is no more fashionable a form today than it was in 1928. Certain writers, chiefly Americans, make handsome livings from big fat best-selling books, to be sure, but these are seldom novels of any consequence. The contemporary

current of the novel proper runs through thickets of introspection
and closely-observed relationships; set the big fat books next to
this, and they seem pathetic things, scarcely existing as works of
the imagination at all. Once they have dropped out of the best-
seller lists, they vanish completely with astonishing speed. But
The Good Companions, fashionable form or no, has survived
success, survived the critical reaction to success, and has been sail-
ing serenely down the older mainstream of literature now for
forty years.

It is a crowded book, of dense texture: so is *Festival at Farbridge*.
In this respect these two show better than any of Priestley's other
novels how peculiarly observant he has always been. He loves
inventing minor characters, filling whole books with them;
populating the background of his plot in the same deft delight
with which Shakespeare scattered about the stage a pompous
official here, a bone-headed yokel there, a pert servant somewhere
else. Behind these brief sketches of appearance or character, there
can be as much insight as in portraits which support an entire
book.

> There was a large bright fire in the lounge, and there was also
> a large bright woman. She stood out from the other guests, the
> assorted 'motterists', like a cockatoo among thrushes. Indeed,
> she was not unlike a cockatoo. A tiny curved beak of a nose
> jutted out of her purply-red face; she had big staring eyes and
> a little round mouth, daubed a fearsome vermilion; her clothes
> were gaudy and expensive, every time she moved there was a
> glitter of jewellery: and she seemed to have enough flashing
> odds and ends of handbags and little boxes to stock a small shop.
> She sat alone, not far from their table, and was easily the most
> conspicuous person or object in the room. . . .[1]

> Where it was the train stopped, shortly after ten, Inigo never
> knew. It seemed a fairly large station. Susie opened her eyes,
> sighed, then went to sleep again, leaving Inigo praying that
> nobody would disturb them. At the very last moment, how-
> ever, when the whistle sounded, the door was flung open to

[1] *The Good Companions*, p. 361 (Heinemann 1966 edition).

admit some raw November night and a large man. Inigo looked at the man in despair. The man looked at Inigo with cheerful interest. He sat in the middle of the opposite seat, removed his hat, mopped his brow, re-lit the stump of a cigar, put a fat hairy hand on each knee, and blew little benevolent clouds of smoke at Inigo and the sleeping Susie. He was a well-developed specimen of a type of large man seen at all race meetings, boxing matches, football matches, in all sporting clubs and music-hall bars. His head was pear-shaped, beginning with an immense spread of jaw and ending at a narrow and retreating forehead, decorated by two little loops of hair, parted in the middle. His eyes protruded; his nose shone; his little moustache was ferociously waxed. There was a suggestion that innumerable double whiskies were hard at work illuminating his vast interior. All these details Inigo noted with distaste.

The man removed the stump of cigar and winked slowly, ponderously, at Inigo. 'Just caught it,' he said companionably. 'In the bar of the White Horse at ten, and here I am. That's moving, y'know, that is.'

Inigo merely nodded, but this seemed quite enough to establish a firm friendship with this genial intruder.

'Here,' he said, producing a flask as unexpectedly as a conjuror, 'have a drink of this. Go on, there's plenty for all. No? Well, will your wife have one? No, she's not your wife, is she? She's your sweetheart. Our wives and sweethearts,' he proclaimed, holding up the flask, 'and may they never meet.'[1]

He tiptoed forward, feeling horribly clumsy, uncertain. One hand, held behind him, was tightening, tightening, until its nails were digging into the horny palm. Then he stood by the bedside, looking down into the face of Number Twenty-seven.

'Eh, lass,' he said huskily. He tried to smile, but could only make a grimace. 'Nay—nay.' And there seemed nothing more he could say.

Her face was all bone and sharp wrinkles and seemed as brittle as egg-shell. Her mouth was a short line, dark, bitter. But her eyes, though they wandered with an awful slowness, still

[1] *Ibid.,* pp. 369–70.

gleamed in their hollows, and there looked out from those eyes, the soul, stubborn, unflinching, ironic, of Mrs. Oakroyd. He himself could feel this, though he had no words for it. But an inner voice was saying, 'Eh, she'll nivver give in,' and he stared at her in mingled pity and awe.

Her eyes roamed over him. She stirred a little and there came a sickly sweet smell. A hand travelled over the folded sheet and he sat down as he grasped it. His face was working desperately but to no purpose.

'Jess? What—what—you doing here?'

'Our Leonard sent.'

At the mention of Leonard those eyes changed, softened. They would not do that for anything else now, it seemed.

'I didn't tell him to.' Her voice was clear but slow, a voice speaking out of a dream.

'He thowt he'd better send word. He's been a good lad. I told him he's been a good lad to his mother.'

'Time you thowt so,' she said, with a flash of the old sharp spirit. 'Ay, ay, a good lad . . . our Leonard. Is he coming soon?'

'Soon as he can or whenivver you want him,' he told her.

She nodded, very slowly, so that it hurt him to watch her doing it. Then she looked away, at nothing it seemed, as if he was no longer there. He waited through a shrinking and numbing silence. At last, however, she looked at him again, and it was as if she had returned from far away and was faintly surprised to find him still there. He tried to think of something to say, but there seemed to be nothing he could say and somehow his voice too had rusted away.

'I'm bad, Jess,' she said finally. . . .[1]

One of the most remarkable things about *The Good Companions*, and all Priestley's major novels, is the closeness of its weaving. There are no loose patches; no points at which one strand of the story flays wildly about and destroys the balance of the rest. And of all those crowds of minor characters, each one is in his particular place for a particular purpose; Priestley, like all good story-tellers, manages to seem relaxed while being very

[1] *Ibid.*, pp. 586–7.

much aware of what he is about. He has been likened *ad nauseam* to Dickens, but as a craftsman he is closer to Thackeray; though Priestley shares a number of qualities with Dickens (notably his ferocity as a social critic), he has never in any novel shown the Dickensian tendency to charge off on some rhetorical steed for a page or two and leave his narrative waiting patiently behind.

'In all good literature,' Priestley once wrote, 'there is a certain satisfying balance of sharp criticism of our common life and an escape from it.' He maintained his balance uncommonly well in *The Good Companions*; better than those who recall only the book's popular success might believe. His three fugitives come from three species of common life: Jess Oakroyd, a middle-aged Yorkshire joiner from back o' t' mill in Bruddersford, who bursts suddenly away from his shrewish wife and spoiled son on the spur of thinking himself pursued by the police for an illusory theft; Miss Elizabeth Trant, slim, erect and thirty-seven years old, driving out breathless and alone on a holiday from the shelter of The Hall, Hitherton-on-the-Wole, where she had looked after her father the Colonel for fifteen years until he died; and Inigo Jollifant, twenty-five, three years out of Cambridge, dashing owner of hopeless literary pretensions and sparkling musical talent, who sets out with a knapsack after getting himself joyously sacked from brief usherdom at a deadly prep school. For perhaps a third of the book Priestley shows his reader each of these three in turn, on their separate adventures; until it becomes apparent that the travels have all been gradually leading towards the same point—to merge in the bemused discovery of a stranded concert-party, which is translated by their arrival from The Dinky-Doo, into The Good Companions. When the show returns to the roads Inigo is its pianist, Mr. Oakroyd its carpenter and handyman, and Miss Trant is financing it with the proceeds of the sale of effects from The Hall, Hitherton-on-the-Wole.

For the rest of the book, the stories of these three intertwine with the fortunes of the group as a whole. Against a background of battered theatres and music-halls, cramped theatrical digs, and train journeys between places with names like Middleford and

Tewborough, Priestley charts the lives of his ten Good Companions to their eventual distribution between security and
success. Inigo, forever enraptured by the star Good Companion,
young Susie Dean, is like her wafted by his talent to the bright
lights and the big money; Miss Trant marries a Scottish doctor
who has astonishingly reappeared out of her past, and becomes a
respectable Edinburgh matron occasionally to be found affec-
tionately reading the small advertisements in *The Stage*; Mr. Oakroyd emigrates to Pittford Falls, Ontario, to join the family of his
beloved daughter Lily, whose disappearance over the water had
been the chief cause of his disenchantment with life in Bruddersford at the beginning. The romance is ended. Jack has his Jill, in
most cases, and perhaps he and she are happy and perhaps not.
'We must leave it at that. In this place, whether we call it Bruddersford or Pittford Falls, perfection is not to be found, neither in
men nor in the lot they are offered, to say nothing of the tales we
tell of them, these hints and guesses, words in the air and gesti-
culating shadows, these stumbling chronicles of a dream of life.'[1]

Thus in the Victorian manner Priestley ended his first large
book. While it was as modern as anything else being published
then (and a great deal more modern than some), the whole thing
was in structure and attitude a genial continuation of the tradition of the Victorian novel, with chapters headed, tongue in
cheek, '*Inigo Jollifant Quotes Shakespeare and Departs in the Night*',
and '*In Which Colonel Trant's Daughter Goes Into Action, Sticks to
her Guns, and May Be Considered Victorious*'. There was even a
chapter composed of letters from each Good Companion, en-
titled, '*All Stolen from the Mail Bag*'. If Priestley had been writing
in instalments, for publication in periodical form, as Dickens and
Thackeray did with nearly all their novels rather less than a
century before, the public of 1929 would have been panting for
each month's new allowance, just as the public of the 1850's
had clamoured for their instalments of *Nicholas Nickleby* or *Vanity
Fair*. As it was, of course, they greeted it with a single roar of the
same kind of rapturous discovery. It was, is, that kind of narra-

[1] *The Good Companions*, p. 604.

tive: a romance, artfully involving the reader in the emotions and lives of a particular clutch of individuals, and bringing him the satisfaction of observing those lives—as he has probably despaired of ever seeing his own—brought to a secure, restful and unlikely plateau for conclusion.

There is, however, one vital difference between Priestley and the Victorians. They and their readers found genuine enjoyment, and a kind of sticky catharsis, in plunging now and then into undiluted sentimentality; Priestley, like most of us in this bleaker century, does not. He could easily have given his Good Companions a kind of idealized troubadour existence, all warm and glowing; after all, the background of the book was all of his own invention, since he didn't know the first thing about life on the lower rungs of show business—not at any rate beyond a little picked up from members of concert parties on the pier at Deal, where he worked on the book for a whole summer in a furnished house taken as holiday accommodation for his rapidly growing family. But the tinge which he gives it is not rosy, but grey: as realistic and disenchanted as if he had himself been prancing wearily in obscure music-halls for forty years. This is nicely encapsulated in a proposal scene which would have been a sad disappointment to a Victorian reader: in which Mr. Bert Dulver, a large pink hotel manager with prospects, enquires solemnly of Miss Elsie Longstaff, a Good Companion who sings and dances with more energy than talent, whether she has ever thought of abandoning her stage career in order to get married.

> 'Oh, I've been proposed to a good few times, I don't mind telling you,' cried Elsie, who didn't mind telling him.
> 'No doubt. Suppose you were asked now, though?'
> 'Depends on who did the asking.'
> 'I'm doing the asking.'
> 'You try me.'
> 'Go on then. What d'you say? Coming to Eastbeach as Mrs. Dulver of the "Black Horse"?'
> 'Oh, Bert——! Are you sure——?'
> 'Shouldn't be asking if I wasn't.'

Then Mr. Dulver found himself being kissed. Into that kiss went a whole captured ecstatic vision of the future and a glorious farewell to cheap lodgings, bad meals, old clothes, cramped dressing-rooms, bored audiences, and long Sundays in the train; and it took his breath away, almost frightened him. . . .[1]

The newly popular novelist may have been creating, for himself as well as his readers, a great escapist romance, but he was letting no one wallow in false emotion; here was one of the occupants of the escapist world delirious with glee at the prospect of escaping not into, but out of it. Priestley's view of emotions and relationships, people and situations, was already as firmly unsentimental as it has generally been even in his most relaxed tales. This is a negative attitude, of course, and gives rise to one of his early weaknesses as a novelist. His aversion to the idea of appearing sentimental in those first few novels is not only strong, but stronger than any positive idea of appearing to be something else instead (just as the moments when he does actually fall into sentimentality are those at which he is trying very hard to be grand, like a man trying to play too many instruments of the orchestra all at once). When Jess Oakroyd stands at the bedside of his dying wife, in the scene quoted earlier, Priestley writes with an unerring bleak poignancy; his generation had seen too much death too recently for him to be in any danger of turning out the kind of treacle with which Dickens—very successfully, at the time—coated the death of Paul Dombey. But in other situations, mostly those dealing with romantic love, he does seem to sense a peril of sentimentality, and sometimes even apologizes for creating the situation at all. Inigo Jollifant and Susie Dean, the nearest approximation to a pair of young lovers in *The Good Companions*, are twice briefly twitched into an embrace. The first is a light matter, when Inigo, seized comically with wrath at hearing Susie describe him as 'feeble', takes the natural course of at once kissing her in public. The second is not. Inigo, given the chance to sell some of his songs to a giant of the music-halls, refuses to sell unless this giant will make a safari to the Gatford

[1] *Ibid.,* pp. 455–6.

Hippodrome to hear Susie singing them; the time taken for this bargain makes him miss Susie's twenty-first birthday party. She is at first chilly; then, when she hears him out, overjoyed.

'. . . I forgot your present——'

'You didn't. The great Monte's my present. Marvellous present!'

'And I never wished you anything. It isn't too late, is it? Many happy returns of the day, Susie.'

'Thank you.' She said this quietly, demurely. But then, with a glorious rush: 'Oh—I'm an idiot—but I'm so happy. Inigo, you are a darling.' And her arms were about his neck and she had kissed him, all in a flash.

For a minute or two he held her there. No, not for a minute or two. These were not minutes, to be briskly ticked away by the marble clock on the mantelpiece and then lost for ever; the world of Time was far below, wrecked, a darkening ruin, forgotten; he had burst through into that enchanted upper air where suns and moons rise, stand still, and fall at the least whisper of the spirit. Let us leave him there. We must remember that he was a romantic and extravagant youth and very much in love—a young ass. Nor must we forget that such asses do have such moments. Isis still appears to them as she once appeared to that Golden Ass of the fable, and they still feed upon her roses and are transfigured.[1]

Inigo is in the enchanted upper air; fair enough, most of us are lucky enough to visit that region now and again, and possibly even honest enough to admit that this is what it felt like. But having got him there, Priestley feels impelled to remind us that his condition is that of a young ass. 'We must remember——' the phrase is affectionate but patronizing, and not obliterated by the final sentences which bring us back in a circle to the enchantment again. The whole thing is commentary, from a narrator who keeps himself deliberately detached; who will invent pairs of young lovers but never let himself become or seem involved in their emotions, for fear of inadvertently falling into the trap of writing sentimental slosh.

[1] *Ibid.*, p. 517.

This is part of the truth; the rest of it, I suspect, is that Priestley is simply never really very interested in the young lovers he invents. *The Good Companions*, his first major novel, is primarily a romance of character and situation; like the four or five other major novels which have stood out of his work over the forty years since, it contains no juvenile leads who could be played straight. Jerry Jerningham is a caricature, a kind of junior Liberace with feet instead of a keyboard. Inigo Jollifant is one of those bouncy but uncertain young men who survive by deliberately caricaturing themselves. Susie Dean is Priestley's nearest approach to a straightforward *jeune première*; she is a bright, shrewd little bird, but although we hear a great deal about her charm and wit we are not given a great many examples of either, and her sparkling dark eyes and flashing changes of mood have to make up for them instead. I have never been sure whether Priestley quite gets away with Susie Dean; though she is admittedly often described through Inigo's love-sick eyes (but again without any real involvement), she is adorned too often with words like 'adorable', 'maddening' and 'delicious' not to seem dangerously close sometimes to the young women in some of Priestley's less notable books, who are no more than objects of emotion, and themselves only sketches or shadows. The same judgement can be applied to *Festival at Farbridge*, the second of Priestley's three mammoth novels, written more than twenty years later than the first. Laura Casey, also a young woman of bright dark eyes and uncertain moods, similarly seems to possess little else; and her lover Theodore Jenks is an amiable golden-haired ox unlikely to haunt the dreams of even the most impressionable young female reader. This is not to say that Priestley is incapable of writing well about love, desire, sex appeal and the innumerable nuances of relationships between men and women; he can portray all four with extreme sensitivity, though it is his much later novels, particularly those of the 'sixties, which really bring them into proper focus. But his most successful characters are always those who are playing 'character' parts, or who are old enough to have a more positively definable personality than is possible to anyone under, say, twenty-five. He would have done a great deal better with Antony and Cleopatra than with Romeo and Juliet. In many respects, of course, so did Shakespeare.

★   ★   ★

There are no golden lovers in *Angel Pavement*. Priestley began work on his second major novel two months after the first was published; by the time *Angel Pavement* was in turn published, less than a year later, its hefty predecessor was still selling more than 1,000 copies a week. Probably a large proportion of his gigantic new public expected a repeat performance, especially when his next book followed so soon after what was, as far as most of them were concerned, his first. From a commercial point of view alone it made good sense for a newly triumphant writer to send a second book rushing along to success on the back of the wave created by the first. But although Priestley, never lacking in common sense, was as aware as anyone of this elementary rule of business, his speed was of a different kind. The flow of royalty cheques from *The Good Companions* had relaxed the financial pressures which for the last few years had led him to write so much so quickly; but at the same time they had given the real writer his head. Now that he was more widely known, a hot property instead of a safe bet, the surge of his own creative imagination could be let loose. And it was the confidence of knowing this which sent him, not to London to bask in the popular success of his exploding fairy story, but to South Devon to write a darker novel about the darker side of London itself, which he had been mulling over for some time.

Angel Pavement provides in its mood and atmosphere the London end of *English Journey*, that 'rambling but truthful account of what one man saw and heard and felt and thought during a journey through England during the Autumn of the year 1933'. Like *English Journey*, it showed with grim vividness the bleak uncertainty of England during the Depression years. Another novel written between these two books, *Wonder Hero*, has more claim to the position of companion piece to the travel book, to the extent that it too described the despair and poverty of the depressed areas in the Midlands and the North. But *Wonder Hero*, now almost forgotten, was a topical and rather belligerent book with a plot hinging on the circulation-catching antics of the popular daily press; the descriptions of the ground-down North from which its hero is whisked by one of these papers after winning some idiot contest, are bitter and memorable, but the book itself is—to use the distinction Priestley tends to make in private if compelled to survey the better and worse ends of his ranging work—no more than a tale. If history had not drowned its chances, it might have been turned into an uncommonly good tragi-comic film; René Clair and Priestley were working together on a screenplay when the war broke out. But in the publication sequence of *Angel Pavement* (1931), *Wonder Hero* (1933) and *English Journey* (1934), the real link—one of quality—is between the first and last of the three.

Angel Pavement is a novel of a totally different kind from *The Good Companions*. This time, Priestley was not plunging into a gigantic undertaking that would become, if it worked, a professional *tour de force*, an edifice of a book—or if it didn't work, a long rambling chaotic bore. This time, he was simply a professional novelist, confident and accomplished, sitting down to write a novel. Once more he followed his own currently unconventional path in the patterning of his story; he took no individual as his focus, and used no one as a pair of spectacles through which to show a subjective view of all that happened in the book. In this one respect *Angel Pavement* is like *The Good Companions* after all; it deals in the Victorian tradition with a group of several characters and gives more or less equal attention to each. But this time, no device is needed to bring the characters together. This is a novel of place, of a small community invaded and destroyed by a dark stranger—whose coming and going on London River, between suitably questionable ports in the Baltic and South America, begin and end the book. James Golspie, businessman-adventurer, erupts into the little City office of Twigg and Dersingham, dimly surviving dealers in inlays and veneers, bringing his beautiful and bitchy daughter Lena with him; and the handful of Twigg and Dersingham employees who are alternately caught up and tossed down in his tumultuous wake make up four of the five main supports of Priestley's novel.

The fifth is London itself. In the brief space during which he had lived permanently in London, he had absorbed the feel of it —especially, it now emerged, one dusty, obscure ageless corner of it in which he had never lived—as only a natural artist can. And with popular success roaring him along, to a peak which had not yet shown itself as belonging to the wrong kind of mountain, he was free to let loose that particular talent, somewhere between the art and the craft, which can merge observation and imagination so effortlessly into one that after a while not even the writer himself can tell the difference. There are always some readers, of course, who will try. 'After *Angel Pavement*,' Priestley says, 'a man wrote to me and said it was a lot of damn nonsense, I could never have written that book if I had any idea of what the veneer business was really like. . . .' But nobody wrote to complain that he didn't know his London.

> Many people who think they know the City well have been compelled to admit that they do not know Angel Pavement. You could go wandering half a dozen times between Bunhill Fields and London Wall, or across from Barbican to Broad Street Station, and yet miss Angel Pavement. Some of the street maps of the district omit it altogether; taxi-drivers often do not even pretend to know it; policemen are frequently not sure; and only postmen who are caught within half a dozen streets of it are triumphantly positive. This all suggests that Angel Pavement is of no great importance. Everybody knows Finsbury Pavement, which is not very far away, because Finsbury Pavement is a street of considerable length and breadth, full of shops, warehouses, and offices, to say nothing of buses and trams, for it is a real thoroughfare. Angel Pavement is not a real thoroughfare, and its length and breadth are inconsiderable. You might bombard the postal districts of E.C.1 and E.C.2 with letters for years, and yet never have to address anything to Angel Pavement. The little street is old, and has its fair share

of sooty stone and greasy walls, crumbling brick and rotting
woodwork, but somehow it has never found itself on the stage
of history. Kings, princes, great bishops, have never troubled it;
murders it may have seen, but they have all belonged to private
life; and no literary masterpiece has ever been written under one
one of its roofs. . . .

It is a typical City side-street, except that it is shorter, nar-
rower, and dingier than most. At one time it was probably a
real thoroughfare, but now only pedestrians can escape at the
western end, and they do this by descending the six steps at the
corner. For anything larger and less nimble than a pedestrian,
Angel Pavement is a *cul de sac*, for all that end, apart from the
steps, is blocked up by *Chase & Cohen: Carnival Novelties*, and
not even by the front of Chase & Cohen, but by their sooty,
mouldering, dusty-windowed back. Chase & Cohen do not
believe it is worth while offering Angel Pavement any of their
carnival novelties—many of which are given away, with a
thirty-shilling dinner and dance, in the West End every gala
night—and so they turn the other way, not letting Angel Pavement have so much as a glimpse of a pierrot hat or a false nose.
Perhaps this is as well, for if the pavementeers could see pierrot
hats and false noses every day, there is no telling what might
happen.

What you do see there, however, is something quite different.
Turning into Angel Pavement from that crazy jumble and
jangle of buses, lorries, drays, private cars, and desperate bicycles,
the main road, you see on the right, first a nondescript blackened
building that is really the side of a shop and a number of offices;
then *The Pavement Dining Rooms: R. Ditton, Propr.*, with R.
Ditton's usual window display of three coconut buns, two
oranges, four bottles of cherry cider picturesquely grouped,
and if not the boiled ham, the meat-and-potato pie; then a
squashed little house or bundle of single offices that is hopelessly to let; and then the bar of the *White Horse*, where you have
the choice of any number of mellowed whiskies or fine sparkling
ales, to be consumed on or off the premises, and if on, then
either publicly or privately. You are now halfway down the
street, and could easily throw a stone through one of Chase &
Cohen's windows, which is precisely what somebody, mad-

dened perhaps by the thought of the Carnival Novelties, has already done. On the other side, the Southern side, the left-hand side when you turn in from the outer world, you begin, rather splendidly, with *Dunbury & Co.: Incandescent Gas Fittings*, and two windows almost bright with sample fittings. Then you arrive at *T. Benenden: Tobacconist*, whose window is filled with dummy packets of cigarettes and tobacco that have long ago ceased even to pretend they have anything better than air in them; though there are also, as witnesses to T. Benenden's enterprise, one or two little bowls of dry and dusty stuff that mutter, in faded letters, 'Our Own Mixture, Cool Sweet Smoking, Why not Try it.' To reach T. Benenden's little counter, you go through the street doorway and then turn through another little door on the left. The stairs in front of you—and very dark and dirty they are, too—belong to *C. Warstein: Tailors' Trimmings*. Next to T. Benenden and C. Warstein is a door, a large, stout, old door from which most of the paint has flaked and shredded away. This door has no name on it, and nobody, not even T. Benenden, has seen it open or knows what there is behind it. There it is, a door, and it does nothing but gather dust and cobwebs and occasionally drop another flake of dried paint on the worn step below. Perhaps it leads into another world. Perhaps it will open, one morning, to admit an angel, who after looking up and down the little street for a moment, will suddenly blow the last trumpet. Perhaps that is the real reason why the street is called Angel Pavement. What is certain, however, is that this door has no concern with the building next to it and above it, the real neighbour of T. Benenden and C. Warstein and known to the postal authorities as No. 8, Angel Pavement.

No. 8, once a four-storey dwelling-house where some mer-chant-alderman lived snugly on his East India dividends, is now a little hive of commerce. For the last few years, it has contrived to keep an old lady and a companion (unpaid) in reasonable comfort at The Palms Private Hotel, Torquay, and, in addition, to furnish the old lady's youngest niece with an allowance of two pounds a week in order to design scenery for plays that are always about to be produced at the Everyman Theatre, Hamp-stead. It has also indirectly paid the golf club subscription and caddie fees of the junior partner of Fulton, Gregg and Fulton, the solicitors, who are responsible for the letting and the rents. As for the tenants themselves, their names may be found on each side of the squat doorway. The ground floor is occupied by the *Kwik-Work Razor Blade Co., Ltd.*, the first floor by *Twigg & Dersingham*, and the upper floors by the *Universal Hosiery Co.*, the *London and Counties Supply Stores*, and, at the very top, keeping its eye on everybody, the *National Mercantile Enquiry Agency*, which seems to be content with the possession of a front attic.

This does not mean that we have now finished with No. 8, Angel Pavement. It is for the sake of No. 8 that we have come to Angel Pavement at all, but not for the whole of No. 8 but only for the first floor. No doubt a number of tales, perhaps huge violent epics, could be started, jumped into life, merely by opening the door of the *Kwik-Work Razor Co. Ltd.*, or by trudging up the stairs to the *Universal Hosiery Co.* and the *London and Counties Supply Stores*, or by looking up at the grimy skylight, and giving a shout to the *National Mercantile Enquiry Agency*; but we must keep to the less mysterious but more respectable first floor—and *Twigg & Dersingham*.[1]

There are few other passages in *Angel Pavement* in which you hear the narrator's voice. In the one above, vivid memorial to a thousand, even a hundred thousand, obscure little alleys which have criss-crossed the heart of London for several centuries, and are vanishing now beneath bigger, cleaner, more efficient and boring places for life and work, you hear the Priestley of the essays. The tone is calm, reflective, occasionally whimsical; as with that angel and his trumpet. But none of these takes precedence over the scene-setting. There are no other whimsical asides, of the 'Dear Reader' variety, in *Angel Pavement*, though there were a fair number in *The Good Companions*. And there is none of the affectionate, detached contemplation of the characters—this time, Priestley put himself inside their various skins, and as a result made them both vaguer and more satisfying than he had ever done with his characters before.

[1] *Angel Pavement*, pp. 15–19 (Heinemann 1969 edition).

Five people make their daily way to the office of Twigg and Dersingham at No. 8, Angel Pavement: Howard Dersingham, a 'weakly unfinished sketch' of a smart younger City man; Smeeth, his cashier, an anxious, grey little family man who loves his not altogether dependable job; Turgis the young clerk, weak in chin and worldly experience but strong in imaginary longings; Stanley the office boy; and the first of Priestley's more carefully drawn and convincing women—Miss Matfield, haughty and dissatisfied and nearly thirty, impatient yet vulnerable, typing efficiently away in a job she despises. Mr. Golspie too is strongly drawn; tough, self-confident and vulgar, he electrifies the little firm and the ineffectual Dersingham with a vision of prosperity to be brought by his cut-price Continental contacts, and by the time he vanishes, switching off this illusory excitement and leaving Twigg and Dersingham to totter shocked into ruin, he has destroyed the livelihood of Dersingham and Smeeth, brought self-contempt to Miss Matfield, and—through his daughter Lena —so broken the spirit of the miserable Turgis that he attempts suicide. The suicide is, mind you, a notably unsuccessful attempt. After a fearful evening during which he has half-throttled the seductive Lena Golspie, for revealing to him that the great love of his life has been no more than a game played by a bored tease, Turgis rushes home and grimly stuffs paper into the cracks in his windows and door—only to discover, as he turns to the gas-fire that shall waft him into the next world, that he hasn't a shilling for the meter. And before the next day is out, he is playing the wronged hero to a small but admiring audience consisting of the new little typist from the office.

Life goes on. It does not, as in *The Good Companions*, reach as agreeable a resolution as possible for all concerned; instead it plods its way along the same tragi-comic path taken by life in the larger world to which a man's readers return when they put down his novel. '*Men have died, and worms have eaten them.*' '*Aye, but not for love.*' And not for disappointment or betrayal or dismay either; not often. At the end of *Angel Pavement* little Mr. Smeeth goes home to his wife with the bleak news that through the swift and efficient trickery of Mr. Golspie, and the clumsy and ineffectual counter-trickery of Mr. Dersingham, he and everyone else in the Twigg and Dersingham office will shortly be without a job. At the beginning of *The Good Companions* Jess Oakroyd had gone home to his wife with similar news, and in that book of encountered coincidence and seized chance, the lost job, combined with an illusion of being wanted by the police, had split open an already cracking marriage and sent Mr. Oakroyd steaming off on his travels (as of course something had to do, if he was to become a Good Companion). But Mr. Smeeth, for all his greyness, is a more complicated man with a sounder and more complicated marriage, and although his doom-laden journey home erupts briefly into bellowing rage when he finds his wife entertaining some thirsty friends who have caused arguments before, the sturdy centre of his marriage stands firm. 'Here, Dad,' his wife is saying in shaky concern as soon as they are alone together, 'are you sure, really sure, about your job?'

He tried to tell her what had happened, and at least succeeded in convincing her that he was entirely serious. 'And if you think I'm going to get another job as good as that, or a job worth having at all, in a hurry, you're mistaken, Edie. I know what it is, with office jobs; and it'll have to be an office job, because that's what I've always done. I'm nearly fifty, and I look it. I dare say I look older——'

'That you don't, Dad.'

'Well, that's your opinion, but you won't be employing me. I know what it is.' And there came back to him, suddenly, poignantly, the memory of that tiny scene outside the office door, several months ago, when he had said to that anxious man, the last in the line of applicants, 'Good luck!' and had received the ghost of a smile. 'There are four of us here. George is out of work, though he might get something soon. He's a good lad, really. There's Edna. She's earning nothing now.'

'She will be before this time next week,' said Mrs. Smeeth quickly. 'I'll see to that.'

'She might be, and then again, she might not. And in a week or two I'll be among the unemployed. And we've got about forty-odd pounds saved up, that's what we've got, all told, unless you count this furniture.'

'I can work,' cried Mrs. Smeeth fiercely. 'You needn't think there'll be me to keep in idleness. I'll get something. I'll go out charring first.'

'But I don't want you to go out charring,' Mr. Smeeth told her, almost shouting. 'I didn't marry you and I haven't worked all this time, never missing a minute if I could help it, and we didn't save and plan to get this home together, so you could go out charring. My God, it's not good enough. When I think of the way I've worked and planned and gone without things to get us in a decent position——!' His voice dropped.

'We'll manage somehow.' And having said this, Mrs. Smeeth, the gay and confident partner, suddenly and astonishingly, burst into tears.

'Manage? We'll have to manage,' Mr. Smeeth had begun, grimly. Then he changed his tone. 'Here, Edie. That's all right, that's all right. Now then, now then. . . .'[1]

In *Angel Pavement* Priestley was using subtler colours, dwelling more on nuances of relationship, than he had allowed himself time to do before; now, he had relaxed into his craft and ceased to be self-conscious. Except in a few slight incidental characters there are no grotesques in this novel, nor even any 'Characters'; merely a set of unremarkable people put under the spotlight of testing circumstances, with their behaviour there charted compassionately and with truth. You are not particularly likely, in the streets of London, to encounter a young man resembling Inigo Jollifant whose private life is totally dependent on a young woman resembling Susie Dean—which of course is not only one of the reasons why Priestley wrote *The Good Companions*, but one of the reasons why it was so popular. But you are likely to pass—without a second glance—a dozen dim young men resembling Harold Turgis, two or three of whom may even have had a few brief hours of glowing frustration being tantalized by a miniskirted Lena Golspie. And Priestley treats poor Turgis, whose appearance and behaviour are sadly unheroic, with a humorous

[1] *Ibid.*, pp. 598–9.

compassion he does not give to his *jeunes premiers*, the Inigos and Theodores whose love affairs turn out well. Home goes the un-hero from his second and last evening with Lena, a hot-and-cold session which would have driven a more confident young man to rage or rape:

> Turgis was still dazed, still aching, still hot and pricking above the eyes, as he went out into the street and turned to have a last look at the enchanted window above; and desire burned and raged in him as it had never done when he had vainly searched the long lighted streets for an answering smile, had stared at red mouths, soft chins, rounded arms and legs in tube trains and buses and teashops, had felt those exciting little pressures in the darkness of the picture theatres, had returned to his little room, tired in body, but with a heated imagination, as he had done so many times, to see its dim corners conjure themselves tantaliz-ingly into the shapes of lovely beckoning girls. The flame of this desire was fed from the heart. He was now in love, terribly in love. The miracle had happened; the one girl had arrived; and with this single magical stroke, life was completed. He merely existed no longer; but now he lived, and, a lover at last, was at last himself. Love had only to be kind to him, and there was nothing he would not do in return; he was ready to lie, to beg, to steal, to slave day and night; to rise to astounding heights of courage; all these trifles, so long as he could still love and be loved.
>
> The conductor of the 31 bus, noticing the young man with the rather large nose, the open mouth and irregular teeth, the drooping chin, whose full brown eyes shone as they stared into vacancy, whose face had a queer glowing pallor, might easily have concluded that there was a chap who was sickening for something. But Turgis was alight with love. He sat there in a dream ecstasy of devotion, in which remembered kisses glittered like stars.[1]

And the novelist, though smiling, neither mocks him nor apologizes for him; there was no need to fear sentimentality here. With *Angel Pavement* Priestley had broken through for the first

[1] *Ibid.*, pp. 376–7.

time into realism; the escapist entertainer, the experimental symbolist, the whimsical essayist, had the chance now to reveal more of himself and his central talent: the kind of story-telling which is also a commentary on the condition of man. He allowed himself one glance over his shoulder: Mr. Golspie and Miss Matfield, in the course of a brief affair conducted on a more worldly level than that of Lena and Turgis, but with an equally unsatisfying conclusion, go out one evening to 'the new Jerry Jerningham musical comedy'. It was a flicker of a private joke between the novelist and all those hundreds of thousands of readers of his first successful novel—most of whom, to judge by the similarly astronomical sales-figures, bought the second as well. But it was the only direct link between the two books. Jerry Jerningham and his good companions were not cut from the same cloth as these new tragi-comic figures, each isolated by his anxieties from the great humming indifferent city all around.

Angel Pavement was published in 1931. Fifteen years went by before Priestley published his next major novel, *Bright Day*. Nothing could have been more typical of him, both as man and as writer. Having established himself as one of the best essayists in England, he went on to the novel; having published two enormously successful novels within the space of ten months, he turned his attention to the theatre, and wrote more than twenty plays before the end of the Second World War. Accomplishment in one medium, as usual, was never enough to shut out ideas which would lure him away to others. His seduction by a new form never meant that he had left its predecessor behind; he always took it with him—so that after about 1940, when he had been writing professionally for eighteen years, and had produced essays, criticism, biography, novels, plays, and autobiography, he never stayed with any one of these forms for more than two or three works at a time, but danced continually from one to another and back again.

It had been the same from the very beginning. This progression from the essay to the novel to the theatre was not as clear-cut as it sounds; the different forms were interwoven all the way. When Priestley wrote *The Good Companions* he was at the height of his powers as an essayist, certainly; but he had also already written the two earlier novels and experimented with dramatic technique by turning Peacock's *Nightmare Abbey* into a play. (The play, like so many by so many playwrights, never quite reached the West End, but it was a useful piece of apprenticeship.) He then continued to write essays while at work on his subsequent bigger novels; the essay collection *The Balconinny* was published in 1929 with *The Good Companions*, and *Self-Selected Essays* a year after *Angel Pavement*, in 1932—the year which also saw his first play proper, *Dangerous Corner*, on the London stage. And though the seven years remaining before the war were those of his deepest involvement with the theatre, they included much else as well. He wrote four more novels; *Faraway*, *Wonder Hero*, *The Doomsday Men* and *Let the People Sing*. He went off on his English Journey, and wrote that; he spent two five-month periods in the United States, worked on screenplays for Hollywood, gave dozens of lectures, and wrote the two volumes of what should have been—and perhaps one day may yet be—an autobiographical trilogy: *Midnight on the Desert* and *Rain upon Godshill*. And all this time his plays were appearing, at the rate of about two a year. His output of creative energy during that period was astounding: 'In the middle 'thirties,' he wrote later in *Margin Released*, 'I was a kind of three-ring circus of authorship. I had undertaken to do so much that almost everything I did was hit-or-miss.'[1] But the decade as a whole produced some very palpable hits, and the hardworking ringmaster of the circus was growing in stature all the time. 'Go to your desk, no matter how high or low your mood, face the icy challenge of the paper, *write*.' Nobody could ever accuse him of having failed to follow his own advice.

Once the war began, of course, he complicated his output still further by adding to it a large quantity of broadcast talks; not only the celebrated *Postscripts*, but the far greater number of others delivered to audiences overseas. And though the overall quality

[1] *Margin Released*, p. 191.

of his work dropped markedly during the war years, this was due more to the personal strain of wartime living than to the professional effort of mastering yet another new form. War, like tyranny, can sometimes invigorate a nation but will generally repress the imagination of artists; they are, like everyone else around them, too much occupied with the complicated matter of staying alive. And Priestley, being the kind of man who was also much involved with the fate of his own society, not only by temperament but by action (he had written repeated warning articles about the Nazi menace throughout the 'thirties), was more preoccupied than most.

He went on writing just as hard as ever between 1939 and 1945, turning out—between broadcasts—five plays and at least seven assorted books; but few of them are remembered today. One or two of the books, with titles like *The Man-Power Story* and *British Women Go to War*, were straightforward propaganda of the kind which patriotic writers are inevitably expected to produce uncomplainingly in times of national stress. To find one of those today you would probably have to visit the Reading Room of the British Museum, or go hunting in obscure little second-hand bookshops. The best of the bunch is a novel, *Daylight on Saturday*; a sturdy, well-peopled piece of work whose entire action takes place in an aircraft factory; whose background is exceedingly well-observed (and taken from life, since Priestley the Popular Broadcaster had been allowed to visit a good many aircraft factories) and whose handling of the relationships between people in their place of work is more ambitious and perhaps more sensitive than that in *Angel Pavement*. One or two critics at the time stated baldly that it was in fact better than any of Priestley's earlier novels; still, today it is gone where most of our memories of life in wartime go. Having fought during the First World War with a rifle, he fought during the second with a typewriter, and managed in the course of it to entertain and encourage so many of his beleaguered countrymen that in the long run he may well have contributed as much to civilization as if he had written fifty great but untimely books. And when the pressures of war were released, his talent was released with them; it is more than coincidental that 1946, the first year after the war, saw the emergence of Priestley's first really good play for seven years, and his first really good novel for fourteen. The play was *An Inspector Calls*, an artfully constructed suspense drama masking a sober examination of the human conscience; and the novel was *Bright Day*.

No part of this sequence of darting from one form to the next was a result of any professional plan. A sensible and cool-headed professional, mindful of his reputation and epitaph, would never have begun such a zig-zag path, but would have chosen one, two, or at the most three literary forms and stuck to those. Looking back with some (but not much) regret in 1960, Priestley wrote: 'Restless, impatient, easily bored by any routine tasks, touchily independent but not really ambitious, mentally indolent except when roused, I have enjoyed hopping from one field to another, even if it meant missing some of the harvest. But I would not advise any young English writer to follow my example. Better to keep to one field and year after year describe the same three brown cows in it. Then people know where they are with you, cows and all. Ours is an age of specialization.'[1] But if some demiurge had swept him up and dropped him immediately in the past of twenty years earlier, he would not have followed this advice. Twenty years earlier he had in fact been giving almost exactly the same kind of advice, at the beginning of *Midnight on the Desert*.

> I have a restless nature, easily bored, and so I flit from one kind of work to another, partly sustained by a very genuine interest in the technical problems of all forms of writing. I have always wanted vaguely to be an all-round man of letters on the eighteenth-century plan, which allowed or commanded a man to write essay or poem, novel or play, just as he pleased. This is good fun, but it may not be good business. If you want to play for safety, keeping the career on a steady course, you will do the same thing over and over again—painting two cows in a field,

[1] *Margin Released*, p. 180.

two cows in a field—until at last they write, for the school books, 'Nor can we omit a consideration of the leader of the two-cows-in-a-field group ...' And there you are in your pigeon-hole, and not unlike a stuffed pigeon.[1]

In twenty years, even a very crowded twenty years of professional authorship, he had not changed in the least. He had always known the disadvantages of the course he was taking; but it was the course he wanted, and he proceeded to go on taking it. His plan for living consisted of deliberately avoiding all plans. There are not too many men who could come out with the same piece of self-knowledge on either side of a twenty-year gap, and feel it to be equally true at both times. Even the image of specialization remained the same: the same cows in, presumably, the same field.

When you listen to him reflecting on the past now, in his seventies, the focus broadens to embrace the situation of writers in general.

'I've never in any sense planned a career—just gone from one thing to another. In that sense I've never really had a career. If I were starting again, ideally I'd do less. But I've never really worked at pressure, you know. Well—in the early 'twenties I did, there were so many bills to pay. But after that, it was just this one thing; that I always had a lot of ideas and they amused me. My muse goes to bed with whoever she likes. I'm fascinated by difference. Differing forms—as in *Daylight on Saturday*, with all the action of the novel happening in one place—or differences in what action can contain. It's always been the same. I make no claims for myself on a higher level, but I do make the claim of being a craftsman.

'A lot of people who express themselves in criticism rather than creative writing just don't understand writers like me. They talk of the writer feeling out popular moods—but he doesn't; the awareness of an audience doesn't exist in my mind except when I'm reading these chaps. If I happen to write broad humour at some point, it's because I like broad humour. Poets often tend to plan their careers, but writers in general really can't.

[1] *Midnight on the Desert*, pp. 9–10 (Heinemann 1947 edition).

They can be ambitious, some of them—Bennett said a successful writer should be mentioned in the papers every day, and by
that point in his life he really believed it. That was fatal. He even
reached the stage where an entry in his Journal about the funeral
of Wells' wife said: "Very few A-1 people there." He never
got lower than that one. Hugh Walpole—he wanted desperately
to be liked, after that awful boyhood—he used to wake from
nightmares about his childhood even when he was staying with
me. As a result he thought in terms of a career. But he had
many good qualities that have been passed over. . . .

'I very much dislike negative criticism; this business of not
being content to judge a man by his best work, but worrying
about all the rest. It's entirely donnish, treating writers as if they
were trying to pass exams, and giving them marks for each work.
There's no reason why Bennett shouldn't have written lighter
novels like *The Card*, if they were good of their kind. After all we
don't judge Shakespeare by *The Two Gentlemen of Verona*, or
The Merry Wives of Windsor—which is a play so lazily constructed
that I wouldn't have put my name on it.'

And by implication: there was no reason why J. B. Priestley
shouldn't have written a book like *The Good Companions*, which
was undeniably good of its kind; but equally no reason why he
should be judged by it. The one work on which he would stake
his reputation, if it came to the point, would in fact be *Bright Day*
—'If they said, you can only come in here with one book,
that's the one I'd choose.' But every one of his major novels was a
different kind of challenge, which is why, having once come to
grips with the form, he has never really left it, but returned to it
again and again. 'I didn't see myself as a born novelist,' he wrote.

Had I been, obviously I would have been writing novels from
the first, nothing would have been allowed to stop me. But this
was not a literary form in which I could work instinctively and
at ease, as I had done in the essay, as I came to do in descriptive-
cum-autobiographical books like *English Journey* and *Midnight
on the Desert*, and as I discovered later, to my astonishment, I
could do in the supposedly more difficult dramatic form. I enjoy
the neglected little art of narrative, sheer story-telling, my own

or anybody's else's. I can cope with a scene, in the direct dramatic manner. It is easy for me to write those descriptive bridge passages that most novels demand. What I find hard and wearisome to do is precisely what the born novelist has not even to think about at all.

This is the trick of maintaining an even flow of narration, steadily moving on no matter how thick or rich it may be. If a man can do this instinctively—and, let me add, very few men can—then God intended him to be a novelist.[1]

Whatever God may have intended, the fact that Priestley found this particular trick 'hard and wearisome to do' probably has something to do with the fact that he went on doing it. He has always been a writer incorrigibly attracted by the challenge of a form which he finds in some way difficult, or which he has not tried before; one reason why he eventually stopped writing essays, after proving himself a master essayist, and wrote them only in occasional spurts during the next forty years or so, was the fact that he found the essay form too congenial, too undemanding. He felt that if he relaxed into this comfortable rut, his work in the form concerned would sooner or later deteriorate, his muscles grow slack; and as far as essays are concerned he was right. It is not difficult to think of numbers of promising young authors who have found themselves a comfortable niche in the small world of newspaper and magazine 'columns' and have sat there for so long that their talent and promise have gently wasted away. But there was about as much chance of this happening to Priestley as of his joining an advertising agency or retreating into the House of Lords. 'When you start seeing life as a series of essays fourteen hundred words long,' he says, 'it's time to turn to something else.' So he did. The form of the novel was a challenge; each idea he had for a different approach to the novel was an extra challenge; so throughout his life he has given a large proportion of his talent to the battle with the novel, and the talent grew as a result.

'Of course,' he says today, 'in a way I've never been a novelist

[1] *Margin Released*, p. 177.

at all. A real novel doesn't take itself beyond its own action. Bennett's *Old Wives Tale* and *Clayhanger* are pure novels in the sense that Wells's and mine aren't. Take Dickens, Thackeray and Trollope—the last two were novelists, but Dickens, though a much greater writer, really wasn't. His books are gigantic poems, like Gogol's *Dead Souls*. And Turgenev is a novelist in a way that Gogol and Dostoevsky aren't. Turgenev and Bennett were both influenced by the French—seeing the novel as a pure work of art, like a picture or a piece or music. I remember Mencken saying that only women wrote novels: that Conrad's novels, for instance, were all really metaphysical sonatas. Many of us are writing fables, parables, myths, legends—not novels at all.'

But he says it in parenthesis. It is, after all, the kind of distinction that only a professional novelist could draw.

III

THEATRE

He was first bewitched, as I suppose most of us were, as a young-ster up in the gallery. For him, it was the gallery of the Theatre Royal, Bradford, about the year 1911; that lad in the tug-o'-war team photograph sat there week after week, hot, uncomfortable, and enchanted. He watched, and delighted in, an enormous range of plays from *Oedipus Rex* to *The Merry Widow*, with Sir Frank Benson's touring Shakespeare company coming regularly to town and a succession of howling Edwardian melodramas at Bradford's second theatre, the Prince's.

But on the other nights when he sat in his attic study at home, scribbling devotedly away in his little home-made brown note-books, it never occurred to him to attempt to write for the stage. The magic was too strong. Since he was still a boy, it had to do not only with the plays themselves, with the bright-rimmed edge of the dark rising curtain, with the small brilliant second-world of the stage, but with those minor gods called actors and actresses. They used to pass him on their way to the stage door as he stood in the gallery queue, and he would watch them with the mingled devotion, envy, awe and ambition of all stage-struck adolescents as they strolled by: 'their trilbies perched on their brilliantined curls, their outrageous overcoats barely clearing the ground, fabulous beings far removed from the wool trade.'[1] He was in love with all the powerful emotions aroused by the theatre, and from time to time inevitably he focused his devotion on one of these demi-gods who represented the magic world. One of his cousins was a 'gallery boy', a member of the energetic local élite who were admitted to the theatre free during the run of a panto-mime, to wedge themselves into the corners of the gallery and

[1] *The Art of the Dramatist*, p. 84 (Heinemann 1957).

lead the chorus-singing and applause: 'It was he who told me,' wrote Priestley in *Margin Released*, 'when I was about fourteen and distantly infatuated with the principal girl, Mabel Sealby, that she might be soon leaving the pantomime, weeks before it was due to close; and I remember how miserable I felt then, how such light as Bradford had in January retreated before sudden shades of darkness.' And as he wrote elsewhere, of his evenings in the gallery, in *The Art of the Dramatist*: 'It was then and there, and never again, I took my portion of honeydew and the milk of paradise.'[1]

By the time he was settled in London, the evenings may no longer have tasted like honeydew, but there were even more of them, and each brought at least a taste of delight. He wrote, in 1957:

> Good theatre seats were comparatively dear then, just as they are comparatively cheap now, so if we could not find somebody, a dramatic critic or friendly editor, to give us complimentary tickets, we went in the pit or gallery. I remember paying about ninepence or so at the old Alhambra to see the most astonishing galaxy of prima ballerinas that ever blazed on one stage. And the Lyric, Hammersmith, was cheap enough, and there Nigel Play-fair's production of *The Beggar's Opera* was running. We knew every word and note of it, used to roar them out round the piano, but still returned, time after time, to the Lyric. It seemed to me then—and after a quarter of a century of work in the Theatre, I am not prepared to change my mind—an enchanting production, the best in its kind we have ever had in this country, never beaten by later attempts to get away from Playfair's style, Lovat Fraser's décor, Frederick Austin's modest but rather luscious arrangement of the music. On the other hand, although I saw the production, I was never an enthusiastic admirer of the other long run, *The Immortal Hour*, at another old theatre brought out of shabbiness and neglect, the Regent, near King's Cross. But if you wanted perfection of a very different theatrical style, extreme naturalism, there were the productions of Galsworthy's plays by Basil Dean at the St. Martin's, where so many good actors learnt

[1] *The Art of the Dramatist*, p. 84.

their trade. You might dislike this kind of play, this method of production, yet could not deny Dean the triumph of his formidable qualities which we are beginning to miss in the Theatre. There was also some good new work being done up at the Everyman Theatre, Hampstead, by Norman Macdermott. And Gerald du Maurier, who as actor-manager had every virtue except the courage necessary for experiment, was still at Wyndham's. . . .

And of course, there was still the music-hall.

. . . It had already passed its peak even then, but some of the ripe old turns were still with us. You could look in at the Coliseum, as I often did on a winter afternoon, and see Little Tich and Harry Tate, and there were still some glorious drolls at the Holborn Empire (a sad loss: it had a fine atmosphere of its own), the Victoria Palace, and the rest. There were no microphones and nobody needed them. There were no stars who had arrived by way of amusing farmers' wives and invalids on the radio. There were no reputations that had been created by American gramophone records for teenagers. The men and women who topped the bills had spent years getting there, learning how to perfect their acts and handle their audiences. Of course there was plenty of vulgar rubbish, but all but the very worst of it had at least some zest and vitality. And the audiences, which laughed at jokes and did not solemnly applaud them as BBC audiences do now, were an essential part of the show; they too had vitality, and were still close to the cockneys who helped to create, a generation earlier, the English music-hall of the great period, the folk-art out of which, among other things, came the slapstick of the silent films, especially those of Chaplin.[1]

But by that time his delight was of a different kind. He was no longer stage-struck. 'It was an advantage to me long afterwards, when I came to work in the theatre, that I had left this complaint far behind, like the measles and mumps of my childhood.'[2] When he did begin to think about writing for the theatre, the spell which at first overtook him was that simply of another new

[1] *Coming to London*, an anthology edited by John Lehmann, page 69 (Felix House 1957).
[2] *Margin Released*, p. 41.

medium for the professional writer who hadn't yet tried it—
though his involvement with it, like the medium itself, became
rapidly more complicated once he had turned in that direction.
He recounts the beginning in an appendix to *The Art of the
Dramatist*, published in 1957 (the major part of the book is the
text of the first commissioned lecture delivered at the Old Vic
under the Hubert Henry Davies Fund the previous year, and the
appendices are extracts from a seminar held the next day. He was
a long way from the gallery queue by then).

> My first job, for which I had had no real preparation, was to
> collaborate with Edward Knoblock in dramatizing my novel
> *The Good Companions*. Knoblock had done a lot of this work;
> he was the 'play doctor' type. From him I learnt a number of
> useful technical points—to delay an entrance here, to hurry an
> exit there, and so forth—but I made a discovery that was more
> important. We had a scene at the end—I think it was my idea
> originally but will not swear to it—showing Oakroyd boarding
> the liner that would take him to his daughter in Canada, so
> fulfilling his heart's desire. And for this short scene I refused to
> write any dialogue. What with the liner hooting, our orchestra
> playing, the audience cheering and clapping, I argued, no dialogue
> could be heard. Knoblock did not agree, and when I still per-
> sisted, he appealed to our manager and producer, Julian Wylie,
> who strongly supported him. They were old hands, I was
> a new boy, I must be reasonable, and so forth. But I would not
> give in; for once I knew in my bones I was right and they
> were wrong. So, with much shaking of older and wiser heads,
> the scene went in exactly as I wanted it, with not a word of
> dialogue. And what happened was exactly what I had told
> them would happen: the liner hooted, the orchestra played,
> the audience cheered and clapped, a little man walked up the
> gangway into a big ship. I decided then that at times, when
> my imagination was hard at work, when I felt excited about
> what I was doing, I might have an instinct, an insight, an
> intuition, worth more than years of experience and a knowledge
> of all the technical tricks.[1]

[1] *The Art of the Dramatist*, pp. 84–5.

He discovered, that is to say, that on top of everything else he was a dramatist as well. The next thing was to prove it, not only to himself but to managements, actors and audiences. He did this very simply: he sat down and wrote a play. It was called *Dangerous Corner*.

Not quite so simple as all that, of course. The idea had to come first, and it came out of his fascination with theories about Time, which had first taken hold of him several years before when he reviewed J. W. Dunne's book, *An Experiment with Time*, and had been developing ever since. *Dangerous Corner*, like *An Inspector Calls*, is a play which presents two time-schemes, the possible and the real, and leaves its audience uncertain which is which. With the sound of a musical cigarette-box acting as trigger for the switch from the real to the might-have-been, it explores the behaviour of a group of people gradually compelled to unravel the truth from a network of falsehood in their background and relationships. Its effectiveness lies in the way it draws the audience into an enormous tension of involvement with the explosive result of such revelations, and then drops them with a great jolt into uncertainty over whether the falsified behaviour had ever happened at all. 'I think telling the truth,' says one character, 'is about as healthy as skidding round a corner at sixty.' To which another enigmatically replies: 'And life's got a lot of dangerous corners—hasn't it, Charles?'[1] For a first play, *Dangerous Corner* was a perilously ambitious bit of juggling with technique; it depends a great deal on a jig-saw-puzzle structure of changes of mood, revelations of hidden relationships, and so on, and before he went to his typewriter Priestley had the jigsaw fairly well worked out in his head. When he did sit down and write the play, it took him ten days.

This was typical. He has always written rapidly, once begun: no chewing of the thumb-nail, no gloomy staring into the type-writer keys for fifteen minutes between every couple of lines. Occasionally something emerges in the wrong shape, and has to

[1] *Dangerous Corner*, Act I. P. 5 in Vol. I of *The Plays of J. B. Priestley* (Heinemann 1948).

be done again, but always it emerges at speed. With novels, as he says, 'I am not a synopsis man.' The rough pattern of the book is there before he starts to write it; so are certain key scenes, and probably most of the major characters; but for the rest, he claims to have no very clear picture of the novel except its beginning and its end. 'Once I've started, I let the characters take over. I do always know the kind of atmosphere the book has—there's an overall tone to a good novel, as to a good picture. But if you're sticking to a synopsis, you depend too much on the front of your mind. I rather like to let it go a bit. And it's just the same with a play. You know where you're going, and where you're leaving from, and who's going with you—but you don't really know the route.'

There was a crafty and complex route mapped out in *Dangerous Corner*, which was produced by Tyrone Guthrie and opened at the Lyric Theatre in May 1932, with a good cast led by Flora Robson. James Agate wrote in the *Sunday Times* four days later, of the play's time-corner trick: 'If this is not a brilliant device, I do not grasp the meaning of either word, and if the plot is not a piece of sustained ingenuity of the highest technical accomplishment, I am not an impercipient donkey but an ass who has perceived too much.' Ivor Brown also praised the play in *The Observer*, and A. V. Cookman, for many years dramatic critic of *The Times*, wrote later in the *Oxford Companion to the Theatre* that 'it is perhaps the most ingenious play ever put together.' But the notices in most of the dailies held no such praise. They may have been flavoured by a certain resentment: a feeling that this over-confident novelist (and essayist, and journalist, and critic), who now appeared to think himself a dramatist as well, should be cut down to size. *Dangerous Corner* can hardly have seemed to lack all merit, since from a technical point of view it is one of the few plays whose construction is strong enough to enliven even the clumsiest amateur production, and to achieve the intended theatrical effects however patchy its acting may be. (As a result it has been performed professionally at intervals in almost every country in the world, and is a still a favourite standby among amateurs.)

At all events it very nearly folded after three days, and was kept on the stage only by Priestley's own belligerent persistence, with some help from the warmer notices in the Sunday papers. He made loud and determined noises of dissent when it was suggested that the play should close. It may only have taken him ten days to write; it may have been, as he commented later in *Rain upon Godshill*, a play of the kind 'which, once you have laid down the main lines of action, almost writes itself';[1] it may not have been a play of which he was afterwards particularly fond. But it was *his* play, his first play, and he had professional pride in it—together with the kind of confidence which had earlier led him to argue obstinately with Messrs. Knoblock and Wylie over the scene of the little man climbing into the big ship. Also, of course, he was J. B. Priestley, Yorkshireman, and nobody was going to knock down something he had built unless he himself felt that it deserved to come down. So with his friend and agent, A. D. Peters, and capital from the sales of *The Good Companions* and *Angel Pavement*, he formed his own production company and took over *Dangerous Corner*, which then had a respectable run. In his arrival in the theatre, nobody could accuse Priestley of creeping gently in from the wings and putting one toe gently on the stage; he took a running jump from the front of the house, and landed on both feet.

★   ★   ★

He was made for the theatre, in some ways. When young Jack Priestley sat entranced up there in the gallery, the part of his nature which responded so enthusiastically to the magic of the theatre was not so much the potential writer as the potential actor. Though capable of silent melancholy and morose gloom, he was for the most part 'an extremely robust lad, a loud emphatic talker, a notable clown at parties'.[2] The mixture of introvert and extrovert endured, varying only its proportion as the years

[1] *Rain upon Godshill*, p. 181.
[2] *Margin Released*, p. 47.

passed. He has certain kinds of shyness in him, but they are not those of the traditional shrinking violet; Priestley is not the kind to cringe away from the risk of making a fool of oneself in public. (He once wrote to me, after an amiable reprimand for just such a cringing: 'I am afraid of large fierce dogs, bulls and even bullocks, small boats in rough water, and so forth, but I have never been afraid of people, not even when I was much younger than you are.')

He has the capacity to shrug off—or perhaps magnify—self-consciousness at will, and is thus one of those useful family members who are good at charades, good at playing enormously complicated and solemn games with small children, good at the deadpan self-confidence necessary for entertaining smaller and larger children with conjuring tricks. (With fifteen grandchildren, he is kept in practice.) In the days when he used to make music regularly as well as listening to it, he was one of those dashing pianists whose enthusiasm makes up for their sketchiness of technique, and he sang in a rich baritone which is still pretty good today, if someone can manage to lure him with a phrase of lieder, or a snatch of tune from the Edwardian music-halls. (One evening during his Hollywood period, Priestley had dinner with Charlie Chaplin, Paulette Goddard and H. G. Wells. A Boswell with a tape-recorder under the table might have expected to immortalize some piquant clashes of personality, but he would instead have found himself with miles and miles of uproarious music, as Chaplin and Priestley sat for hours delightedly swapping music-hall songs.) Even something as unremarkable as a game of tennis brought out the same cheerful abandon: 'On my day I might fairly be described as one of the best bad players in the world,' he wrote solemnly in Delight.[1] His daughter Mary, reminiscing of her childhood, has expanded this statement a little: 'Not content with being able to concentrate superbly on his own game, he would undermine our efforts by shouting things calculated to reduce us to a state of hopeless giggles, just as the ball was being thrown up for a service.' She adds one or two other nice illustra-

[1] *Delight*, p. 183.

tions of an essential part of Priestley—the feeling for broad
humour which could tumble over the edge into schoolboy farce
if it weren't so ingeniously daft. 'He would call: "Your break-
fast's here," outside the weekend guests' room, and then drop his
metal plate-crashers on the floor—to their horror and our infinite
amusement. And once he put a banana through my sister's toy
mangle, just to see what could happen.' Not the most striking
piece of wit imaginable, but it isn't difficult to think of one or two
other middle-aged novelists who would have been greatly improved by feeling a sudden surrealist impulse to put a banana
through a mangle—though the shock of feeling it would probably
have sent them reeling to a psychiatrist. Priestley, however, is
seldom far from humour. Though he is, unlike many such positive persons, an extremely good listener, he can without raising
his voice a decibel above its normal slow rumble tell a story well
enough to hold a score of people taut with attention, and then
slip in some droll image that makes them collapse into laughter.
If he is, by his own description, a mild manic-depressive, when
the manic side is uppermost he is extraordinarily good company.
'Jack,' the friends will say contentedly as they go home (or 'J.B.'
if they are under forty or so), 'was in good form tonight.'

From being 'a notable clown at parties' it is not a great step to
becoming a notable performer—clown or otherwise—before
larger audiences. Priestley has done an enormous amount of public speaking in his time; mention any kind of speech, lecture or
address that you can imagine, and you find that at some time or
another he has delivered one of that brand: lectures at senior
English universities or before gaggles of the blue-haired, keen-
eyed members of American women's clubs; ceremonial speeches
at the Mansion House or rousing bits of political campaigning in
some remote Northern town; joky chats to audiences in theatres
or deeply-felt appeals to thousands of nuclear disarmers at protest
rallies. He knows all the tricks; they are so close to his finger-tips
that for decades now he has hardly had to give them a thought.
Nobody listening gives them a thought either; they are dissolved
so deftly into the matter of what he says that none of them is ever

noticeable. It makes no difference how hard you may be looking. There is only that first twitch of surprise—felt every time, and every time forgotten—that comes when you are listening to any good public speaker whom you know better through his normal speaking voice: the launching of the public voice, deeper, slower and more resonant than you expect it to be. Then within a moment or two the surprise is forgotten. In the case of a few particularly successful speakers like Priestley, and of all good actors, it is less a matter of getting used to the public voice than of being wheedled by it; by the deft pauses, accelerandos, diminuendos, crescendos, and switches in tempo, tone, depth, mood and force which can all be learned but which are also at best infused with something that comes, as the song said, naturally.

> 'I remember being with Gracie Fields once before the war; a night when she was due to appear at the Palladium. She'd just had an operation, and wasn't over it—she looked terrible. We had our supper, and she asked me if I'd like to come along to the show. I looked at her, so very pale and weak, and I thought: my God, she'll never make it, what's going to happen? But I went along, and stood there in the wings—and you know, the moment she got on that stage something happened to her, she wasn't the same person, she took energy from that audience and gave it back to them.
>
> 'Of course that was Gracie—all great performers are like that, have that quality. But all effective actors and speakers have it too in different degree. And I've got something of it, I think. It comes with experience to some extent. And if you're giving a lecture, you must remember, you've got the audience on your side: they don't want to be bored, they're hoping the thing's going to be a success. Unless it's a political speech you're giving, that's something else. I've had fireworks thrown at me in my time. . . .'

Thus Priestley reflecting on his performing self; after all, any kind of public speaking is a performance, and any speaker who forgets this small fact is heading for disaster. Broadcasting is a matter of performance too, though of a much simpler kind, and

the success of the wartime *Postscripts* is an index of his abilities in
that medium. Only a year or two ago he casually accomplished
the seldom-successful feat of combining the two, by delivering
to an audience in the Town Hall at Stoke-on-Trent a centenary
lecture on Arnold Bennett which was simultaneously broadcast
live by the BBC. Since he never writes or reads a lecture, he
spoke fluently for precisely the required fifty-five minutes without using a note. 'It wasn't difficult,' he said afterwards, cheerfully and inaccurately, and went on to sum up the process of
public speaking in almost exactly the same words as he describes
the business of writing a novel or a play. 'All you need to have
is your beginning and your end—and thirty-minutes'-worth of
talk inside you for every ten minutes that you actually speak.'

All these things—the self-confidence of the extrovert side, the
delight in performing, the 'feel' for an audience—make it inevitable that Priestley, as a wide-ranging author, should sooner or
later have become involved with the theatre. He never seriously
considered becoming an actor, he was the wrong kind of man:
'Most actors and actresses,' he said once, 'are good at being someone else but bad when you put them on a platform where they
have to be themselves. I'm the opposite.' All the same, twice
in his seventy-five years he has appeared caparison'd on the
stage.

The first was no more than a bit of fun: a single evening in 1919
which is engagingly recorded in an essay called 'My Debut in
Opera'. The Beecham Opera Company was playing in Bradford,
and Priestley, newly returned from the war and currently writing
articles and reviews for the local paper at a guinea a column,
arranged with a friend to take the place of a local 'walk-on' for
one evening's performance of Gounod's *Romeo and Juliet*. The
friend was an old hand at walking-on, and had appeared with all
kinds of visiting companies; Priestley—'so eager, so rash are we
amateurs'—was so far from such weary professionalism that he
was even ready to hand over his one night's pay, two-and-six-
pence, to the man whose place he was to take.

So into the theatre he goes with his friend, passing for the first time through to the other side of that magical stage-door, and winds his way to a dressing-room that contains one long mirror, several large theatrical baskets, an overpowering smell of grease-paint, and one bored little man in his shirt-sleeves.

I find myself wearing a yellow and black doublet or whatever it is, and one black tight and one striped yellow and black tight; and I look like a rather plump wasp. The little man takes our faces, one by one, and rubs red and brown into them. Then we put on brown or black wigs, thick and bobbed, and crown them with little round hats, Beefeater style. To complete our discomfort—for the wigs are very hot and the hats do not feel as if they were on—we are now given pikes about eight feet long. We are, it seems, the town guard of Verona, and I have no doubt we look the part or, indeed, something better than the part. We have all been in the army, and I will wager we could have mopped up the real town guard of Verona—and Vicenza and Padua—in a jiffy. But not, I must confess, with those pikes. When an opera company as big as the Beecham concern is playing in a provincial theatre there is no room behind the scenes for a walking stick, let alone half a dozen eight-feet pikes. As we trail our pikes down steps and up steps and along corridors, we are cursed by Montagues and Capulets together. 'A plague on both your houses!' we mutter, trying in vain to disentangle ourselves.

We arrive in the wings. The opera has begun, but we are not wanted for some time. To walk into that brightly lit space looks a fearsome enterprise, yet we see fellows dashing on and off and never turning a hair. Mercutio—or some other bearded gallant—waves his arms and reaches a top note, then comes out into the wings and lights a cigarette. But now we are summoned. The stage manager has remarked our existence. He is the most worried-looking man I have ever seen. Everything he does appears to be one last desperate effort. Night after night he dies a hundred deaths. Now he seizes a pike and shows us how it should be carried.

Our duties, he explains, are simple. We make two appearances. The first time we march on, we stand, we march off. Nothing could be easier, though it is clear that as he says this he does not believe we shall find it easy. He only means that if this were the world he thought it was when he first undertook stage management, it would be easy. As it is, if we were to go prancing round the stage, tearing the scenery with our pikes, he would not be really surprised. He alone is sane in a lunatic world. Now comes a big scene. More and more people crowd on to the stage and make more and more noise. At last we are the only performers left in the wings. Is it our turn now? It is. Affairs in Verona are at a crisis. There is nothing for it but to summon the town guard. But will the town guard come? They will. At this moment they are fearfully carrying their six pikes in the tiny space between the drop and the back wall of the theatre, to appear through a central arch. There we were. No applause greeted us; nobody paid much attention to us. either on the stage or in the audience. But we did what we had to do manfully. We marched on; we stood, we marched off. Half the opera was saved. Back in the wings I hear a thunder of applause, and I wonder if the audience is aiming some of it at us, if they are saying to one another: 'The principals and chorus are not very good, but the town guard is magnificent, especially the third one with the black tight.' What would happen if I insisted on taking a curtain with Romeo and Juliet? I see myself standing between them, pike in hand, bowing gracefully. What I do, however, is to retire to our subterranean dressing-room with the other five. The little man is still there, sinking into a more profound boredom. He must always have been there. Perhaps the theatre was built round him.

It is almost time for our second and final appearance. We are back in the wings, and the stage manager, now far beyond hope, a man resigned to his fate in an idiotic universe, gives us our instructions. There is to be an admirable little variation in our movements. This time we have to march on, *to spread ourselves*, to stand, to march off. Before, the audience saw us in a dense mass: now, they will see us in scattered groups. No doubt there will be a great deal of talk afterwards, some people preferring us in a solid body, others delighting in the scattered effect, in which individual features, the fit of a black tight, for example, are brought into greater prominence.

Here is the second big scene—the wedding. All Verona is turning out. We see to it that our hats are not on straight, we grasp our pikes and on we go, spreading ourselves superbly. The post of honour falls to me. I am on guard at the church door itself, actually between it and the footlights, which are not two feet away. I am standing gracefully at ease. I am also wondering what would happen if I dropped my pike, which now seems about twenty feet long. Would it brain the *cor anglais* player in the trench below? Very busy they are too, down there. I can see them all quite plainly. I can see rows of faces in the stalls and the circle. All the people in the chorus are singing now, so I join in, finding Gounod well within my powers. It is absurd perhaps that the pikemen on duty should sing, but then it is equally absurd that anybody else there should sing. The drama moves. I have a strong desire to drop my pike or alternatively to play a bigger part in the action. Why shouldn't a humble member of the town guard— the one with the black tight—suddenly becomes the hero of *Romeo and Juliet*? Again, why shouldn't we pikemen take charge of the whole drama, begin by clearing the stage? That would be a welcome diversion. What would happen if we passed a note on to the management saying that we would clear the stage with our pikes unless we were given five pounds apiece? After all, we hold the opera in the hollow of our hands. We also hold our pikes, and I for one am tired of mine. . . .[1]

I re-read all Priestley's books of essays in succession a year or two ago when editing a representative collection of them. His most fertile years as an essayist, those between 1923 and 1932, were also years which, by his own account, one should expect to have been free of any involvement with the theatre. After all he was no longer stage-struck, having allegedly outgrown that in youth like the mumps or the measles; he was not yet writing for the theatre; it would have been logical to find the stage occupying no greater place in his mind and imagination than in those of any other intelligent regular theatre-goer. But the essays of those years, when read in sequence, told a different story. Here was a small brightly-lit scene, there a memory of an actor or a clown:

[1] 'My Debut in Opera', from *Essays of Five Decades*, pp. 131–3.

on this page a character from Shakespeare, on that page a deliberately theatrical metaphor. In 'Different Inside' he could be found describing himself as 'a man with a calm philosophic mind but with a face that long ago decided to go on the stage, and the melodramatic stage at that';[1] in 'The Illyrians', a piece from the *English Comic Characters*, he was writing of *Twelfth Night* not as a scholar studying printed pages of literature, but as an observer of three-dimensional beings seen on a stage. And over and over again he seemed to be seeing life itself, in the manner of Jaques, as a great stage. The theatre, like cheerfulness, would keep breaking in. When I looked at my first over-long selection of essays from the whole span of fifty years or so, I found plays and stages and theatrical images everywhere—and particularly in the first period. This would not do in a collection representative of the whole wide range of J. B. Priestley interests and topics, so I diligently cut down the more obviously theatre-tuned pieces until they made a total of about ten in a collection of seventy-nine. But if I had been presenting a cross-section of Priestley's private— perhaps subconscious—hauntings, instead of a gambler's choice of his best essays, I should have used three times as many of these pieces. During those early years, the period of essays, reviews, criticism and the first novels, he was not really out of the theatre at all. He was no longer the boy in the gallery; he saw actors and actresses not as demi-gods but as human beings; but whether he knew it or not, the theatre had got inside him, and was simply waiting to get out through his typewriter keys.

The second and last time that he appeared as a real actor on a real stage, it was not purely for fun. One day in 1938, when Priestley was an established and highly successful dramatist with *Johnson Over Jordan* in his typewriter, *Dangerous Corner* enjoying a revival at the Westminster Theatre, and *When We Are Married* beginning its run at the St. Martin's, one of the principal actors in the third of these, Frank Pettingell, was involved in a car smash and whisked into hospital. With less than twenty-four hours to go before the next performance, Priestley and his producer, Basil

[1] *Essays of Five Decades*, p. 171.

Dean, somehow came up with an engagingly dotty idea. The prostrate Mr. Pettingell should be replaced, temporarily, with the play's author.

The part was that of one Henry Ormonroyd, a bibulous West Riding photographer, and it involved no great subtlety but a 'mixture of fruity character-acting and sheer clowning', the kind of thing Priestley had been indulging in at family parties for years. It also involved, of course, far more than that: this was the professional stage, not a family party or even a lecture platform, and even after some hasty and concentrated rehearsals with the rest of the cast, Priestley faced his first performance knowing that he was risking not only making a fool of himself and wrecking his own play, but spoiling the careful work of all the professionals. When the curtain went up on the Monday night, it marked probably the only time in his long life when he has faced an audience with a sensation resembling terror, 'feeling like a man condemned to an early execution'. But all went well. That first performance was no great shakes, but he learned as he went along, never 'dried', got his laughs in all the right places and even one or two new ones; and filled the gap without dishonour for twelve performances until a real actor took over the part.

He hadn't really enjoyed it much. Certainly he was proud of himself for having behaved creditably within an artistic discipline that was not his own; as an author he subscribes to no press-cuttings agency, and, like many, never keeps any book-reviews that he does happen to see; but he preserves to this day a small book containing all the cuttings from his ten days as an actor. All the same, this 'curious and rewarding experience', as he later called it, was notable chiefly for proving to him something that he already knew: that his instinctive understanding of the theatre was more suited to the making of plays than to the performing of them. Having the innate 'feel' for an audience which makes you a natural public speaker is one thing; devoting your whole life, talent and personality to the service of the professional stage is quite another. And Priestley, when plunged briefly and suddenly into the life-pattern of a successful professional actor without having gone through any of the long gradual years that normally lead up to it, found that it wouldn't have suited his personality at all.

> What surprised me most when I was acting was the odd way in which the whole day steadily worked itself up towards a climax that never came. You climbed up to a peak that somehow was not there. You might reasonably expect the first rise of the curtain to be that climax, towards which a jerking finger of excitement had pointed. But no, it was not. Then you might expect with even more reason that the peak of the evening would be reached during those moments when you stand bowing to the applause and the curtain falls for the last time. It must have been that you had been waiting for all day. But no, it was not even that. Nor was it for the friends who would come round to the dressing-room for a drink and a chat. Nor for the supper you ate afterwards. So you were left—or I had better be more accurate and say, *I* was left—somwhere in mid-air, off the earth but not soaring heavenwards, feeling queerly unsatisfied. . . .[1]

It all set him to brooding over the nature of acting, and actors—whose honest professional devotion he now preferred even more than before to the cavortings of other 'born actors' who take their talents to the wrong place. ('It is the intrusion of this temperament into political life, in which at this day it most emphatically does not belong, that works half the mischief in the world.')[2] Given now some first-hand understanding of the performer's problems and outlook, he intended for a while to make use of it in a long serious novel; but if that novel ever did appear it was not until thirty years later, with *Lost Empires*. The understanding illumined other books, more incidentally; most of all, of course, it went into the rest of his plays.

Dangerous Corner, The Roundabout, Laburnum Grove, Eden End, Duet in Floodlight, Cornelius, Bees on the Boat Deck, They Walk in the City, Time and the Conways, I Have Been Here Before, People at

---

[1] *Rain upon Godshill*, pp. 196–7 (Heinemann 1939).
[2] *Ibid.*, p. 200.

*Sea, Music at Night, When We Are Married, Johnson Over Jordan,
The Long Mirror* . . . Some of the plays which Priestley wrote and
presented during the 'thirties are completely forgotten now, by
their author as well as everyone else. The man-in-the-street today
would probably not automatically describe J. B. Priestley as a
dramatist. But at that time he was more dramatist than anything
else, and like the man himself, the plays were, and are, a curious
mixture. Excluding a few bits of froth, they deal often with
powerful themes, but are written with such intense theatrical
skill that their effectiveness as entertainment has tended to over-
shadow the theme itself, sometimes even obliterating it altogether.
Unless your play has the quality of genius to fuse its several
aspects into a whole, it is possible in the theatre to be too effective
for your own good; to make people think, but at the same time
to entertain them so successfully that they carry away with them
not a continuation of the thoughts, but merely the cheerful
memory of having been entertained. Audiences, who go to the
theatre to enjoy themselves, tend naturally to react like this.
Critics do not. Priestley nearly always pleased the audiences, but
sometimes displeased the critics; it is after all their job to criticize,
rather than to observe comfortably 'I enjoyed that' or 'I was
bored', and so they were more likely than the audiences to look
beyond the skill of entertaining and spot the idea or message
Priestley was artfully seeking to illustrate. Having seen it, some
of them would then accuse him of preaching, or of pretentious
experimentalism; he should, the implication went, have stuck
instead to the business of entertaining for its own sake. It was not
an unfamiliar pattern; the shade of the Good Companion was
flitting past the playhouse.

But the critics in general were as friendly as the audiences, and
even if he had been critically lynched Priestley would at this
stage have had little time to worry about it. He was very much
the busy man of the theatre, writing, casting, rehearsing, caught
up in a flurry of congenial work. As a paterfamilias he could not
earlier have staked so much of his life on the theatre, but by this
time the risk was minimal. Life was less complicated for the suc-

cessful young dramatist then than it generally is today, and he was as nearly his own master as it is possible to be in the theatre. After *Dangerous Corner* he had his own production company, English Plays Limited, and an arrangement with J. P. Mitchelhill, owner of the Duchess Theatre, which meant in effect that he had a theatre available whenever he wanted it. In this situation he and his colleagues could put on a play for as little as £800, knowing that if it enjoyed a reasonable run their 'get-out', or net profit, would be about this same amount every week. Nobody was likely to become an instant millionaire in this kind of operation, but equally nobody had to be a millionaire in order to start it off. Priestley looks back to the 'thirties now with a kind of practical nostalgia.

'Where it cost us about £800, today you need about £8,000 to put a play on in London—an economical play at that, with one set and a small cast. On Broadway you'd need about 120,000 dollars. And managements everywhere are so extravagant now. Take one small thing. There used to be a huge second-hand shop at a corner of Euston Road, gigantic, with chairs and wardrobes and things spilling out over the pavement like air from a cushion, and we used to go there and buy whatever we wanted for a set, very cheap. But today the managements hire all their furniture. and after a few weeks, they've paid out in rent the amount it would have cost them to buy it in the first place. . . .

'A. D. Peters handled all the business side of things. We had some very happy times in the theatre. I'd write a play, choose the producer, and get down with him to the casting—I've always had a lot to do with productions of my plays, even directed some. I don't attend a lot of rehearsals—only at the beginning, when I make them read to me, and at the end. You make a lot of small changes as a production goes along. I can't understand how people can publish plays before performance—comedies especially need a lot of adjustment in timing. With others, it's not so vital. *Time and the Conways* opened dead cold in London, without a try-out. So did *I Have Been Here Before*. . . .

'We used to take things off after eighteen months or so. The production gets loose then, and there's an end of it. Nothing was

as involved as it's become since then. In the 'thirties I could write
a play like *Time and the Conways* and be in rehearsal within two
months of finishing it. Today, with everyone tied up in film and
television commitments as well as stage work, you'd be two
years finding a decent cast, let alone a theatre.'

'Team plays', Priestley calls his successes of the pre-war
theatre, and accurately enough: they were well-written, well-
acted, well-produced. Guthrie had produced *Dangerous Corner*;
Cedric Hardwicke produced *Laburnum Grove*; Basil Dean *When
We Are Married* and *Johnson Over Jordan*; Irene Hentschel *Eden
End* and *Time and the Conways*; Lewis Casson *I Have Been Here
Before*. The general quality of the casting can be judged from the
fact that when the curtain went up in 1936 on an effective but
forgettable satirical farce called *Bees on the Boat Deck*, it revealed
not only the actor-producers of the piece, Laurence Olivier and
Ralph Richardson, but a sequence of glowing performances from
Richard Goolden, Kay Hammond, Raymond Huntley, Alan
Jeayes, John Laurie and Rene Ray. Flora Robson illumined
Dangerous Corner, Wilfred Lawson *I Have Been Here Before*;
Laburnum Grove was a star part for Edmund Gwenn. So it went
on; by the time World War Two broke out, Priestley had worked
with almost every major actor or actress on the English stage.

Of them all, Ralph Richardson was the one he found most
congenial. Perhaps the two have similar kinds of talent, in their
respective arts: each of them darting up, from time to unpredictable time, out of a rocklike professional excellence into an
eruption of wild brilliant fantasy, an explosion of the unexpected.
They worked together on five plays in all, of which two—*Eden
End* and *Johnson Over Jordan*—were written especially for Richardson. In his engaging memoir, *It All Began with Growcott*, published in 1960 in the *Sunday Times*, Richardson observed, after
listing a dozen dramatists 'I have jockeyed for', ranging from
Anouilh to Shaw, that 'J. B. Priestley has been to me the most
indulgent of all, both as an author and as a friend.'[1] And after

[1] Article reprinted in *Encore: The Sunday Times Book*, p. 95 (Michael Joseph,
1962).

analysing the reasons why *Peer Gynt* is his favourite among all the
longer parts he has played, he wrote: 'Much as I like *Peer Gynt*, I
must qualify my "favourite" to "a favourite", because, after all,
it must be spoken in translation, and it seems that Norwegian,
especially Ibsen's idiom, is difficult to render into English. I have
been favoured by much beautifully-written English to speak on
the stage, and perhaps my favourite is the dialogue of J. B. Priestley: his seemingly simple diction is rich in melody. The best
shorter part I have ever had was that in *Eden End*. There I was
given wonderful jokes all set to music—what more could one ask?'

His period of intense involvement with the theatre did not, of
course, induce Priestley to drop all, or even any, other forms of
literary activity. Nor did it keep him in Highgate Village, where
the family now lived, or in the summer home on the Isle of
Wight, to which they shortly moved. It was in the middle of this
period that the Priestleys twice departed *en masse* to spend the
winter in Arizona; initially because Priestley's wife's health demanded a dry winter climate, but afterwards because every member of the family promptly fell in love with that curious Western
moonscape. The second and longer visit, late in 1935, began for
Priestley with work on the New York production of *Eden End*—
the fourth of his plays to be produced in the United States, but
the first in whose production he had personally taken a hand—
and was then spent largely on writing the not-very-successful
novel *They Walk in the City*. *Dangerous Corner* had been followed
by *The Roundabout*, a play which has been performed on many
stages but never in London, and by the first of the plays which
Priestley presented with J. P. Mitchelhill at the Duchess, *Laburnum
Grove*. This, a firmly-constructed and very English suburban
comedy which still turns up regularly in repertory and amateur
productions, was one of those which he had written cheerfully
and at speed (having planned it in a nursing home and written it
during his convalescence), and the fates had also beamed on its
production, giving it a very long run.

Eden End had come next, and he took the trouble to supervise its New York production because, as he wrote later in *Midnight on the Desert*, it was his favourite.

> It was not simply that it was my best play—it still remains that—but that also I had for it a special tenderness, like that which some parents feel for a certain child. I had thought about the people in it for years, had lived with them, so when the time came to write it, I went into the country in the summer of 1934, and after a week or two of happy absorption, that utterly self-forgetful creative zest which more than pays for all the sick vanity and vexation of an author's life, I began and finished all its three acts. Its production in London had been a success; not a 'smash hit' because it was not that sort of play; but it had been generously praised, in and out of print, by people whose opinion I valued, and it had run at a profit for over a hundred and fifty performances. Afterwards, all the repertory and Little Theatre companies in the country had given performances of it. A lot of people did not like it at all, but the people who did like it found something more than an evening's entertainment in it, were caught and held by the life that I had imagined, were moved as I had been moved; and no writer can reasonably ask more than that.[1]

Nevertheless, *Eden End* sank without trace on Broadway, after a few weeks of struggling survival. By the time Priestley read the glum telegrams reporting its poor reception, he was a long way from Broadway: standing on the platform of Albuquerque railway station, New Mexico, a windy place where civilization seems to have been swallowed up by a great embrace of open sky—as indeed it has in one respect, this being several thousand feet higher than most of the United States. After a brief resentful rage he accepted the bad news with a shrug—a characteristic reaction which must have been even easier than usual in that environment—and went on to join his family on the Arizona ranch where the owners obligingly built him a small hut, a little way off in a thicket among the coyotes and the cactus, to serve as a study.

Here he worked at the ill-fated novel *They Walk in the City*—

[1] *Midnight on the Desert*, pp. 28–9.

producing, though not the major work he had hoped for, at any rate some vividly remembered scenes of London life—and at an assortment of pieces of screen-writing. Hollywood, then a frenzied golden city in its heyday, was in fairly easy reach, and for a while he paid it regular visits (later reporting that his happiest hours there were those spent playing tennis, and his best evenings those spent with Charlie Chaplin or Groucho Marx). He travelled a great deal throughout the South-West. And he read, in the timeless, alarming and not altogether unsuitable surroundings of Death Valley, a book called *A New Model of the Universe*, by the Russian mathematician P. D. Ouspensky, and thought a lot about Time. As a result, on the way back from the United States, aboard a freighter travelling from Los Angeles, he began to write a play called *I Have Been Here Before*.

This one did not burst forth fully-armed and battling into the theatre; it was not even finished for several months, and by the time it did reach the stage Priestley had re-drafted it three times. He worked at it intermittently. After resettling himself in the Isle of Wight in the spring of 1936, he wrote *Midnight on the Desert*, the first part of his still-unfinished trilogy, using his stay in the United States as a framework for a kind of self-portrait of the author as dramatist, and for numerous reflections on America and the world in general. He also wrote several other plays before setting off again after Christmas on a boat to Port Said. ('My wife still had to spend part of the winter in a desert climate, so this time instead of Arizona we were trying Egypt and the Sudan.') When he came back two months later—his time flashing by, as it did throughout the 'thirties, in a zigzag of writing, rehearsing and travelling—he set off again almost at once on a rather shorter safari, to the Liverpool Playhouse, where a try-out of one of the earlier clutch of plays, *The Bad Samaritan*, was in rehearsal. He never liked this play very much, probably because he had uncharacteristically written it from a synopsis, and even after re-writing its third act he decided in the end that it did not deserve either a London production or publication.

The Bad Samaritan thus disappeared; and so, even more rapidly than before, did Priestley—on an urgent mission to Italy, where his wife was nursing their 17-year-old daughter through a sudden serious illness. By the time the patient was beginning to recover, he had managed to become mildly ill himself, and the family trio ended up in a Fiesole nursing home run by Irish and Australian nuns. In this unaccustomed environment Priestley re-wrote *I Have Been Here Before* yet again. It was better than it had been before, but it was still not right. In some ways it never did become quite right; from the beginning the strongest element fermenting in Priestley's imagination had been not—as it was in the making of all his other major plays—the plot or the people, but the idea. The basic concept of *I Have Been Here Before* had been dropped into his mind by Ouspensky's time-recurrence theory in *A New Model of the Universe*, and he was never really able to escape from the strain of having to fit the story into the theory and explain the theory itself at the same time. There are places in *I Have Been Here Before* where the signs of his effort bulge through the seams. All the same, it did finally reach a form which satisfied him—with some help from a mysterious American producer named Jed Harris, who had great enthusiasm for the play, burst into Priestley's life with a shower of useful suggestions for cuts and improvements and plans for an American production, and then burst bafflingly out again without making further contact. Unpredictable characters of this sort are far from rare in the theatre, and Priestley was used to meeting them; but he was not at all used to needing or accepting help with a piece of his own work, and as a result you can find a deliberate, if somewhat baffled, acknowledgement of the advice given by this Mr. Harris appended to any mention of *I Have Been Here Before* that Priestley has made since. It is the twitching of that same sensitive literary conscience that has always taken such care to express gratitude to Hugh Walpole, who first gave him the chance to become an author in his own right.

I Have Been Here Before is in shape a straightforward three-act play with eight characters; it is set in the sitting-room of the Black Bull, an inn in the North Riding of Yorkshire, and its action spans three days. The fixed pillars of the place and of the play are the landlord of the inn, an elderly, contented Yorkshireman called Sam Shipley, and his daughter Sally, a competent youngish widow who lost her husband in World War One. It is Whitsun weekend, and before long four guests are installed in the Black Bull: a young public-school headmaster named Oliver Farrant; a prosperous businessman, Walter Ormund, and his young wife, Janet, and a vaguely mysterious German professor of mathematics, one Dr. Görtler. An atmosphere of strange influences from the unknown is set from the beginning, when Görtler appears out of the blue at the inn enquiring about the guests who are expected for the weekend.

> DR. GÖRTLER (*gently, tentatively*): Two of them—perhaps—are married people—the man older than his wife—he might be rich —and then—perhaps—a younger man?
> SALLY (*who has listened to this with some surprise*): No. We're expecting three ladies.
> DR. GÖRTLER (*rather taken aback*): Three ladies?
> SALLY: Three teachers from Manchester.
> DR. GÖRTLER: Oh! Perhaps there is another inn here, eh?
> SAM: Nay, this is t'only one. There's t'Lion at Dale End, but that's eight mile from here.
> SALLY: But there's one or two here that lets rooms. You might try Lane Top Farm—Mrs. Fletcher—it's just a bit further on.
> SAM: Not five minutes in a car—if you've come in a car.
> DR. GÖRTLER (*still showing signs of disappointment*): Yes, I have a car. I will try this farm but I do not think it will be any use. (*Smiles rather forlornly.*) This must be the wrong year.
> SAM: Don't you know what year your friends are coming?
> DR. GÖRTLER (*with a slight smile*): They are not my friends. (*He goes to the door.*) How do I find this farm?[1]

He departs. Odd, one thinks. Soon it is odder still. The three ladies from Manchester telephone to cancel their reservation.

[1] *I Have Been Here Before.* Act I. P. 205 in Vol. I of *The Plays of J. B. Priestley.*

Farrant, the young schoolmaster, appears dusty from a long walk; he is clearly already staying at the inn. A few minutes later there is another telephone call, heralding the unexpected arrival of the Ormunds. When Dr. Görtler shortly returns, this time also to stay, the pattern of his group of fellow-guests has become exactly that which he had described in his first enquiry. 'Ich bin glücklich!' he says (*triumphantly, with a touch of wonder, really to himself*). 'I am fortunate.'

The atmosphere grows odder yet. Görtler, on meeting Oliver Farrant, appears to recognize him; Farrant in turn looks at him with a puzzled sense of half-recognition. ('You know, I must have seen your photograph somewhere.') When Janet Ormund enters this room that she has never seen before, she is overwhelmed by so curious a sense of familiarity that for a moment the emotional impact makes her feel faint; and it returns momentarily later when she is listening to something Görtler says. ('Suddenly I felt . . . I could have sworn . . . you'd said all that to me before . . . You and I . . . sitting, talking, like this.') And when Farrant meets the Ormunds for the first time, there is a sudden shock of indefinable emotion to which none of them refers specifically, but which clearly throws each of them off balance in some way. And the mysterious Görtler, rousing uneasiness particularly in Sally's very feminine mind, seems in unspoken ways to know more about his three fellow-guests than a stranger could possibly know.

It is a good first act, leaving its audience involved in the characters and caught up by a nebulous feeling of tension. Priestley had reinforced this with a gentle trick, charted in his stage directions. There is a pause near the beginning of the play before Dr. Görtler's first entrance. '*In the empty room we hear the clock ticking.*' When Görtler enters, the clock chimes. Later, on Janet Ormund's first entrance, with her startled reaction to the sight of the room, '*the clock chimes at her.*' When she and Ormund have been alone in the room for a while, they have their first sight of Oliver Farrant. '*FARRANT enters, and stops short, and he and JANET look at one another. Then ORMUND looks too, and the clock joins in*

*with its tick and chime, as if it had been expecting this. An odd tense-
ness for a moment. . . .'*[1] And the clock chimes once more, towards
the end of the act, when Farrant says casually of Görtler: 'I
thought I'd met him somewhere before,' drawing a sharp reaction
from Janet Ormund of something like alarm.

This clock continues to take some part in the rest of the play,
but nowhere so pointedly as in the first act. Once he was into the
building and resolution of his crisis, Priestley needed no mere
hint of the part played by time; he had come to grips with the
Time theory itself, which had to control the action after this
point, with the puzzling Dr. Görtler at its helm. And this was
where his problems with the play had been focused all along.
Ouspensky's theory of Time was not the relatively simple pro-
position of reincarnation; it put forward instead the idea of a
three-dimensional Time in which movement takes place in a kind
of spiral. We live our lives not once, it suggested, but again and
again: entering the same dilemmas, making the same mistakes,
coming to the same crossroads and always, after much anguished
weighing of possibilities, taking the same road as before. We
encounter the same delights and the same miseries, every time as
fresh as they were before—though sometimes, at some apparently
meaningless moment, there may come like an echo of a familiar
phrase of music a sudden momentary flash of memory from some
point along the spiral we have already travelled, bringing with it
the *déjà vu* sensation that Priestley put into his title, and that
almost everybody has experienced at some time: *I have been here
before.* And then the flash is gone, and our lives go on, repeating
their pattern over and over again. But not all of them.

> Some people, steadily developing, will exhaust the possibilities
> of their circles of time and will finally swing out of them into
> new existences. Others—the criminals, madmen, suicides—live
> their lives in ever-darkening circles of their time. Fatality begins
> to haunt them. More and more of their lives are passed in the
> shadow of death. They gradually sink——[2]

[1] *Ibid.*, p. 217.
[2] *Ibid.,* Act II, p. 242.

Thus Dr. Görtler, the mystic, commentating—and ending that piece of commentary abruptly, as he is interrupted by the successful but unhappy Walter Ormund, the play's nearest approach to Everyman, who finds in the 'ever-darkening circles' an image intolerably close to the shadowy dreads and despairs that lurk within his own mind. Priestley makes Görtler far more than a simple device figure for explaining the rules of the game. He does explain, certainly—a matter presenting a large technical problem for dramatists, particularly the writers of thrillers, who usually give up all idea of trying to avoid it and instead assemble their entire cast dutifully onstage to hear the clever detective explain whodunit (or if not who, at least how, and why). Priestley craftily solves his own version of the problem, and avoids nearly all awkwardnesses of the 'do tell us' kind, by putting the most dangerous hurdle offstage. Both Görtler and the first perilous plunge into explanation are thus invisible and inaudible, and we are led on instead by the gentler device—as old as the drama itself—of reported speech.

> SAM: Well, it started with me saying last night: 'If I'd my time over again,' which seemed to right tickle Dr. Görtler. Because he comes to me this afternoon and tells me I'm going to have my time over again. He started on about time going round i' circles an' spirals, an' i' two minutes, what with his dimensions and eternities and what not, he had me dizzy. He says we all go round like dobby-horses.[1]

And after Sam has added that he himself would not object to this system in the least, Görtler enters and is led smoothly and naturally into the key piece of extra exposition quoted earlier, which Ormund brusquely interrupts: the point that for some men this long spiral of existence is not endless, but can lead either to a higher or a lower plane. It is a key because it leads on to the more active part which Görtler takes in the play. Priestley's eerie German doctor is more than a commentator; he is the personification of the other side of Ouspensky's theory of Time—that of

[1] *Ibid.*, Act II, p. 241.

an intervention which can break the recurring spiral of a man's life.

In his two earlier versions of the play Priestley had written Görtler as a kind of transient being from another sphere of existence, but this hadn't worked. It was only when he replaced the *deus ex machina* with a rootless mystic, a man who has 'lost everything except the love of knowledge—and faith and hope', that his treatment of the idea of intervention became acceptable to him (and, as it turned out, to his audience). Half way through *I Have Been Here Before*, the schoolmaster Farrant and Ormund's wife Janet realize that by a *coup de foudre* as inexplicable as the chiming clock they are fiercely in love, and it is at the point of their departure together, to break up the Ormunds' already uncertain marriage, that Dr. Görtler first intervenes. He is, if you like, a kind of experimentalist yogi, who has been able to capture like vivid remembered dreams certain scenes from the spiralling of his own life. And the one such scene which sent him in the first place to look for these three strangers at the Black Bull Inn was one in which he had seen himself, a year or two older than he is now, meeting in London a bitter young couple trapped in a disastrously unhappy marriage.

> This was not the woman's first husband. She had been the wife of a rich man, older than herself, with whom she had fallen out of love. But they had gone on a little holiday together, at Whitsuntide, to a small inn, which they described. There she had instantly fallen in love with a younger man—the one now her husband—and they had run away.... Then there came out of this, as they now realized, the ruin of many innocent lives.... But what made them so bitter was that though their love for one another had compelled them to take this course, had made them poor and lonely and neglected, it had given them nothing in return. This love of theirs, it had died.
>
> JANET (*very sharply, painfully*): No, it couldn't have done that.[1]

But Görtler has such inexplicably accurate evidence written in his little notebook, out of his memory-dreams, that it is not very long before Janet, at least, accepts that what he has seen is in

[1] *Ibid.,* Act III, p. 257.

fact a future part of her own life. From there it is a short step to the idea of changing the doomed course of that life. But surely, she says to Görtler, we are not all marionettes: 'We can make our own lives, can't we?'

> DR. GÖRTLER: Once we know, yes. It is knowledge alone that gives us freedom. I believe that the very grooves in which our lives run are created by our feeling, imagination and will. If we know and then make the effort, we can change our lives. We are not going round and round in hell. And we can help one another.
>
> JANET: How?
>
> DR. GÖRTLER: If I have more knowledge than you, then I can intervene, like a man who stops you on a journey to tell you that the road ahead is flooded. That was the further experiment I had hoped to make. To intervene.
>
> JANET (*pointing to the notebook*): Recurrence and Intervention.
>
> DR. GÖRTLER: Yes. That seemed possible, too. I discovered some things I did not know before. Two of you, troubled by memories, were instantly attracted to one another. That I expected. But the third——
>
> JANET: You mean Walter?
>
> DR. GÖRTLER: Yes. The one I had not met before, I soon discovered that he was a man who felt he had a tragic destiny and was moving nearer and nearer to self-destruction——
>
> JANET (*startled*): Suicide?
>
> DR. GÖRTLER: Yes, that was why the great business collapsed, why so many were ruined, why everybody knew the story. You told me when you left him, your husband went into the garage here and shot himself. . . .[1]

By this point, the future course of the action is clear to the audience. Through Görtler's intervention, Janet Ormund will not leave her husband after all, Ormund will not shoot himself, the sudden lovers will part and all will—not yet, but in the long run—be well. And indeed if Priestley had been a lesser dramatist, concerned with the Ouspensky theory only as a basis for an entertaining play, he might have let it go at that. But there was more

[1] *Ibid.*, Act III, p. 260.

in his head: the focus of his concern in *I Have Been Here Before* is not the lovers, or even Görtler, but the Everyman figure of the businessman Ormund.

Suddenly the dramatist picks up his audience and sets them, astonished, facing in a new direction. Janet Ormund and Farrant go out to say good-bye to one another; Görtler challenges the suicidal Ormund with Hamlet's argument against self-destruction, and there follows the real scene of intervention, for which the first was only a preparation.

> DR. GÖRTLER: We do not go round a circle. That is an illusion, just as the circling of the planets and stars is an illusion. We move along a spiral track. It is not quite the same journey from the cradle to the grave each time. Sometimes the differences are small, sometimes they are very important. We must set out each time on the same road but along that road we have a choice of adventures.
>
> ORMUND: I wish I could believe that, Görtler.
>
> DR. GÖRTLER: What has happened before—many times perhaps —will probably happen again. That is why some people can prophesy what is to happen. They do not see the future, as they think, but the past, what has happened before. But something new may happen. You may have brought your wife here for this holiday over and over again. She may have met Farrant here over and over again. But you and I have not talked here before. That is new. This may be one of those great moments of our lives.
>
> ORMUND: And which are they?
>
> DR. GÖRTLER (*impressively*): When a soul can make a fateful decision. I see this as such a moment for you, Ormund. You can return to the old dark circle of existence, dying endless deaths, or you can break the spell and swing out into new life.
>
> ORMUND (*after a pause, staring at* DR. GÖRTLER, *then with a certain breadth and nobility of manner*): New life! I wish I could believe that. They've never told me yet about a God so generous and noble and wise that he won't allow a few decisions that we make in our ignorance, haste and bewilderment to settle our fate for ever. Why should this poor improvisation be our whole

existence? Why should this great theatre of suns and moons and starlight have been created for the first pitiful charade we can contrive?

DR. GÖRTLER: It was not. We must play our parts until the drama is perfect.

ORMUND (*very slowly*): I think what I've resented most is that the only wisdom we have is wisdom after the event. We learn, but always too late. When I was no longer a boy, I knew at last what sort of boy I ought to have been. By the time we are forty, we know how to behave at twenty. Always too late. So that the little wisdom we get is useless to us.

DR. GÖRTLER (*very quietly*): In your world. Not in mine.[1]

Not in Priestley's either, though his universe is not that of this play. Ormund does not shoot himself; the lovers are not parted; and Everyman goes out into the world alone much as Johnson, at the end of Priestley's later play *Johnson Over Jordan*, goes out into eternity; perhaps they are treading the same road. *I Have Been Here Before* is by no means Priestley's favourite play, and not really one of his best pieces of work; when one contemplates the range so far of his half-century of accomplishment, he seems to be right in his contention that the things he produced with the greatest speed and conviction, and the least number of technical problems, also turned out to be the best.

But in a curious way this play, which gave him so much trouble, seems now to have marked the beginning of a new stage in his life. For the first time he was dealing sufficiently seriously with a serious theme to risk the whole of a piece of work on the chance of making palatable an intellectual idea; he had accomplished ambitious enough projects of other kinds before, goodness knows, but this was the first time he had grappled with one so extremely ambitious that it had made him wonder at times whether he had bitten off more than he could chew. His sticky progress with the play, through ups and downs of cutting and writing, was a fairly accurate indication that this would not emerge as a major work, but at the same time it was a sign of a new kind of maturity.

[1] *Ibid.*, Act III, pp. 264-5.

Priestley was now in his forties, and as far as his mental development was concerned this was perhaps the most important decade in his life. Often it seems to be during the first few years after passing the age of forty that a man realizes whether he has now discovered all that there is to be known about his allotment of ability, creative or otherwise. He knows the sum of himself now, and which dreams are within his reach and which beyond his capabilities. If he feels subconsciously that he has reached a kind of limit of new growth, like a tree which has come to its full height, he tends after this point, without rancour, to set himself to polishing the ability he has, broadening his field of work rather than trying to push it ahead. Having found what it is he can do, he now concentrates on doing it as well as he can. But for other men—as for most women—the forties mark instead a kind of shift in development. Their mental capacities and their work continue to grow after this point, perhaps taking a slightly different direction; and though they do not necessarily climb any higher in the long run than the man whose mind was 'mature' at forty— the tree, as it were, is no taller—they do continue to develop and to change in the way that is generally expected only of younger men. Perhaps such men are simply slow developers. At any rate the uneasy forties are for them important years, in which the foundation for this second stage of development is laid. And the forties for Priestley were the years in which his thinking was influenced by Gurdjieff, Ouspensky, and perhaps most of all by Jung; his busiest decade was also the one in which he became more deeply reflective. It didn't change the nature of his work— that had been changing all the time—but it did deepen the colours, a process which has continued ever since. The colour of *I Have Been Here Before* is not deep, any more than the play is itself, but it is significantly deeper in this rather nebulous sense than that of any play before. And another aspect of the change it reflects is visible in another play, both similar and different, which was first produced at about the same time.

He was still finishing the last details of *I Have Been Here Before* when he had, suddenly, what seemed to him a glorious idea.

I can remember the very moment when it came. I was lunching with my sister, who was staying with us in Highgate during Whitsuntide, and we were idly discussing old acquaintances and especially a family I had known before the War. Suddenly I saw that there was a play in the relation between a fairly typical middle-class family and the theory of Time, the theory chiefly associated with J. W. Dunne, over which I had been brooding for the past two years. The idea was not the usual possible good idea one jots down in a notebook and then leaves for a year or two. It excited me at once, and I had to begin sketching out the general action of the play. Within a day or two, having come down here to the Isle of Wight, I had made out a list of the characters and told myself what sort of people they were. The first and third acts were set in 1919, and I needed some 'period' details for these scenes; but I could not wait until we returned to London, where I could do my little bit of research, so I left the two 1919 acts and plunged boldly into the contemporary one, Act Two. With almost no preparation, without any of the usual brooding and note-making, I wrote this Act Two of *Time and the Conways* at full speed. It seemed to cost me no more thought and trouble than if I were dashing off a letter to an old friend. Page after page, scene after scene, went off effortlessly, with hardly a correction on my typescript. I did not stay up late at night, drink strong coffee, put wet towels on my head; I kept a bank clerk's hours and almost behaved liked one; and yet within two days I had almost finished this long and complicated act; and what I wrote then, with only two or three tiny alterations, was rehearsed, played and afterwards printed.[1]

Time and the Conways, on the face of it, is a fairly simple play with no convoluted plot. It is the story of a family, one of those close, gay, self-sufficient families which have always fascinated Priestley; in this one there are two sons, four daughters, no father, and a bitchy and altogether feminine Juno of a mother. As far as demonstrable action goes, we are shown simply what this family is like in 1919, and then what it has become by 1937. But we are not shown it quite like that. In letting this play explode

[1] *Rain upon Godshill*, p. 43.

around him before he had properly finished work on *I Have Been Here Before*, and then putting it on the stage only a few weeks before the other opened, Priestley put himself in what seemed the typically audacious position (though really it was no more than a kind of creative accident) of presenting simultaneously in two different London theatres two plays based on contradicting theories of Time. The fates of the two plays themselves differed too. *I Have Been Here Before* had been a problem child; there were difficulties not only over its writing but over its theatre, director, cast and nearly everything else. *Time and the Conways* was born under a brighter star; the rest of the writing went almost as smoothly as the astonishing emergence of that second act; the right theatre, director and cast were all immediately available, everything went well in rehearsal and in production, and the houses were enthusiastic and full. It is, as Priestley once observed, small wonder that theatrical persons are nearly always highly superstitious: 'In the Theatre nearly every enterprise, from start to finish, either goes wonderfully right or dreadfully wrong.'

But the most significant difference was of course in the plays' content. Although *Time and the Conways* is based on a theory about Time—J. W. Dunne's 'serialism', which had been buzzing in Priestley's head for so long—there is no point at which the theory has to be explained. Nobody anywhere gives one word of explanation, only a few brief hints. There is no need for any of the dramatic trickery which has to smooth out the obviousness of planted ideas, announcements, exposition and so forth in *I Have Been Here Before*. This time, the play is its own explanation. Everything that needs to be said about *Time and the Conways* is said by its shape, by the transposition of years in which Act I is set in 1919, Act II in 1937, and then Act III back in 1919 at the moment when Act I left off. Dunne's theory is as complicated as Ouspensky's spiral of existence; it involves an assumption that each of us is, in a sense, two selves: Observer One, who inhabits your waking mind and sees the fourth dimension as Time, and Observer Two, who sits behind One as a deeper self-consciousness, taking over the mind completely only in dreams, and whose

Time is the fifth dimension. Observer Two surveys human life not only in its three dimensions but along the fourth as well, backwards and forwards in the past, present and future of the time that we ourselves call Time. With this as a basis Dunne's philosophy produces a view of immortality as a transition from life with Observer One to life with Observer Two: the survival, that is, not of you as you are at any particular instant, nor of some central 'immortal soul', but of the whole course of your life from the moment of birth to the moment of death. Nothing that has existed in the first four dimensions ever stops; it continues in the fifth, from which all four are always visible without real beginning or real end.

The peculiar vividness with which Priestley manages to convey this idea in *Time and the Conways* comes from the way in which, by switching his time-scheme from past to present and back to past again, he turns his audience during the third act into a kind of composite Observer Two. They have met the Conways; they have looked ahead along the fourth dimension and seen what the Conways will become; now they are put back in the poignant situation of watching the Conways set gaily off along the road to their various mistakes and miseries, without being able to show them the way round the pitfalls that lie ahead. The effect is powerful; *Time and the Conways* does not 'read' particularly well on the printed page (chiefly because Priestley did not surreptitiously heighten the tone of its dialogue as the play progressed, in the way that he did with some others) but can provide a most moving experience in the theatre. Obviously an audience watching any tragedy whose outcome they already know must be in the position of an Observer Two—a Tiresias, able to foresee doom but unable to use his knowledge to avert it. (I think it was Paul Dehn who envisaged a performance of *Macbeth* in which a small-part actor, overwhelmed by this sensation just as he was due to enter to Macbeth with the news: 'The Queen, my Lord is dead,' came on and announced joyfully instead: 'The Queen my Lord, is much, much better.') But it was not the traditional cathartic effect brought by the awful inevitability of high tragedy that Priestley was after in this play; he wanted to show the kind of dramatic irony which is visible all round us in every day of ordinary life. He was, as it were, writing a fantasy in order to produce a realistic effect.

He gave his audience only one small signpost to the underlying idea of the play, at the end of the deep disillusion of Act Two, in which all the bright Conways have been seen among the messy wreckage that they made of their lives within twenty years. The quiet brother Alan, who has 'made nothing' of his life, yet is the only one to have preserved his serenity, is comforting Kay, the sister who had the most brilliant dreams and ideas and who has ended in the bleakest despair.

> KAY: . . . Remember what we once were and what we thought we'd be. And now this. And it's all we have, Alan, it's *us*. Every step we've taken—every tick of the clock—making everything worse. If this is all life is, what's the use? Better to die, like Carol, before you find it out, before Time gets to work on you. I've felt it before, Alan, but never as I've done tonight. There's a great devil in the universe, and we call it Time.
>
> ALAN (*playing with his pipe, quietly, shyly*): Did you ever read Blake?
>
> KAY: Yes.
>
> ALAN: Do you remember this? (*quotes quietly, but with feeling*):
>
>> Joy and woe are woven fine,
>> A clothing for the soul divine;
>> Under every grief and pine
>> Runs a joy with silken twine.
>> It is right it should be so;
>> Man was made for joy and woe;
>> And when this we rightly know,
>> Safely through the world we go. . . .
>
> KAY: Safely through the world we go? No, it isn't true, Alan— or it isn't true for me. If things were merely mixed—good and bad—that would be all right, but they get worse. We've seen it tonight. Time's beating us.
>
> ALAN: No, Time's only a kind of dream, Kay. If it wasn't, it

would have to destroy everything—the whole universe—and then remake it again every tenth of a second. But Time doesn't destroy anything. It merely moves us on—in this life—from one peep-hole to the next.

KAY: But the happy young Conways, who used to play charades here, they've gone, and gone for ever.

ALAN: No, they're real and existing, just as we two, here now, are real and existing. We're seeing another bit of the view—a bad bit, if you like—but the whole landscape's still there.

KAY: But, Alan, we can't be anything but what we are *now*.

ALAN: No . . . it's hard to explain . . . suddenly like this . . . there's a book I'll lend you—read it in the train. But the point is, now, at this moment, or any moment, we're only a cross-section of our real selves. What we *really* are is the whole stretch of ourselves, all our time, and when we come to the end of this life, all those selves, all our time, will be *us*—the real you, the real me. And then perhaps we'll find ourselves in another time, which is only another kind of dream.[1]

If Alan were to produce the book he mentions, it would of course turn out to be Dunne's *An Experiment with Time*. But he does nothing so obvious. To be fair, Dr. Görtler didn't mention Ouspensky either, but he did have to spend rather a lot of time charting the Ouspensky ideas. There is no getting away from the fact that the real reason why *Time and the Conways* is a more effective play than *I Have Been Here Before* is not that one theory is less complicated than the other, or one plot better-made, but that one was written in what was for this particular writer the wrong way. Priestley's best pieces of work seem to emerge fully-grown from the back of his head. The failures are those which had a more difficult birth, and his descriptions of such works are always chilly and disapproving; like that of the play *The Bad Samaritan*. 'It was a sardonic comedy, with a good basic idea, but it had a messy third act, and indeed needed not only re-writing but entirely re-shaping. Ironically enough, this was the only play I have ever written in the manner of the text-books, first building

[1] *Time and the Conways*, Act II. Pp. 176-7 in Vol. I of *The Plays of J. B. Priestley.*

up a detailed synopsis, then clothing each scene with dialogue. The result was that my real imagination never got to work anywhere; it was all done with the surface of the mind, like a film script; so craftily and coldly put together that nowhere was there any life in it.'[1] When he describes the writing of the other plays, though, the ones that not only turn out better but *feel* better while they are pouring out of the typewriter, he becomes almost metaphysical in his reflections on the nature of the creative energy which infuses them—in *Rain upon Godshill*, his description of that rapid second act leads him to Jungian wonderings about the possibility of artists, who are particularly deeply immersed in some piece of a creative work, being sometimes able, 'without being then aware of it, to "tap" a reservoir of creative energy and skill, which reservoir is really the source of all so-called inspiration.'[2]

There was one other kind of strength which made a difference to the quality of the overall conception of *Time and the Conways*. The play was produced, remember, at the end of 1937, when the shadows were beginning to creep again over Europe, even though they had not yet quite blotted out the sun. To people who —like Priestley—were beginning to feel dark and dreadful forebodings of approaching disaster, the contrast between the young Conways and their later selves had much in common with the contrast between the hopeful years after World War One and the ominous disillusioning years now, twenty years later, lying under what was beginning to look like the threat of World War Two. And an earlier contrast than this was burned more deeply into Priestley's own unconscious mind than anything else that had happened to the society in which he lived; the old loss, the vanishing of his early golden world, trampled for ever into the mud of the First World War. With that dark memory always lurking behind his conscious thoughts, and the world in which he now lived proving every day its failure to produce anything to take the place of the lost world, it was small wonder that he gave

[1] *Rain upon Godshill*, p. 31.
[2] *Ibid.*, p. 45.

Time and the Conways an overall atmosphere that was, some said, 'too pessimistic'—and equally small wonder that he was able to give it genuine quality as a work of art. It is not as good of its kind as *Bright Day*, but the two share a particular poignancy which gives them their strength.

*   *   *

From a purely practical point of view, Priestley had need of speed in his writing; he was now existing, in this decade of the theatre, in a more manic whirl of work than ever. In the autumn of 1937 *I Have Been Here Before* was running at the Royalty Theatre, and *Time and the Conways* at the Duchess—the last of the five plays which Priestley and English Plays Limited presented there in association with J. P. Mitchelhill, who was about to sell the theatre. At the same time he was working on a try-out production, at the Bradford Civic Theatre, of yet another play, *People at Sea*, which had been bought by a Shaftesbury Avenue management and was shortly due to join the successful plethora of Priestley plays in the West End. He was also writing a series of articles for a Sunday paper and preparing for a breakneck lecture tour of the United States—his wife and children having already sailed for another winter's visit to the South-West. He made some changes in *People at Sea*, and took a hand in the casting, but by the time rehearsal began he was already in America and could take none of his usual active interest in the making of the production; so it was not altogether surprising that this third play of the year, which had been hastily written in the first place, met a fairly rapid end. As he escaped aboard the *Queen Mary* Priestley swore to himself that he would never again plunge into such a maelstrom of work: 'Nothing less than the certain salvation of the human race would justify such an existence, and until I am called upon to save my species I do not propose to work like that again.'[1] But he still had to deliver twenty lectures in four weeks, travelling thousands of miles in American trains; to make arrangements for

[1] *Ibid.*, p. 54.

the New York production of *Time and the Conways* (which promised well but turned out to be a failure); and to experience a number of those assorted side effects of literary celebrity which ranged, this time, from delivering a lecture at Columbia University to finding himself sitting in Radio City discussing the fourth dimension with Rudy Vallee on the *Royal Gelatine Hour*.

His little hut was still waiting in Arizona, and in it he wrote the better part of a play he had been brooding about during his lecture tour, *Johnson over Jordan*. This did not slacken his life-and-work tempo for long. After a gleeful sightseeing car journey through Arizona and Nevada with his wife and three friends, he sat down in his hut and in the space of three happy weeks wrote a novel called *The Doomsday Men*, which employed all five of them as characters, under various suitable disguises, and told a story of three mad brothers who wanted to destroy the world. Then, when he was back in London in the spring of 1938, he accepted an invitation to be one of six writers contributing new plays to be produced at the Malvern Festival—he knew that he had no new play written, and that rehearsals were to begin within a month, but there was an idea that had come to him in Arizona. . . .

The idea was for *Music at Night*, an experimental piece about the moods and thoughts of a group of people listening to the first performance of a piece of music; taking each of them in turn into gradually deepening levels of his own consciousness and eventually merging them into a kind of subconscious dream in which they seem to be all partakers of one great world mind. It was a Jungian idea comparable to the way in which he had begun to think of the process of artistic creation, but in the event it did not work. In trying to write so ambitious a play so quickly, Priestley had offered Time a challenge, and Time threw it straight back at him.

> . . . It was very hard work, and I had to do it against time, with one eye on the calendar. It had to be cast long before it was finished, and though the cast, with a few exceptions, was reasonably good, I could not help feeling uncomfortable. I fairly sweated at the piece, and once weakly telephoned Ayliff that it

could not be done in time. He was so alarmed, for now the Festival had been announced, that I promised to have another try, and after a day or two's rest I grappled with the tortuous thing again. It was like wrestling eight hours a day with a gigantic eel. In the final scene, where I wanted to suggest the deepest level of consciousness, I used verse that the characters had to chant, sometimes singly, sometimes in chorus, and I soon discovered that after years of prose my verse, which did not pretend to be poetry but only heightened dramatic speech, was wretched stuff. I chopped and hacked and changed it about, with the production almost waiting round the corner, but it was still wretched stuff, and when finally the actors spoke it, which they did very badly, it remained wretched stuff. This whole enterprise of writing a difficult experimental play, with the minimum amount of time for reflection and revision, was a desperate business.[1]

This was the wrong kind of speed, something imposed on him by an external deadline rather than the force from inside of a work of the imagination kicking away in its determination to be born. But before *Music at Night* was in its second rehearsal Priestley was back in the kind of haste that was his more natural habitat: writing, 'very happily and at a furious speed', the farcical comedy *When We Are Married*. This cheerful piece, the story of three solidly respectable Yorkshire couples who discover on the day of their joint silver wedding that they have never been legally married, was a chance to let out all the Northern drollery that had warmed his youth, and he enjoyed it hugely. 'Often I laughed while I was writing, not because I thought I was being very witty, but because memories of favourite words of that period, such as "flabbergasted", came back to me, and it was such fun introducing them all into the text.'[2] The audiences had fun too when the play opened later at the St. Martin's; so did the Press when Priestley gave his twelve emergency performances in it as the drunken photographer Henry Ormonroyd; and the merry-go-round of his busy theatre life went on.

Michael MacOwan and Thane Parker, who had been working

[1] *Ibid.*, p. 182.
[2] *Ibid.*, p. 184.

together for some time at the Westminster Theatre, suggested that Priestley should help them to finance and direct a semi-permanent company there in a season of revivals; the playwright Ronald Jeans joined them; and together the four founded the London Mask Theatre. 'We put on some very good stuff there for fourpence,' says Priestley now in affectionate reminiscence; and it was truly a labour of love, since the company was set up on a non-profit-making basis in order to avoid entertainment tax and keep ticket prices low. Thus although Jeans and Priestley could get their money back (or for that matter lose it), they would not be able to make any. The company's first effort was a modern-dress production of *Troilus and Cressida*, which had as side-effect one of Priestley's brief rumbles of discontent about newspaper criticism when he complained that 'one of our senior dramatic critics' had wasted half the space of his review of the piece in grumbling about the name the quartet had given their company. ('It is as if you had given a present to somebody and there came back instead of thanks a long complaint about the brown paper in which it had been wrapped.')[1]

The autumn of 1938, that uneasy autumn of the Munich crisis, was full of rehearsals. There is not a great deal that an author can do to express dissatisfaction with his country's policies, other than write about them, and Priestley had done that, being almost as prolific a journalist as dramatist in these years. So having done it, he tried not to look at the darkening skies and deliberately pushed still further into 'the tiny crisis-ridden exciting world of the Theatre' while it was still there to provide its tiny crises. He had a hand in the rehearsals of *Troilus and Cressida* at the Westminster; more than a hand in the rehearsals of *When We Are Married*, which needed the usual hard work on adjustments in timing and dialogue before its imminent three-week try-out in Manchester and its London opening in October. And he worked too on another production which was already playing in Manchester: a new *I Have Been Here Before*, which was about to depart with an improved production and cast for New York. Inside the playhouse,

[1] *Ibid.*, p. 186.

Priestley's spirits were high, as he watched Wilfred Lawson giving 'a performance to make your hair stand on end' in his original part of Ormund, the Everyman; but outside, the sky grew darker yet. 'As soon as my Yorkshire tragedians moved out of Manchester, on their way to New York, my Yorkshire comedians moved in; and now as Basil Dean and I watched the play in the Opera House every night we could hear the news-boys crying outside.'[1]

The news-boys went on crying. Priestley went on working on *When We Are Married* during its try-out, and did his bit of acting in it when it had opened in London. All this time he had been writing and polishing *Johnson Over Jordan*, the most ambitious and experimental thing he had ever done, with its key part written for Ralph Richardson, and at the beginning of 1939, when Richardson had finished work on a film, the work of bringing this largest of all J. B. Priestley projects into the theatre began.

Johnson Over Jordan is a morality play—and in a way also the most advanced of all Priestley's so-called Time plays, since it de-thrones Time altogether and examines the life of Robert Johnson, businessman, Englishman, Everyman, through the fragmented fantasy of an after-life dream. Basil Dean was the right producer for it, since technically it was an immense undertaking. It made great use of music, specially and very effectively written by Benjamin Britten, and this demanded a sizeable orchestra; the more stylized and fantastic of its sequences involved dancers; in one act most of the cast wore huge hideous masks with movable mouths; there were constant changes of costume and scenery; and the lighting plot alone must have been a document as com-plicated as the score of a Mahler symphony. But for all the com-plexity, Priestley had not over-reached himself; he had been steeped in the world of the working theatre for so long now that he had a highly professional knowledge of everything that can or cannot be effectively shown on a stage—and, more important, precisely how to show it.

[1] *Ibid.*, p. 191.

'*After some music, which begins fiercely and frighteningly and then sinks into a funeral melancholy, we find ourselves looking at the hall of* ROBERT JOHNSON'*s house, somewhere in one of the pleasanter outer suburbs.*'[1] It is the day of Johnson's funeral. Ushered by a hovering Undertaker's Man, the Johnson family appear briefly in deep mourning, and the funeral service then begins in the next room. You can hear the Clergyman's voice through the door: '*I am the resurrection and the Life, saith the Lord; he that believeth in me, though he were dead, yet shall he live; and whosoever liveth and believeth in me shall never die. . . .*' Two mourners arrive late, and reminisce about Johnson; we learn that he was only fifty-one years old, carried off suddenly by pneumonia: a careful, steady fellow who always understood his responsibilities, and who was happily married, with a son and daughter, all comfortable, all nicely settled. 'No sense in it, no sense in it at all . . .' Then they go outside to wait, rather than be caught hovering:

> *. . . and now the door opens, not because the service is over but because* RICHARD *is there, opening it, ready to sneak away himself but also to give his sister* FREDA, *who is taking it very hard in there, a chance to slip out and recover. We do not see her, however, but only catch this glimpse of* RICHARD, *for now the lights are beginning to fade and through the growing dusk comes the voice of the* CLERGYMAN *continuing the service:* 'For man walketh in a vain shadow, and disquieteth himself in vain; he heapeth up riches and riches, and cannot tell who shall gather them. . . .'
>
> *Now it is completely dark and the music has begun again, but it does not continue long in that strain but changes into something quicker and fiercer. Obviously the real Johnson is not lying in that oak box which the* UNDERTAKER'S MAN *is now having conveyed to the waiting hearse. What is happening to the real Johnson? Just as we are wondering this, we see him. That is all we see—*JOHNSON'*s face strongly illuminated against a background of darkness. He is talking away in an odd confused manner, like a man in a delirium.*

Johnson talks: about the hospital he is in, about what will become of his wife if anything should happen to him; perhaps, he

[1] *Johnson Over Jordan*, Act I. P. 273 of Vol. I of *The Plays of J. B. Priestley*.

muses, he should write a letter to his insurance company, just in case. He imagines himself in his office and calls for his secretary; at once he is surrounded by four secretaries, 'blank-faced girls all wearing tortoiseshell glasses and dressed alike', carrying notebooks from which comes the light that illuminates their faces. He stammers out the beginning of his letter; he cancels it; they disappear. He babbles again to himself; a letter won't do, he must go and see the insurance company himself; 'May have a little difficulty . . . businessman myself, so quite understand . . . But I must have my money. . . .'

> *As soon as he has said this, the music bursts into a fast, clattering, nattering, nervy strain, and we see that* JOHNSON *is now surrounded by a number of clerks and secretaries, male and female, who are all busy exchanging documents, making notes, and so on, making very quick movements in a stylized fashion. Moreover, they are lit from below, and it is not easy to see them properly and they throw big confusing shadows. The total effect is irritating and then exhausting, as if we had been given a whole modern businessman's day within one minute. And now through the clatter comes a loud, harsh, impersonal voice from a loud-speaker, bellowing:* 'The time is four-twenty-five—four-twenty-five. All forms K.R.T. three-seven-nine to be returned to Room Eighty-Two by four-thirty-five. All forms K.R.T. three-seven-nine to be returned to Room Eighty-Two by four-thirty-five. The time is now four-twenty-six.' *And now the ballet of clerks hurries off.* JOHNSON *tries to stop the last of them but is not successful.*
>
> *The whole scene is now illuminated by a hard white light, almost dazzling. It is quite a big and high room, with enormous silvery swing doors at each side, and in the middle, the only furniture it has, a tremendous silvery desk raised on a dais, with a very big swivel chair at each side and one at the back. In front is a kind of settee made of the same silvery material. It all looks very modern, efficient and opulent, and quite inhuman. Seated in the big chairs at each side of the desk are two old men, worried old men with white hair, tinted spectacles, morning coats, and the look of dyspeptic millionaires. They have forms and enormous ledger-like volumes in front of them, and they turn the pages of these volumes in a quick desperate sort of fashion. . . .*

They are adding and subtracting and telling tall tales of money;

they are filling in impossible forms against impossible deadlines
(perhaps Priestley was remembering the writing of *Music At
Night*); they are men of the world of money in their own busy
little hell. A clerk brings Johnson too a form to fill in. The disturbing ballet of clerks and secretaries rushes back in, and then
out, and is replaced by two tall bald men in spectacles and frock
coats, First Examiner and Second Examiner, who put Johnson
through a cross-examination made up of all the contradictory
advice and admonitions and inquisitions that ever were. His wife
appears, a changed wife, shrill and complaining and poorly-
dressed, accusing him of having neglected every duty to her, to
his children, to his work. 'All application forms to be completed
within the next fifteen minutes,' booms the Voice from the loud-
speaker, 'only fifteen minutes more.' The irritating ballet again
comes and goes; then the white light is back, and with it Johnson's old schoolmaster, reproachful, and then a succession of
others in small scenes: newsboys prophesying inflated disaster;
Johnson's old employer reprimanding him as a young clerk; his
mother-in-law coldly considering his inadequacies as a prospec-
tive husband; a convict who is a friend who did wrong; a police-
man warningly listing every small piece of deceit Johnson has
ever committed; the Examiners again, contemptuous; and then
finally Death, offering him his money—or not Death, but a
figure wearing a terrifying death's head, behind which is the
face not of terror but wisdom and calm. Before he turned round
to show his face, the Figure had seemed to be a workman, in
that great mad office, stuffing into a furnace all the paper and
money handled there each day. Johnson has his money from him,
having now forgotten what it was for, and as he takes it he slides
into another mood; proud, swaggering, brash.

> *While he is stuffing the last of the notes into his pockets, what seemed
> before the small opening down into a furnace is now revealed as a
> decorated and brightly-illuminated corridor, and along this corridor
> comes the sound of a dance band.*

JOHNSON: Listen! What's that music? Sounds good to me.

THE FIGURE: Oh—that! It's the night club—the *Jungle Hot Spot*.
Bright lights. Hot Jazz. Dinners, suppers, drinks, beautiful girls.
JOHNSON: They'll take this money there, eh?
THE FIGURE: They'll be delighted to take it.
JOHNSON: That's the place for me, then. Let's have some fun
while we're alive, I say; we're a long time dead. What do you
say?
THE FIGURE: (*rather sadly*): I say what I've always said, Robert,
that there isn't much harm in you, but nevertheless you're rather
a fool. . . .

'*Let us eat and drink, for tomorrow we die.*' The Clergyman's voice,
with a phrase here and there from the funeral service, lightly
frames the rest of the play, flickering in this same way through
Johnson's life—and at the same time, as in a dream, through
every kind of mood and passion, good or evil, felt not only by
Johnson but by any man. On it goes, through the disturbing
fantasy of the second act in the sinister night-club; through the
glowing warmth of the third act in a place that is called the Inn
at the End of the World. Here Johnson meets again all those who
have brought him—or have been brought by him—happiness;
something which Priestley accomplishes with triumphant success
because his feeling for things magical prevents him from ever
slipping into sentimentality, and because his own feeling for
people as individuals has an effect far more moving than, say,
Maeterlinck's thin and idealized personifications. This third act
of *Johnson Over Jordan* can stand against any other parallel kind of
fantasy-morality play; all Priestley's feeling for the theatre focuses
there to convey those most difficult of all emotions, genuine delight and warmth and a kind of innocence, which no technical
tricks on their own can create. It does not take any great theatrical
imagination to be able to read this last act and realize, without
ever having seen it produced on the stage, that this is the stuff of
which moments of real enchantment in the theatre are made.
Somehow the words and the music and the lighting manage to
coalesce and work their magic even in cold print, and so does a
certain strange window in the strange Inn, through which those

who care to look can see any number of places, people, things
that have been important to them—through which Johnson sees
a farm where he stayed as a boy, the lake where he and his wife
spent their first days together, the garden of the house in which
they lived. He thinks he catches a glimpse through it of the stage-
coach of the Pickwick Club driving down the road with Tony
Weller up on the box (a glimpse that Priestley had once put into
an essay, and that has perhaps been haunting his dreams all his
life). He does most certainly see Don Quixote, armour, jutting
beard, long lined fantastic face and all, who not only appears in
the bright moonlight suddenly streaming through the window,
but steps forward into the room—with, shortly, something to say
which has the whole of *Johnson Over Jordan* in it and perhaps also
a great deal more of Priestley himself than ever turned up in the
less fantastic Time plays.

> Your great poet once said that the best of our kind are but
> shadows, though I think he knew that your kind too—who
> appear so solid to yourselves for a little time—are also shadows.
> And perhaps you too take life from the mind that beholds you
> and your little tale, so that you live as we must do, in another
> and greater being's imagination, memory and affection.[1]

It is the only explicit hint that Priestley offers concerning the kind
of dimension that Johnson is existing in now; and from it the
play mounts, through that glowing last act, to a dream experience
of Johnson's first meeting with his wife at a dance. Suddenly the
orchestra is playing the *Valse Bleu*, and all the characters of the
play, all the characters of Johnson's life, are waltzing there, filling
the stage—until Johnson turns happily to sweep his wife into the
dance, and she is not there. The music stops, the dancers are still;
the Clergyman's voice comes from somewhere far off: '. . . *Lettest
thou thy servant depart in peace according to thy word* . . .' The music
becomes sombre; the Figure, tall and hooded, appears in a golden
shaft of light on the staircase, and all else is in shadow except for a
steely light playing on Johnson's face. 'Robert Johnson,' says the

[1] *Johnson Over Jordan*, Act III, p. 322.

Figure, 'it is time for you to go.' And this is the real moment of transition for Johnson. He will not speak to his wife again, but now there is no need; all is well; he has only a debt to pay in the Inn at the End of the World.

JOHNSON: You said it would cost me nothing.

THE FIGURE: I said no money was necessary.

JOHNSON: Then how can I pay you?

THE FIGURE (*gravely*): With thanks. And then it is good-bye, Robert.

All the people in the crowd, now in deep shadow, begin to drift away, and as they go we just catch their low confused voices saying: 'Good-bye, Robert', and 'Good-bye, Johnson', and 'Good-bye, Good-bye'. And then JOHNSON *is left, a solitary figure in this steely shaft of light, while* THE FIGURE, *shining and golden, waits above on the stairs.*

JOHNSON (*with deep emotion*): I have been a foolish, greedy and ignorant man;

Yet I have had my time beneath the sun and stars; I have known the returning strength and sweetness of the seasons,

Blossom on the branch and the ripening of fruit,

The deep rest of the grass, the salt of the sea. The frozen ecstasy of mountains.

The earth is nobler than the world we have built upon it;

The earth is long-suffering, solid, fruitful;

The world still shifting, dark, half-evil.

But what have I done that I should have a better world,

Even though there is in me something that will not rest

Until it sees Paradise . . . ?

(*With very great emotion*)

Farewell, all good things!

You will not remember me,

But I shall remember you. . . .

THE FIGURE (*gravely*): Robert Johnson, it is time now.

(*And here is the* PORTER, *standing just behind* JOHNSON *with his hat and overcoat and bag.*)

PORTER: Your things, sir. (*Helps him on with his coat*).

JOHNSON (*now with his overcoat on, holding his hat and bag, with an echo of childish accents*): For Thine is the kingdom, the power and the glory . . . and God bless Jill and Freda and Richard . . . and

all my friends—and—and—everybody . . . for ever and ever . . .
Amen. . . .

He puts on his hat and is now ready to go. He looks up at THE
FIGURE, *doubtfully.*

JOHNSON (*hesitantly*): Is it—a long way?

THE FIGURE (*suddenly smiling like an angel*): I don't know, Robert.

JOHNSON (*awkwardly*): No . . . well . . . good-bye. . . .

*A majestic theme has been announced, first only by the woodwind.
As* JOHNSON *still stands there, hesitating, the light on* THE FIGURE
fades, and then the whole staircase disappears, leaving JOHNSON *alone.
He looks very small, forlorn, for now the whole stage has been opened
up to its maximum size, and there is nothing there but* JOHNSON. *The
music marches on, with more and more instruments coming in.* JOHNSON
*looks about him, shivering a little, and turning up the collar of his coat.
And now there is a rapidly growing intense blue light; the high curtains
have gone at the back, where it is bluer and bluer; until at last we see
the glitter of stars in space, and against them the curve of the world's
rim. As the brass blares our triumphantly and the drums roll and the
cymbals clash,* JOHNSON, *wearing his bowler hat and carrying his bag,
slowly turns and walks towards that blue space and the shining constella-
tions, and the curtain comes down and the play is done.*[1]

Johnson Over Jordan was produced at the New Theatre in
February 1939, then not long afterwards was transferred to the
Saville Theatre. But while it cost as much to run as a big musical,
it had not the same attraction—that is for the stalls public, though
all the cheaper seats were filled at every performance. There were
no Arts Council subsidies then, and the play finally closed because
it had lost too much money. Out of that eternally mysterious
layer of the English population which goes to the theatre, some
people were so enraptured by the play that they went to see it over
and over again (one actress went to fourteen performances), but
most of the rich did not go at all.

Priestley has said—like Harold Hobson, J. C. Trewin and a
number of other critics—that the ending of the play, when Johnson turns to depart into the star-glinting, blue-dark depths of the
universe, provided one of the most moving moments he has

[1] *Ibid.,* pp. 335-6.

ever known in the theatre. (He, understandably, said this of the last performance on the last night: '. . . the last farewell, the last glimpse of Johnson against that starry sky, the last sound of Britten's triumphant crescendo—never, never again—and I might have been staring into a grave.')[1] Apart from that, he has scarcely mentioned the play since. At the time, the disappointment must have been appalling, even for a writer with so many other irons glowing cheerfully away in the fire. Almost everything he knew of dramatic technique had gone into this play, and a great many of the things which, at the age of forty-five, he felt about the point and meaning of life. His sense of the theatre was—and is—so intense that as a dramatist he is almost ridiculously lacking in illusion: 'When you've done a play,' he said once, 'that's that. Once it's done, it's gone.' Here was a play which he had done his utmost to make into a stirring dramatic experience and the experience had lasted for only a few weeks, and now it was gone. No wonder he felt he was staring into a grave.

Perhaps *Johnson* was produced at the wrong time, in that uneasy spring of 1939. Priestley felt then that this was a good and suitable time, that a moving play on a serious theme could provide people with a release from months of emergency and stress; but he was probably nearer the truth in his later observation, written in wry hindsight in *Rain upon Godshill*, that 'the typical modern English reaction to any deep emotional stress is to pretend that it does not exist'.[2] The English theatre of 1939, partly by accident and partly by demand, tended to support this remark. There were not many major contemporary writers afloat; James Bridie was as prolific as Priestley, and had been throughout the decade, but O'Casey was now writing few plays, and Shaw was over eighty. Though John Martin Harvey was acting his last Oedipus at Covent Garden, and John Gielgud and Edith Evans orchestrating a revival of *The Importance of Being Earnest* at the Globe, the major names on the list of available entertainments were, though good and even great of their kind, not exactly indicative of a

[1] *Margin Released*, p. 210.
[2] *Rain upon Godshill*, p. 205.

public taste for serious themes. The theatre-going public which was staying away from *Johnson Over Jordan* was finding its release with Leslie Henson, Robertson Hare, Alfred Drayton, George Robey, Bea Lillie, Cicely Courtneidge, Hermiones Baddeley and Gingold, Gracie Fields, Max Miller, Tommy Trinder and Will Fyffe. It was a typical Priestley irony that these were all representatives of the kind of entertainment he had often celebrated, and is celebrating still today.

Whenever critics have written about *Johnson Over Jordan* since then, they have complained of the weakness of its central figure, the lack of real challenge offered him by the dream-rehearsal of his life, and most of all of derivative technique. The words 'German expressionism' pop up every time. Certainly Robert Johnson is not a striking hero; he is ordinary; he was intended to be ordinary. Perhaps he is too passive in his reactions, too bewildered by the whirl of incident and sensation around him; but then, given that he is ordinary, simple survival of all these is in itself not an unremarkable accomplishment. As for 'expressionism', it is a word which tends to be applied with sweeping vagueness to any pre-war play which is not strictly naturalistic. Some of the devices Priestley used in *Johnson Over Jordan* are certainly out of the expressionists' anti-realist box: the arrival of this or that obviously symbolic figure; the grotesque masks; the stage furnished with spotlights rather than furniture. But at the same time there is a major difference between Priestley's play and any of those clumped together beneath the expressionist label. Despite the sprinkling of character types, and the anti-bureaucracy propaganda, *Johnson Over Jordan* makes use primarily of the people in Johnson's life, and of his relationships with them. And the characters of the expressionist plays are not people; they are symbols, emotions, attributes, ideals, sins, as inhuman as the stark personifications of Lust and Avarice and Pride in the early morality plays, to which all such fantasies owe their birth. Priestley was not intellectually capable of writing a performable play about such abstracts, and he didn't want to; so he didn't. Much of the commentary which has been written about *Johnson Over Jordan* is based on the assumption that this is what he was trying to do, that this was what he shouldn't have been trying to do, and that this is what he failed in doing. It is a hard judgement for a play designed as an emotional experience, not so much because it is inaccurate as because it is totally misconceived.

The failure of a play never troubled Priestley for long—and not only because he nearly always had another one about to come to the boil. He is almost unique among dramatists who have been equally eminent in other literary fields (though admittedly there are not many of them) in that he has always been, during his periods of most concentrated play-writing, a genuine man of the theatre. He became a dramatist not as an author seeking a new kind of literary outlet, but as a man fascinated by the theatre and the things that could be done with the theatre. We are back again at the boy in the gallery, perhaps; the boy watching those larger-than-life actors sauntering up to the stage door. When Priestley talks about his writings today, he tends to refer to his novels more often than his plays; not because he feels that he has done better work as a novelist than as a dramatist (though perhaps he does, and perhaps he has), but because he retains this intensely professional vision of the theatre as a medium for which one is creating first of all not a literary work but an experience.

The audience, for him, was not a collection of individuals who might later go home and buy his play in order to see how it was done; the audience was rather a single entity, a composite mind capable of feeling only one mood at a time. And it was the idea of manipulating the reactions of this one mind which particularly fascinated him—as it was his instinctive ability to do it which enabled him so often to write a theatrically effective play at a great speed. The basic reason why he felt it necessary to participate in the direction of his plays—sometimes indeed doing the entire job himself—was a simple matter not of egotism but of professional common sense; since he wrote with an actor's approach to the theatre and to audiences, his plays were not so much scripts as records of a performance first played in his head. And since he had thus, as it were, directed the first performance, he wanted to make sure that the subsequent performances, in which other people would be playing all the parts, got things right. You can see this reflected in his stage directions, which are almost as detailed as Shaw's: liberally sprinkled with adverbs (*grimly, bitterly, hastily, miserably, thoughtfully, darkly*—all from one random page of *When We Are Married*), and with careful pieces of instruction here and there which are more than directions of action or 'business': '*There must now work up a definite suggestion of a very intimate group being merry together. The atmosphere is more important than the speeches. Everybody must relax.*'[1]

His attitude to the whole world of the theatre reflected it too. He has never had any patience with what he refers to gruffly as 'the glamour thing': the gloss and the gossip and the first night parties, *Darling, I loved it . . . Darling, you were marvellous. . . .* On his own opening nights in the 'thirties he used to dodge about uneasily between the back of the house and the street: never quite reaching Sir William Gilbert's restless habit of disappearing for a long walk between the overture and the final curtain, but never able to stand preening himself in public during the intervals, among the compliments that would come showering whether the complimenters meant a word of them or not. In this respect he was certainly more of a Gilbert than a Sullivan, just as Arnold Bennett had been more of a Sullivan than a Gilbert. The alternately fluffy and ego-supporting side of the theatre was not for him; he did not need it, in the way that many actors and actresses inevitably do, since he knew that his real work was done in the lonely study, where the only audience was inside his head and totally independent of public applause. In any case, he had a pretty fair idea of his own worth, and was by nature—perhaps it was the Yorkshireman coming out—more inclined to believe his own judgement than that of anyone else. He used to phrase it, then, a little more belligerently than he does today; the same words of self-portrait

---

[1] *Music at Night*, Act III. P. 390 of Vol. I of *The Plays of J. B. Priestley*.

come at the end of both *Midnight on the Desert* and *Rain upon Godshill*. 'A popular author, who considers himself not quite as good as most of his readers think he is, but a damned sight better than the remainder imagine.' The touch of mischief in that 'not *quite*' is pure Priestley, the same quality which can make him break off in the middle of some account of a past success and observe with a grin: 'That's what my children used to call "the braggies".' His sense of humour disqualifies him from being vain. It has not always saved him from appearing so. The bitterest attack or loftiest disdain can pass by and leave him unruffled, but make some point about his work which he feels is inaccurate, in an otherwise favourable review, and up will come the objection. But these occasional disputations with critics have never been as frequent or heated as Priestley's image in the Press once upon a time made them out to be, and they were prompted always by professional pride rather than self-love. The genuinely vain man —who would certainly not have disliked 'the glamour thing'— enjoys flattery; he may take care not to be seen actually purring, but his enjoyment is clearly visible beneath the mild protestation and the deprecating smile. You will not see Priestley using these. Like any other practitioner of the arts, he likes praise—we are all vain up to a point, or we should never dare to write or paint or compose at all—but face him with a comment that smacks even a little of flattery, and the jutting eyebrows will twitch and all the lines of the face droop downward an extra half-inch, and there will be nothing there except a disdainful silence retreating behind a cloud of smoke. He acquired a certain reputation for grumpiness during his theatre-focused years, and most of it came from the sequence of such reactions which repeated exposure to fulsome camp-followers inevitably brought out. The rest came from a tendency to brusqueness which was fairly predictable in a man so busy with so many things at once. 'You know,' said Ralph Richardson to him once in mild reproof, 'you really shouldn't be so impatient with fellows who are only doing their job.' And though Priestley may not have followed the advice, he remembered it.

'In the 'thirties, I was, I suppose, very quick and impatient. I may not look it, but I'm very quick even in trivial things like changing one's clothes and so on. And with people too. I never meant to be unpleasant, but I tended to brush away people who I knew would be wasting my time. England is full of very nice chaps who are nice to their wives and so on, but who really aren't very *good* at whatever they're doing. A great deal of the reputation I got for being rude came from that. . . .

'And then—when you're living with success, what do you do? You can handle it like X and love every minute of it, or you can pretend not to enjoy it at all—not that there isn't as much affectation in that as in being the successful ever-smiling man. I remember Rupert Hart-Davis saying to me once at a Foyles luncheon: "Jack, you always look so miserable when you think somebody's going to praise you." And I suppose he was right. I'm always so reluctant to be one of those smiling enjoyers of it all. After all, I do come from the West Riding. . . .

'There was one other thing about the 'thirties. I called on Hugh Walpole during the time of the phoney war, when I was doing a tour of England for the *News Chronicle*, and he said later that I was awful then, gloomy and impossible, but that as soon as the war began I became completely happy. It was true, too. We were all like that. Things were only all right once we knew what was *happening*.'

Faster and faster Priestley had whirled through Wonderland, with the theatre as his White Queen, and the speed of the ride slackened only when it became very clear to him and to everyone exactly what was happening in the world. Priestley published the autobiographical *Rain upon Godshill*, using that part of it which was not concerned with the theatre for a discontented examination of his country; then he wrote the novel *Let the People Sing*, commissioned by the BBC to be read in weekly instalments over the air. On the day he went to Broadcasting House to read the first instalment, war was declared.

The lights went out in London. The theatres closed, the audiences sat at home, listening to the shortened evening programmes of the BBC. Fat silver barrage balloons rose into a sky that was

suddenly filled now, at night, with glittering stars that Londoners
had not noticed for centuries. Evenings in the West End were
silent until one night halfway through September, when the
Windmill—of course—reopened. Gradually then the other
theatres followed suit, their performances now beginning an hour
or two earlier than before; Priestley and his colleagues of the
London Mask Theatre at the Westminster were among the first.
('In that September,' he says, 'it used to take me half the night to
find the Westminster—you'd go into a restaurant in daylight and
it'd be pitch black-out when you came out.') They brought *Music
at Night* to London. The Crazy Gang was playing at the Palladium,
Lupino Lane lilting through *Me and My Girl* at the Victoria
Palace—and Drury Lane was the headquarters of the forces'
entertainment service, ENSA, which Basil Dean ran throughout
the war.

London's theatres became very special places during the war
years, providing not only entertainment for the beleaguered
citizens, and the servicemen briefly home on leave, but a refresh-
ment, an escape, a strengthening, a reminder of worlds that had
begun to seem no more than a distant dream. With only one gap,
the theatres remained open throughout the war—the gap being
the thunderous nightmare of the first month of the Blitz, in the
autumn of 1940, when the stars in the sky over London were
again dimmed by light, but this time by the light of flames. Only
one play remained open—for matinées only—during that month,
and it was one of London's wartime symbols: Robert Atkins'
production of *All's Well That Ends Well*.

It was hardly a time for serious advances in drama; everyone, including the dramatists, was too much preoccupied with
other things. Nobody should be surprised to learn that the four
most successful plays of the war, each of them running for more
than 1,000 performances, were Coward's *Blithe Spirit*, Rattigan's
While the Sun Shines, the American Joseph Kesselring's *Arsenic
and Old Lace*, and Esther McCracken's *Quiet Weekend*. Priestley,
of course, was much occupied with broadcasting. But concentration on one medium did not keep him from others, in time of

war any more than it had done in time of peace, and he and James Bridie continued their joint reign as the best contemporary practising British dramatists. The plays which he wrote during the war were a mixed bag; among them *Goodnight Children*, a 1942 satire about broadcasting which was, though in places extremely funny, a failure (this was not really the time to take the mickey out of the BBC), and *They Came to a City*, which ran for a long time at the Globe after a try-out in Bradford. There was in this latter play a lot of Priestley's fiercely optimistic idealism about the kind of world that we could, if we really tried and really cared enough, build up out of the ruins when the war was done: the same belief that sent him to work so feverishly for the Labour cause in 1945 (and that has taken rather a battering since). It was this idealism too which he had tried to introduce into his BBC *Postscripts* during their second period, and which brought them into disfavour with officialdom and eventually into silence. But in the theatre no one felt the need of suppressing his optimism, since it came nowhere near the borders of politics: *They Came to a City* is a play about nine men and women from different levels of British society who find themselves outside the walls of a kind of Utopia; about their reaction to it, and thus about their various capacities for building a better society in the world to which they return. The characters, like those in *Johnson Over Jordan*, represent fairly familiar types but are well enough rounded to impress an audience as real people rather than symbols; and the City, the magical Utopian dream, is never seen and never objectively described. So this time, nobody shouted 'Expressionism', and the play found a warm response in a city which had for some time survived only on determination and dreams.

Two other minor plays were written for specific purposes: *Desert Highway* examines the various ways in which the crew of a stranded tank gradually face the prospect of death, and compares them (he was still experimenting) with a parallel group of Jews beleaguered by Assyrians in the same desert twenty-six centuries before. It was written for the Army Bureau of Current Affairs, to be performed in army camps, though it was also produced in London towards the end of the war. So was *How Are They At Home?*, a topical wartime comedy written for ENSA companies to take overseas: set in an English country house and full of reminders of rationing and billeting and Land Girls. Priestley remembers it now chiefly for the ominous buzzing of V.1 engines, and the even more ominous silences as the engines shut off before the bang, which punctuated many of the play's performances at the Apollo.

He roared into full speed again when the pressures of the war were released. In the first five years afterwards, the bleak years of an austere Britain recovering from the most Pyrrhic of all victories, he wrote five of his—so far, and by my count—nineteen major works: *An Inspector Calls, Bright Day, The Linden Tree, Delight* and *Festival at Farbridge*. Three of his plays were produced in 1946 alone (which was also the year of *Bright Day*) but *An Inspector Calls* was the most successful, the tidiest, the most thoughtful—and also perhaps the timeliest, in its examination of truth, conscience and human responsibility. Like most of Priestley's best plays it has a relatively simple plot: a plain-speaking but somewhat mysterious Inspector investigating the reasons for a girl's suicide calls on a prosperous and self-satisfied family during a party. The course of his questions, and the relationships they reveal, seem to show that each member of the family could have been at least partly responsible for the girl's despairing death. But when the Inspector has gone, a further discussion leaves them wondering whether the whole thing was genuine, suicide, investigation and all; and all but two of them gradually argue their way back out of guilt into their original complacency—until, just before the final curtain, the telephone rings and they learn that a girl has been taken to hospital after attempting suicide, and that an Inspector will shortly be visiting them to begin an investigation. . . . Like *Dangerous Corner*, Priestley's first play, with which it has some parallels in theme, force and deftness of construction (and, as usual, speed of writing), *An Inspector Calls* has had an astonishing history abroad, with frequent performances in almost every country of Europe. These two have also been among the most successful of his plays produced on Broadway, where many of the others proved either too experimental or too English to attract general American enthusiasm.

An Inspector Calls had, too, the rather startling distinction of being given its première not in London but in Moscow, where it played (in two theatres—both at once) to much acclaim while Priestley himself was visiting the USSR for the first time. He was given a three-month tour of the country in 1945, a remarkable distinction, then, for any Westerner: 'I went all over the place, and when I went back later they let me go even further.' The Russians fêted him in the laurel wreath, sit-at-the-feet-of-the-Maestro manner that senior men of the arts enjoy in almost every North European land except ours; his social conscience, his naturalism in the novel and his experimentalism in the theatre had all appealed to them for a long time, and his political attitudes were far enough to the Left not to offend their own. In Leningrad he was told that a Russian translation of his wartime novel *Black-Out in Gretley* had arrived there just before the siege began, and had been publicly read aloud as a way of helping the city through its long dreadful nightmare. So he had been widely published and widely read in the Soviet Union, and he still is today; discuss contemporary English literature with any student or interpreter or teacher you happen to encounter there, and J. B. Priestley is always one of the names they mention with most enthusiasm. (They tend to regard him as the English counterpart of Hemingway: a fact which he might or might not appreciate.) It has been fairly simple for them to deal with the numerous occasions on which he has attacked Communism; one simply fails to publish any work which contains such an attack, and pretends politely that it does not exist.

When it came home from Moscow, *An Inspector Calls* went into the repertory at the Old Vic, and after a couple of unsuccessful productions of other plays Priestley went on to write *The Linden Tree*. His place in the English theatre was solidly recognized by now: J. C. Trewin wrote a couple of years later, in 1950:

'If Bernard Shaw is the headmaster (of the modern theatre), we can call Priestley one of the senior prefects. The young novelist who joined Edward Knoblock twenty years ago in carving out a play from *The Good Companions* is now a veteran dramatist, prolific, vigorous, prickling with theories, desperately keen on the job, never scamping a scene or a line, and ready, at the drop of a hat, to be realist, allegorist, doctrinal playwright, or plain man from Yorkshire.'[1] Trewin added that *The Linden Tree* was 'the best domestic play of our time'.

It was not, however, the play that Priestley had originally begun to write under that title. Eight years earlier, before the war, he had written an intriguing little history of a play that never was: it belonged to the family's last visit to Arizona.

> I re-wrote parts of *Johnson Over Jordan*, and then began a play I had had in mind for some time, a play about a family called Linden. It was to be called, rather prettily, *The Linden Tree*. There was old Linden, an engineer with a touch of genius, who had built up a great firm of motor engineers. In the middle of the first act, which showed a directors' meeting, he returned unexpectedly from a long visit to the East, bringing with him a fantastic Oriental philosopher and a mysterious girl. The old man, who was now more interested in wisdom than in motor engines, threw several bombshells of remarks into the directors' meeting, and really set the play going. Then there were his two sons and their wives, well-to-do middle-aged people of a conventional type, or rather several conventional types. And then there were the young people, the third generation of Lindens, the bewildered or rebellious children of this age. I wrote a good long first act, beginning artfully with this meeting of the board and then bringing in the old man, who was a good ripe character, and his little entourage, and everything went merrily, with nothing wrong anywhere. I waded into the second act, did a very effective little scene between the old man and his elderly chief foreman, a Labour man of the old-fashioned type; discovered one of the middle-aged male characters coming to life admirably: dashed in a scene between the two middle-aged women, mother and aunt, and the girl; and

was working with quite remarkable ease, vigour and mastery when, right in the middle of this fine second act, I had to break off. Then it occurred to me to show what I had done to my wife, to whom I never take bits of work but only fair-sized slabs of it, two or three chapters of a book and at least a whole act of a play. She read this act and a half, which I had turned over to her calmly and confidently, and declared without any hesitation that it was not like me at all and might have been a play written by somebody else. I came out of my dream, and now took a good look at it myself. There was nothing really wrong with it; a sensible and fairly solid play was in the making there; but she was quite right; it belonged to some other man. So I put the manuscript on one side; and though I know it came home with me, now I do not know where it is and do not care. Perhaps one day I shall go to a theatre and discover that it is being played: *The Linden Tree* —with old Linden marching in to the directors' meeting, middle-aged sporting Linden running off with the mysterious girl with whom young Linden thought he was in love; the Linden girl making her appeal to her cousin, this same young Linden; and that fine quiet scene at the very end, when the wise old Linden talks to his grandchildren; and everybody will applaud this sound solid comedy of character and ideas, which will be praised by our senior critics because it will be written in an early Granville-Barker manner, a technique they can now understand, and nobody will applaud more enthusiastically than the man who once typed some of it in his Arizona shack. But who will the real author be?[1]

A curious tale. Though it does not fill one with a burning desire to rush off and recover the lost manuscript—and gives rather the impression that Priestley, favoured by a grateful Time, had been briefly plugged in to the working mind of some worthy but unsuccessful earlier dramatist—it casts an engaging light on the professional who, having found a good title, did not propose to waste it. For the real *Linden Tree*, written eight years after the passage quoted above, has not the least connection with its ghostly predecessor. It was written during the disastrous February of

[1] *Rain upon Godshill*, pp. 132–4.

1947, when Britain was so deep in snow that food rationing, coal shortages and power cuts were grimmer than they had ever been during the war; Priestley had to spend ten chilly days working, eating and sleeping in one small room in the house on the Isle of Wight, and he came out with his play, which begins on the sixty-fifth birthday of Robert Linden, professor of history at the University of Burmanley.

Trewin's description of *The Linden Tree* as a domestic play can be misleading. It is domestic in the sense that it takes place within the structure of a family, and deals with the relationships not only between individuals but between generations, but there is in its overall effect none of the womb-like cosiness that the adjective implies. Linden has in fact to some extent lost both the structure and the allegiance of his family by the end of the play. Having reached the official age of retirement, he is under pressure to leave his university; from his three elder children, from his wife, who is fed up with thirty-seven years of provincial making-do, and from his new young Vice-Chancellor, 'a high-pressure educationalist' who is a particularly efficient and determined new broom. But Linden does not choose to leave. He knows that as a teacher of history, of all subjects, he is not beginning a slow decline but is better now than he has ever been; and that though he represents an older world, he represents those aspects of it which have kept civilization alive for hundreds and thousands of years and which must at all costs be kept from being suppressed by chilly modernism now. Linden knows that he is not being asked to retire simply because of age. 'Really, it's because I'm a nuisance. I'm too free-and-easy. I don't admire the mass-production and conveyor-belt system of education. I say *No* when important personages expect to hear *Yes*. And I propose to go on being a nuisance. . . .'[1]

His only real ally is his youngest daughter Dinah, one of those gay self-contained children who would once have been called 'quaint', but whose undecayed enthusiasm and innocence make

---

[1] *The Linden Tree,* Act I, Scene II. P. 439 of Vol. I of *The Plays of J. B. Priestley.*

a brightness in a gloomy world; Priestley is good at inventing such sprites, without making them either insufferable or sentimental, and Dinah Linden is like a more fully developed portrait of the bubbling, doomed young Carol of *Time and the Conways*. The light of Dinah's youth and promise, still untouched by cold dreams of organized efficiency, is a touchstone for the theme of the play: 'The whole lot of you,' says Linden sharply to his family, 'except young Dinah, are now busy turning away from life, giving it up. The Lindens are leaving the mucky old high road. And somebody's got to stay.'[1] For the whole point of Robert Linden's life, and perhaps of J. B. Priestley's too, is to try to bring to the support of the enthusiastic idealism represented by the young—the only kind of fire and imagination that can build a better world—all the glow and wisdom that infused an older civilized world before it was destroyed for ever. Whether you are talking about the lost Edwardian world destroyed by the conflicts of twentieth-century Europe, or the greatness of a sequence of civilizations back through history that have been destroyed simply by the advance of Time, the fundamental idea is the same. Linden is given it to express when he breaks in on a bitter family argument about religion versus science, superstition versus reason—or as the comic char, Mrs. Cotton, puts it, 'Chapels versus Insecks'—by making them all stop short and listen for a moment to the sound of young Dinah practising on her 'cello upstairs.

> *The door is open behind him, and now we hear quite clearly, though at some distance, the 'cello playing the rich melancholy second subject of the First Movement of the Elgar Concerto. They are all very still. The music dies away. Short pause.*
> MARION (*quietly*): What is that?
> PROFESSOR: First Movement of the Elgar Concerto. I didn't know Dinah was doing the Elgar. She must have just started.
> MRS. COTTON (*softly*): It sounds a sad piece.
> PROFESSOR (*quietly*): Yes, it is. A kind of long farewell. An elderly man remembers his world before the war of 1914, some of it

[1] *Ibid.*, Act II, Scene I, p. 459.

years and years before perhaps—being a boy at Worcester—or Germany in the 'nineties—long days on the Malvern Hills—smiling Edwardian afternoons—Maclaren and Ranji batting at Lord's, then Richter or Nikisch at the Queen's Hall—all gone, gone, lost for ever—and so he distils his tenderness and regret, drop by drop, and seals the sweet melancholy in a Concerto for 'cello. And he goes, too, where all the old green sunny days and the twinkling nights went—gone, gone. But then what happens? Why, a little miracle. You heard it.

JEAN (*softly*): Dinah playing?

PROFESSOR: Why yes. Young Dinah Linden, all youth, all eagerness, saying hello and not farewell to anything, who knows and cares nothing about Bavaria in the 'nineties or the secure and golden Edwardian afternoons, here in Burmanley, this very afternoon, the moment we stop shouting at one another, unseals for us the precious distillation, uncovers the tenderness and regret, which are ours now as well as his, and our lives and Elgar's, Burmanley today and the Malvern Hills, in a lost sunlight, are all magically intertwined . . .

MRS. COTTON (*to the others, proudly*): When he likes, the Professor's a lovely talker.[1]

And the craftsman takes over, giving his audience a chance for an affectionate laugh to release the emotional tension of a solemn speech—and thus at the same time making the solemnity more valid, sealing it off too so that it will be remembered. Priestley wanted to give Robert Linden every chance. Throughout his life and his writings he has been explaining the views of the Priestley-Lindens, and pointing out that they do have a very good chance to help the world make something of itself, if we will let them. So, towards the end of the play, Professor Linden belligerently informs his old friend Lockhart, the University Secretary, that insult or no insult, wife or no wife, he is staying on in Burmanley, at the meagre Emeritus salary that is all the disdainful authorities have offered him.

LOCKHART (*rather angrily, for him*): But why? What in God's name do you think you can do here now?

[1] *Ibid.,* Act II, Scene I, p. 450.

PROFESSOR: Be an old nuisance. Make senile mischief. Throw large spanners into their Godless works. I'll grab the pick of the history honours people and show them what life's done so far with this gaudy little planet. I'll give lectures that have about as much to do with the syllabus as Brock's fireworks. I'll contradict every dreary little lie about humanity that Pearse and Saxon and the rest can cook up. I'll——

LOCKHART (*cutting in, rather sharply*): Don't go on, Robert. Because I think you're bluffing.

PROFESSOR (*who has been on his feet during this last speech, turns away, hurt, but not wanting* LOCKHART *to see he is hurt*).

LOCKHART, *however, guesses this and rises, moving nearer* PROFESSOR. *The latter turns and looks at him, reproachfully.*

LOCKHART: I'm sorry. Even if I thought that, I oughtn't to have said it.

PROFESSOR: If you can think it, then you'd better say it—even tonight. But perhaps I was bluffing a bit—whistling in the dark perhaps. Let's put it like this, then. I've been here a long time—I like the glum mucky old place. And times are hard, Alfred—we've got to keep on if we can. And there might be something I could help to do here, before the light goes. A touch of colour. A hint of wonder. An occasional new glance at old stuff. A bit of insight. Or is it the characteristic vanity of the Emeritus type?

LOCKHART: No, it isn't. You've all that to give. If they'll let you.

PROFESSOR (*a trifle bleakly, at first*): Yes, there's that. And it's not so much men—as machines—that we have to beat. The new educational machine here, for instance. And generally—the capital-industrial machine—and now the Trade Union machine and the Civil Service machine.

LOCKHART: Right.

PROFESSOR: I was telling my family, who don't care a damn, that we're trying to do a wonderful thing here. And so we are. But somehow not in a wonderful way. There's a kind of grey chill hollowness inside, where there ought to be gaiety, colour, warmth, vision. Sometimes our great common enterprise seems only a noble skeleton, as if the machines had already sucked the blood and marrow out of it. My wife and family tell me to go away and enjoy myself. Doing what? Watching the fire die out of the heart, and never even stooping to blow? Here in

Burmanley—with Dinah and her kind—and a few friends and
allies—I can still blow a little—brighten an ember or two.[1]

This might be said by some to be the voice of the middle class.
But though Priestley has a high opinion of the innate, though
often well disguised, merits of the section of society which produced him—'When they are not tangled up in snobbery and false
values, the ordinary English bourgeois middle class are grand
people'[2]—he is setting no such limit on his symbolism here. Symbolism it certainly was, in that 'glum mucky old place', the
England of 1947, and a kind which brought a far readier response
from audiences and critics than some of them had given the more
ambitious stuff of *Johnson Over Jordan*. *The Linden Tree* was one of
the happy enterprises; it was well produced, by Michael Mac-
Owan, well cast, and it ran for a long time. When it was published, Priestley dedicated it to J. P. Mitchelhill: 'You were
enthusiastic about it from the first, and it took us back to the
Duchess Theatre again, in the happiest circumstances, after an
interval of nearly ten years, during which it looked as if we should
never work together in the Theatre again. To have you on the
management once more, together with my friends of the Westminster venture—and Dame Sybil and Sir Lewis Casson playing
so beautifully—this has been happiness when I had almost ceased
to dream of finding it in the Theatre.'

Perhaps he had. The most deeply involved period of his love
affair with the Theatre had ended with the final curtain of *Johnson
Over Jordan*. After that had come the war; after that a brief period
of intense political activity. He was still writing plays, and still
involved in their production, but somehow it was not quite the
same—possibly because he was not quite the same either. *The
Linden Tree* reflects the post-war thoughts which were now pre-
occupying him—the care for the state of society which, after two
wars, was beginning to come out of the middle of his mind and
towards the front.

[1] *Ibid.,* Act II, Scene II, pp. 475–6.
[2] *Rain upon Godshill,* p. 242.

He wrote a few more plays, but they reflected the change too; *Home is Tomorrow*, in 1948, had a United Nations team working on a tropical island; *Summer Day's Dream*, a year later, a different kind of international group investigating—in 1975—a gentle piece of England where deep and tranquil values have survived an atomic war. After that he drifted away from his familiar kind of theatre altogether. He wrote, for Alec Guinness, the only film of which he bothers to make record, *Last Holiday*; he wrote the libretto to Sir Arthur Bliss's music for the opera *The Olympians*. But he became properly caught up again in the theatre only once, in 1952, and even then it was not in the conventional theatre but in an outright experimental form, the 'platform play', written to be spoken without action by actors standing at—and using the particular dramatic capabilities of—microphones. For this he wrote *Dragon's Mouth*, a dramatic quartet in two parts, in collaboration with Jacquetta Hawkes.

The seed of the project came from a reading production by Charles Laughton of the *Don Juan in Hell* section of Shaw's *Man and Superman*, which Priestley saw in New York in 1951. This production, with Sir Cedric Hardwicke, Charles Boyer and Agnes Moorehead, instantly brought out in a rush all Priestley's bubbling response to an exciting idea. 'These performers in evening clothes, pretending to read and using no scenery, costume, make-up, stage lighting, created a feeling of freshness, zest, attack, to which the audience immediately responded. It made recent stage plays I had seen appear by comparison so many faded masquerades.'[1] So before long, of course, with Laughton's encouragement, he was jumping feet first into the challenge of writing a piece especially for this kind of presentation—with the extra challenge of working with another writer whose talent was equal in quality to his own, but totally different in kind. Of the two major books which these two had just published, J. B. Priestley could no more have written *A Land* than Jacquetta Hawkes could have written *Festival at Farbridge*. But the collaboration worked. They made *Dragon's Mouth* a story of four people,

[1] From the Prologue to *Dragon's Mouth*, p. vii (Heinemann 1952).

isolated in a boat, coping with the knowledge that one of them—
we never discover which—has an illness which must shortly
result in death, and they distinguished between their four on a
subtle pattern of Jung's distinction between the Types—emotion,
thought, sensation and intuition.

'Jacquetta did two characters and I did the other two,' says
Priestley in reminiscence. 'We took a man and a woman each.
And nobody could tell who had done which. One critic said that
the way one character, a don, was written showed very clearly
my prejudice against academics. But it was Jacquetta, with her
academic background, who wrote the don. . . .'

The enterprise as a whole, however, did not really work; it was
not one of the fortunate ones. Priestley directed it, and the production itself was effective; but where *Don Juan in Hell* had successfully toured the splendid and expensive halls of America,
Dragon's Mouth was instead forced by circumstance into an
under-organized series of one-night stands chiefly notable for the
way it revealed the dearth of such halls in Britain. It ended its
tour in London at the Winter Garden, which was too big, and was
eventually produced off-Broadway in America. 'I believe', wrote
Priestley in the published version, 'that these platform pieces are
not easy to devise and write, are hard to produce and act well, and
that they demand a great deal of efficient organization (to which
I lay no claim), together with much enthusiasm on the part of
everybody concerned with them. Perhaps we are all feeling too
tired and stale to bother about them. But I am glad some of us
had a try.'[1]

This was why he had enjoyed his brief plunge back into the
taxing life of writer-director in the experimental theatre. It was
a matter of having a try, exercising professionalism, committing
oneself briefly but entirely to an uncertain enterprise—and the
theatre demands total committedness from more people, with
less certainty of the outcome, than any other medium of the arts.
'Our four players, who had had a tough time both memorizing
their lines and reversing much of their stage technique, and our

[1] *Ibid.*, p. xvi.

stage staff, who lived desperate lives on tour, were with us body, heart and soul. . . .'[1]

These were the people, hundreds of them over the years, who had kept Priestley close to the theatre during his Duchess and Westminster periods: the backstage people, the workers of the theatre, the actors and actresses and designers and producers and technicians and all the rest. They had made every play a kind of family enterprise, and he was always by nature a family man. He still dislikes 'the glamour thing', the headlines, the increasing complexities of management; he dislikes first nights and indeed all British audiences; he even dislikes going to the theatre. But he loves working in it. Any reminder of the things a writer can accomplish, given a dark expectant theatre, a bright stage, and a group of devoted professionals, and he is ready to have a try again. In 1963 he helped Iris Murdoch—who, with her husband John Bayley, is a close friend of both Priestleys—to dramatize her novel *A Severed Head*. 'I enjoyed that,' he says cheerfully, 'it was a challenge.' Then the face droops in recollection. 'But then again, it was a year before we got it on the stage, and after that we couldn't get it off, it ran for two and a half years. The whole business of putting plays into theatres is so complicated these days. . . .'

And so of course it is; too complicated for an impatient man, who was at his happiest when he could finish writing *Time and the Conways*, dive instantly into the mechanics of production, and within two months have it on the stage, or at any rate in rehearsal. Today, living in Shakespeare country, with members of the Stratford company on every hand, Priestley is sometimes content to sit and reflect on the theatre, his relationship with it, and its condition now.

'My audience, you know, was—if you can define an audience— mainly made up of the professional middle class, and they aren't so much a theatre-going group as they were; in the last fifteen or twenty years they've got very hard up. I used to cheat them, because my plays weren't slices of life, there wasn't one of them in which the impossible didn't happen. Some people identify me

[1] *Ibid.,* p. xiii.

with Galsworthy and naturalism, but of course that's rubbish, all
my plays are principally fantasies. . . .

'I don't really swallow what people claim about there being a
great post-war renaissance in the English theatre. Too much of
it is sloppy: acting, direction, writing. The old theatre had to
change, it's no good to us now. But looking back at it all while
it did change, you can see an iron rod of theatricality running
through. Today, the change is there but the iron rod's gone.
Pinter understands it best. His range is narrow, of course—he's
a nice man, but all his plays give the impression of a very nasty
chap, with the unknown menace thing . . . But his writing is
very very professional, he knows exactly what he's doing . . .
there's no sloppiness about him, or anything he has to do with.
Some of the others, though . . . hum . . .'

His own way in the theatre has always been that of the professional: there are both good and bad things about it, but the
pattern has always been the same. The bad, unproduced, unpublished play was always the one written in several carefully cor-
rected and worked-over different drafts, and the good play the
piece that was written at enormous speed, the dialogue speaking
itself in his head as his fingers thumped it into the typewriter; the
technique and the solving of rough technical problems came not
through careful deliberate thought but through the instinct of the
professional, the 'feel' for the theatre. It has never been The
Drama, as a literary form studied in schools and universities,
which has had the real hold over him, but the actual magical
Theatre, the building, the institution, the experience, particularly
the creating of an experience, for again, when all's said and done,
it is what people are given to experience that matters to him most.
('You know,' he said to me once, a year or two ago, 'I can still
catch sight of a tumble-down empty theatre in some provincial
town and think'—he gave his knee a great thump—'now, I'd like
to start that up, get it going again.') And he has always written
his plays knowing that he was creating experiences rather than
contributions to Our Heritage, and perhaps he would have
written more enduring plays if he had turned this self-knowledge

the other way round, and perhaps not. Almost undoubtedly not, for the only real dramatists are those who write for the theatre first and for the expression of an idea or style second. Priestley has always done that; always accepted the gentle sorrow that is the inevitable aftermath of any swift magic.

It is hard to avoid melancholy cadences in any account of work in the Theatre. We remember not only the failures that might have been avoided but also the successes already fading in older people's memories. The plays themselves may be in print, but they were written to be seen and heard, not read. And in a Theatre like ours, which asks for something either new or very old, such plays have vanished. A few ageing players, as they wipe the grease-paint and cold cream off their faces, recollect the plays' triumphant first appearances. It is all going, going, gone: a lift of the voice, a gesture, a look, that were marvels and things of beauty in their time. So, thinking about the Theatre, I cling to my belief that in its own time, somewhere along the fourth dimension, everything still exists: that lift of the voice, that gesture, that look, they are still there. Sometimes I wonder how many people, apart from technologists and journalists, are genuinely excited by all the talk about travel in space, by this desire to leave the earth for nothingness. I know that, when I think about the Theatre, I only wonder when at least some part of our minds will be able to travel in time, to recapture the past that has not really vanished at all, to see the old velvet curtains rising and falling again, to applaud once more the brave players.[1]

---

[1] *Margin Released*, pp. 212–3.

IV

ENGLISHMAN

You enter a subtle spell, whichever way you arrive. You can drive there from London, up the roaring impersonal motorway, under its succession of bridges that do not go softly *sha-sha-sha* like Cyril Connolly's passing poplar trees but give sudden gulps with a fierce noise like *cchwup!* as if they were longing to cut off your head—you can drive up that cold efficient strip of waste-land, and within minutes of branching away from it in Warwick-shire you are being lulled and softened by curving hedges and green fields, church spires and country gardens and great single billowing English trees that have for centuries had room to breathe. You can drive from the west, out of the ancient purple-brown mountains and the new dark conifer forests and the secret Celtic names like Llanidloes and Caersws, and then once across the Marches this same green gentle land draws you in to its peaceful self, and the names on the signposts are ageless and English, *Henley-in-Arden, Mickleton, Shipston-on-Stour*; and wherever in England you may have been born, this is, for a part of you, like coming home. Or you can take the train from almost any direction, and rush across the black industrial ant-heap of the middle of England, rocking and swaying under a dirty sky, and find yourself suddenly at rest in little Stratford station, waiting amiably for the last taxi-driver to return from carrying five eager American tourists off to the White Swan; and then lean peacefully back as he drives you in your turn off beneath the chestnut trees, and hear him observe in rounded Cotswold tones that oh yes, indeed, certainly he knows where the Priestleys live. . . .

Kissing Tree House, near Stratford on Avon, is a tranquil white Georgian manor house next to the village church, set behind the kind of summer-warmed English walls where peaches and nectarines grow, and small solid doors look as though they might open at any moment on to an enchanted world in one of those other dimensions of Time. There are wide lawns and great graceful trees, a glow of roses along a fence beyond the broadest lawn, and beyond that again, an archetypal English meadow, where a neighbouring farmer puts his cattle to graze, and hares dart and leap in the spring. Spring at Kissing Tree is a distillation of everything that made Browning glare with such homesick distaste at his gaudy melon-flowers; a great yellow sweep of daffodils flows away from the house and into the distance, as far as you can see; owls call at night among the trees, and every morning early the world is still and misted and new-green, and the grass hazed white with frost. And as a small silent reminder that twentieth-century England does still live and move, out there beyond the meadow, an infrequent red double-decker bus slides past, half-hidden by a hedge.

Priestley walks the hedge-bound roads every day after lunch, wearing a mushroom-flat black beret or broad-brimmed brown hat and carrying a stout stick; and he has the look of a gentler Merlin, benevolent but brooding, unpredictable, thinking no doubt of nothing more remarkable than that it is high time he bought some more tobacco, but seeming to be cogitating deep and sombre matters. It would not be surprising if he were to vanish suddenly in a puff of smoke, like the engaging Master Marlagram in his tale *The Thirty-First of June*. At all events he does not manage, somehow, here or anywhere else, to appear quite ordinary. And he is as much unlike his old persistent public image as these gentle Warwickshire roads are unlike the streets of a Yorkshire wool town.

He has never properly lived in the North of England since he left Bradford at the age of nineteen to join the Duke of Wellington's West Riding Regiment ('known in some circles as "The Havercake Lads", in others as "The Dirty Duke's" '). To be sure he came home on leave from time to time, and passed some months there four and a half years later, after being demobilized and before going up to Cambridge. But he had pulled up his regional roots in 1914, and never replanted them in the West Riding; never really replanted them anywhere, to the extent of becoming overwhelmingly and permanently attached to one region of England, in the way of some other men who cannot feel properly alive if they are away for long from their home ground, be it the Forest of Dean or the Romney Marsh. The feel of the Yorkshire Dales was with him for life, and still strikes some deep chord in his unconscious mind as no other place can (except, somewhat incongruously, the arid part of Arizona to the north of Phoenix, where he spent those two winters in the 'thirties).

For the last fifty-five years, his roots have been not regional, but national; he is very, very English. He has travelled to every civilized country in the world and a number of uncivilized ones as well, but he has never lived voluntarily for more than a few months in any country other than England, and has never wanted to. It is impossible to imagine him departing to spend his old age on a Greek island or in the South of France. ('I have never shared the well-known passion for the Mediterranean common among the educated English,' he said to me once. 'It's too classical and cut-and-dried. Too many damned olives.') No—it is England for J. B. Priestley. Every one of his best novels and plays has been set there; his mind and imagination are essentially English; his work is in a solidly English tradition; his understanding of man has grown out of his uncommon understanding of the Englishman. And though he is not given to overt and emotional celebrations of his land, you can find them here and there.

> Unlike many writers I know, I have no bias against my own country. I am not one of those people who are happy only when they have left their own land. I do not believe—as so many English and Americans do—that anything that happens in a foreign country is more romantic, charming, intelligent, gracious, than anything that ever happens at home. I have travelled often and sometimes travelled far, and I have never been sorry to see the magical white cliffs again. In those boat trains from Southampton I have stared out of the window with tears in my eyes, not because the chop on my plate was half-

raw and the vegetables uneatable, as they always are, but because I was seeing once again the misty trees and the gold-and-white scribble of the buttercups and daisies in the passing meadows. Nobody has praised more enthusiastically than I have the diamond light of the Arizona Desert, but it never catches at my heart as a certain light in England does, the light of a fine morning in June when every leaf or piece of blossom in the foreground is sharply vivid, but beyond them everything is gradually shading and melting away into what is in the far background nothing but an exquisite green tenderness. I say that this occasional English light is not merely magnificent, like the one that you see nearly every morning in the American South-West; it is heart-breakingly beautiful, turning earth and air into music. No wonder we have had such poets. And then the people. Because they are my own people, naturally I prefer them to all others. But not all the English. We have some types that I detest above all others. But the ordinary folk here seem to me the nicest in the world. No people are more fundamentally decent and kind. . . .[1]

He is no mere smug patriot: that passage, written in 1939 in *Rain upon Godshill*, was prelude to half a book of criticism of England and the English. All the same, he meant it. And it is to be noted that he was not writing or thinking of England as a place, a landscape, but as a nation. He begins with that certain summer light, but very soon: 'And then the people——' England and the English are joint subjects of a great deal of Priestley's work and thought; you can no more detach him from them than you can writers like Shakespeare, Chaucer, Dickens, Blake, Kipling, Chesterton, de la Mare, Brooke.

Although the whole of our green and pleasant land has been his subject, it is not the greener and more pleasant parts to which he really belongs. He has a particular feeling for the lonely places, like the Dales, but he is not a rural man; he seldom writes of the life of the villages and countryside. The Industrial Revolution which began in England is to some extent still going on there, so that as a nation we can still be divided more clearly than some into

[1] *Rain upon Godshill*, pp. 211-12.

the two distinct categories of townsmen and countrymen. Some countrymen live uneasily in the towns (or the suburbs, which are no more than towns pretending not to be); some townsmen can live happily in the country so long as it allows them frequent revivifying trips back to town. Priestley lives now in a village set in one of the most beautiful parts of the English countryside; he enjoys its tranquillity, and mutters restlessly if circumstances take him for more than a week or two to any large town; but all the same he is an urban Englishman at heart. You might say, looking back over the geography of his seventy-five years, that on the whole he has done his writing in the country, and his living in the town. And if you consider a dictum of his that it is far better to write about a place in absence, from memory, than when one is sitting on the top of it, then this does not conflict with the fact that his imagination had chosen so often to concern itself with the gaiety, the wretchedness, the bustle, the loneliness, the beauty and ugliness and life and death of urban man.

The sequence of his life's focal points after Cambridge runs thus: London, Oxfordshire, London, Buckinghamshire, London, the Isle of Wight, London, Warwickshire—and still London today, for the flat in Albany to which the Priestleys repair whenever work or friendship brings them to London is the same flat in which Priestley lived much of his life during the war, and which he has intermittently inhabited now for almost thirty years. 'London,' he once wrote, 'is English life in brick, chimney pots, old squares, smoke and mist.' And a part of him still belongs to London, though he could no longer be said to love the place; when he talks about it now, it is with the same kind of distaste with which he wrote in John Lehmann's anthology *Coming to London*, thirteen years ago: 'Because of the intolerable strain of contemporary metropolitan living, the growing defeat of human zest and sympathy by the mere mechanics of existence, London, like New York and Paris, is rapidly becoming a bad-tempered city, filled with the sour smell of that defeat.' But that was in 1957. In the autumn of 1922, when he had first arrived in London, he was only twenty-eight.

We found a seven-roomed flat on the ground floor of King Edward's Mansions, Walham Green, which perhaps I ought to explain is a seedy district between Chelsea and Fulham, their rather raffish poor relation. The rent was about seventy-five pounds a year—and ours was probably the roomiest flat in the building. But for the first few months we shared the flat with our Cambridge friend, Edward Davison the poet, who had edited the *Cambridge Review* and now came to London to edit a Liberal Church weekly called *The Challenge*. We shopped sketchily for odd bits of furniture along the Fulham Road, our one solid piece being a Broadwood grand on hire purchase; we did our own decorating, half poisoning ourselves with white lead; we settled in. Many of our neighbours there were music-hall performers, who were on tour most of the year and did not want to pay much rent for a permanent address in London; Walham Green would do. It would do for me too; in fact, at first I quite enjoyed living there. I do not know what it is like now, but in 1922 Walham Green still seemed to belong to the London of Phil May. It was crowded and noisy with street stalls and barrows, fat women drinking stout at pub doors, young mothers shouting at wizened babies, chaps waiting to learn what won the two-thirty, greasy little eating places; with the Granville Music-Hall and Stamford Bridge (where Davison and I cheered for Chelsea) representing the arts and athletics. We were not long in Walham Green, leaving it for the Chilterns the following spring, and I will not pretend I was sorry to go; but for the first two or three months I certainly relished what seemed to me its thick Cockney atmosphere, very different from anything I had known in the North. To this day there is a certain kind of smoky autumn morning, coolish but with the sun somewhere not far away, with a railway station smell about it, that brings back to mind those first days in London, when I would hurry out of King Edward's Mansions to catch an 11 bus to Fleet Street, hoping to find some books to review.[1]

[1] *Coming to London*, ed. John Lehmann, p. 72.

For a while after that he saw little of London but the route to and from Guy's Hospital, when his life was darkened by the illness and death of his young wife. But he was never away from the metropolis for very long, and there was more to his relationship with it than the fact that it contained publishers, editors and theatres. He lived successively, for varying numbers of years, in Scarsdale Villas, Kensington; Well Walk, Hampstead; The Grove, Highgate Village (where Coleridge used to stay); and then in Albany. He spent the months of the Blitz in London, dodging like every other Londoner between home and street and air-raid shelter; dodging, for his own part, in and out of Broadcasting House several times a week, to deliver not only the celebrated Postscripts but other talks, 'always very late at night, to America, the Dominions, and in fact, through recordings transmitted every hour or so, to all parts of the world where English was understood.'[1] In September 1940 he moved into the old Langham Hotel at the end of Portland Place, a dozen yards from Broadcasting House, so that the perilous business of going home after these late-night broadcasts would be no more than a matter of crossing the road, and a few days later only his professionalism, or his conscience, or both, saved him from a sudden end. 'Grumbling and cursing', he was called away from his bed on his only free evening to do an extra broadcast about the Blitz for Canadian listeners; and while he was sitting in Broadcasting House writing his script the bombs fell all round Portland Place, one of them demolishing the part of the Langham Hotel in which he should have been asleep.

Nearly every Londoner who was alive during the war years has a tale like this somewhere at the back of his memory. And it was during that period that Priestley gave part of his heart to the city; there was no faint praise then.

> 'A lot of us, especially if we are from the North, and thought we knew everything, imagined that that old cockney spirit was dead and gone. We thought the Londoner of today, catching his tubes and electric trains, was a different kind of fellow alto-

[1] *Margin Released*, p. 218.

gether, with too many of his corners rubbed off, too gullible, easily pleased, too soft; and we were wrong. The Londoners, as the Americans are saying, can take it, and London itself—this grey sea of a city—can take it. The fact that the savage indiscriminate bombing of the city has seized the world's imagination is itself a tribute to the might and majesty of London. There was a time when, like many north-countrymen who came South, I thought I disliked London; it had vast colourless suburbs that seemed to us even drearier than the one we had left behind. We hated the extremes of wealth and poverty that we found, cheek by jowl in the West End, where at night the great purring motor-cars filled with glittering women passed the shadowy rows of the homeless, the destitute, the down-and-out.

'The life here in London seemed to us to have less colour, less gaiety than life in capitals abroad, and at the same time to have less character and flavour than the life we remembered in our provincial cities. And so on and so forth. But on these recent nights, when I have gone up to high roofs and have seen the fires like open wounds on the vast body of the city, I've realized, like many other settlers here, how deeply I've come to love London, with its misty, twilit charm, its hidden cosiness and companionship, its smoky magic. The other night, when a few fires were burning so fiercely that half the sky was aglow, and the tall terraces around Portland Place were like pink palaces in the Arabian Nights, I saw the Dome and Cross of St. Paul's, silhouetted in sharpest black against the red flames and orange fumes, and it looked like an enduring symbol of reason and Christian ethics seen against the crimson glare of unreason and savagery. "Though giant rains put out the sun, here stand I for a sign. . . ."

'. . . This, then, is a wonderful moment for us who are here in London, now in the roaring centre of the battlefield, the strangest army the world has ever seen, an army in drab civilian clothes, doing quite ordinary things, an army of all shapes and sizes and ages of folk, but nevertheless a real army, upon whose continuing high and defiant spirit the world's future depends. . . .'[1]

He comes, as always, through the place to the people. That

[1] BBC 'Postscript' broadcast, 15 September 1940.

early world in which he grew up gave him the ideal qualifications for being able to get along with the English. Not every Englishman can do it: not by a very long way. We are—except in time of war or national disaster—the most divided of nations; perhaps it is an inevitable state of affairs, the only way of preserving individuality among forty-five million people crammed into an area of 50,332 square miles. (A statistic which sounds considerably more alarming than the figure for the United Kingdom as a whole, which has fifty million people and 93,024 square miles— ten per cent more people; but almost twice as much space.) Everywhere you look among us, there are barriers, rivalries, senses of difference: between North and South, East and West; between capital and provinces, town and country; differences of accent, manners, heritage, values. These days, there are two sides to the coin that is England, and on one side are the English who still keep all the old barriers firm and high, and on the other those who regard them as nonsensical and undemocratic and feel that they have been torn down by education and travel and general social change. But even the levellers cannot quite escape—even now—an awareness of the ghosts of the barriers; every Englishman who meets another Englishman instinctively 'places' him geographically, intellectually, socially, by his accent, occupation, clothes, address, by the school or university he went to—it's a daft subconscious game, no longer a matter of rousing feelings of superiority or inferiority, but one which we have been playing for so many centuries now that we shall never quite be rid of it. Though we have all been mercifully levelled by common sense, the ghostly divisions still tend to drive most of us to the side either of the snobs or of the rebels, two camps which are both occupied by the same kind of mixture of people either flaunting or concealing their badges of origin.

Priestley is one of the more fortunate Englishmen who have no badge. The world of his Edwardian Bradford was a singularly classless place, and he was never really aware of the existence of the English class system, or any of its parallel pigeon-holing structures, until 1914. As a result he never had to get rid of any deep subterranean sense of being 'better' or 'worse' than anyone else in order to be free to value people for themselves. In dealing with his fellow-men he looks neither up nor down, but all about him, and in so far as he makes judgements about the people he portrays, they are humane judgements only; he is not the kind of man who is able to patronize or sneer or raise a delicate eyebrow, to snarl with resentment and envy, or burrow defiantly into a caricature peasant role. When he says of the North: 'I never felt the compulsion to escape—as Bennett did, so that he spent his whole life breaking out', he might as easily be talking of a level of English society as of a geographical place, since he has always been free of the restraints which handicap so many of the English. Shakespeare, for all his superb perception of the English sense of degree that illuminates the history plays, was this same kind of fortunate free spirit; so was Dickens, whose biting attacks on certain kinds of Englishman were born (like, later, Priestley's own) not out of the resentment of a man sniping up from a lower rung of the ladder but out of pure humanitarian rage at the sight to injustice and cruelty. Men like this are the flowering of the English middle class, the kind of unfettered individualists that if can produce at its best; they can, and do, celebrate or deplore any kind of brick in the wall of the English social structure with complete freedom and objectivity—and if you think this is common or easy, then try to imagine compassionate and convincing passages written by Evelyn Waugh about a mill-hand, by D. H. Lawrence about a senior civil servant, by Virginia Woolf about a music-hall illusionist.

No. If Priestley is identifiable, classifiable, it is only as an urban man; and if he writes principally of the life of men in their cities and towns it is because most modern men, and particularly most Englishmen, live their lives in cities and towns. And it is largely because his writing has so often been of this kind that he has in the last twenty years become increasingly anxious and angry about the direction taken by Western civilization. Gradually he has seen the urban industrialized society, which may well have been at its best in the Bradford of his youth, heading in an increasingly sinister direction: going, not to beat about the bush, quite mad. The Albany flat today is a convenience, a *pied-à-terre* more agreeable than a room in a hotel: no more. Apart from occasional excursions, he will live the rest of his life in rural surroundings which he could never have tolerated for long when he was young; a fact due not to his present age, but to simple revulsion from the nastier side-effects of over-urbanization which a great many men several decades younger find equally alarming.

He had begun to remark the beginnings of this unhappy process a long time ago. The travels through England on which *English Journey* was based were made in the autumn of 1933; they took him on a Chestertonian journey from Southampton to London by way of the Midlands, Yorkshire, Lancashire, the Tyne, the Tees and East Anglia. Things were at a kind of mid-point then. The depressed areas were dreadful, Jarrow and Hebburn and the rest, and he said so with force, and demanded why the devil nothing constructive was being done about 'these decaying towns and their workless people'. But his more prolonged and detailed portrait was that of what the nineteenth century had done to England.

> It had found a green and pleasant land and had left a wilderness of dirty bricks. It had blackened fields, poisoned rivers, ravaged the earth, and sown filth and ugliness with a lavish hand. You cannot make omelettes without breaking eggs, and you cannot become rich by selling the world your coal and iron and cotton goods and chemicals without some dirt and disorder. So much is admitted. But there are far too many eggshells and too few omelettes about this nineteenth-century England. What you see looks like a debauchery of cynical greed. As I thought of some of the places I had seen, Wolverhampton and St. Helens and Bolton and Gateshead and Jarrow and Shotton, I remembered a book I had just read, in which we are told to return as soon as possible to the sturdy Victorian individualism. But for my part I felt like calling back a few of these sturdy individualists simply to rub their noses in the nasty mess they had made. Who gave them leave to turn this island into their ashpit? . . . Cynical greed—*Damn you, I'm all right*: you can see as much written in

black letters across half England. Had I not just spent days moving in the shadow of their downstrokes?[1]

From that he went on to describe the England of 1933: different, improved, essentially democratic, but monotonous and already standardized: 'A large-scale, mass-production job. You could almost accept Woolworths as its symbol. Its cheapness is both its strength and its weakness.' In 1949 he wrote a preface to a new edition of the book; sixteen more years had passed, the Second World War had obliterated—among other things—the depressed areas; we were still, he wrote, making all kinds of mistakes: 'hastily fastening ourselves into a system that lacks flexibility, does not encourage initiative or a general sense of responsibility, and fails to create enthusiasm and release energy.'[2] But at least we were not the 'blind donkeys' we had been in 1933. He was optimistic, as he is always at heart optimistic. But then again, that was 1949. Before the 'fifties were half over, it was beginning to seem unpleasantly apparent that England was still completely in the grip of the cynical greed, unchanged by its passage through democratization, which Priestley had been describing as our nineteenth-century legacy in 1933.

It was all a little like one of the time-spirals of the Ouspensky hypothesis—and indeed again and again, in his writing about his native land, Priestley has seemed not unlike his Dr. Görtler in *I Have Been Here Before*: seeing intuitively things which may happen, in as much vivid detail as if he too had jumped for a moment into another coil of the spiral, and were trying with all his might to head the life of the country into another direction—to intervene. As a writer, of course, the only intervention possible for him was to shout a warning, or to exert every kind of subtlety in efforts to influence men's reasoning; the artist who is not a great genius must change his nature and occupation entirely if he aspires to have any immediate effective power to turn the course of nations and men. But within those limitations, Priestley continually tried. Once, writing of commitment, he described himself

[1] *English Journey*, pp. 400–1 (Heinemann 1968 edition).
[2] From the preface to the 1949 edition of *English Journey*, p. vii.

as 'half an artist and half a damaged man of action',[1] and it must have been an awareness of the monstrous difficulty of this kind of battle that he had at the back of his mind. The very nature of his talent doomed him to a position from which there could inevitably be small chance of accomplishing the thing about which he cared most fiercely. If the course of England, the world, Western civilization, can be turned at all, by anything less perilous than dictators, political ideologies or scientific advance, it can be turned only by statesmen. Priestley is made of a great deal of the stuff which we need—and need most desperately—in our statesmen, now more than ever, but his personality would not tolerate the kind of life which men of action must live in order to gain the power to act; and so the statesman was never born. Instead there was the writer—unable to resist involving himself in as much action as he could take without damaging his chosen course, but for the most part limited by that course, where the future of England was concerned, to shouting warnings into the air.

Consider first the writing, since the actions have always been those born out of it. Priestley has always celebrated, and will celebrate until he dies, the essential, magical nature of the English people; it is patriotism of the deepest—and the only worthwhile— sort, the burning pride of a man looking objectively at his own kind.

> We have been—and still are, at heart—a great race, and we have virtues of our own, almost as hazy and hard to define as our charming landscape, that are perhaps even more valuable now to the world than they have ever been before. There is in us the stuff of which good wise citizens could be made, fit for the City of God.[2]

This kind of pride he will acknowledge any day; it is the fuel which drives the machine, the emotion which can still make any Englishman who lived through the Second World War feel a remembered response when he hears a recording of Churchill's

---

[1] *Margin Released*, p. 229.
[2] *Rain upon Godshill*, p. 217.

voice exhorting us to 'our finest hour'. All the assumptions and standards and institutions of English life are behind it, from Magna Carta onward; Priestley has respect for them all, even—unlike some more indignant members of the Left—the professionalism of the modern Monarchy. 'On the whole,' he said once, 'and in spite of everything, this is still the most civilized place in the world in which to live.' The quality of ordinary everyday life in England is what matters to him most. The last time he was interviewed on American television about a new book, his interviewer led him first into some general topical chat, touching at one point on a very large disturbance which had taken place a day or two earlier outside the American Embassy in London. Grosvenor Square had been filled with thousands of indignant English demonstrators protesting against America's tactics in Vietnam; and the American news media, who seldom find reason to notice affairs in Britain, had carried vivid pictures and films of the leaping hordes of rioters, and the rows of stolid helmeted policemen. Not very long before that, they had been full of other pictures of other riots, as the Chicago police had whacked their way through the crowds of demonstrators filling the streets around the Democratic presidential convention. The interviewer, however, was not talking about Chicago, he was talking about Grosvenor Square, and telling Priestley how startling the pictures from London had been. Priestley sat amiably puffing at his pipe, and listening to the man with an expression of thoughtful benevolence. 'Ah,' he said, 'and I expect you noticed that the policemen in Grosvenor Square didn't raise a finger against anyone. No clubs, no gas, none of that.' Puff, puff: and then a sudden flash of edge in the amiability. 'Now there's *civilization* for you.'

But civilized societies, of course, have a habit of failing to live up to their own high standards; more especially, to the high standards of those who prize them the most. And Priestley, pointing out that the good citizen who loves his country must always insist upon telling it all its faults, has never written a good word about England without following it by several sharply admonitory ones. Consider this, a page or two after the lyrical passage about our 'great race':

> Some deep-seated troubles, indeed the very gravest, we share with the world, but for once we can ignore them. Let us keep inside our island. There, our peculiar vices, which are complacency, hypocrisy, snobbery, stupidity, are flourishing. During the last few years our national life has been riddled with complacency, hypocrisy, stupidity. Never before have we made such a fuss about trivialities. Never have we congratulated ourselves so often about nothing. If we all awoke one morning to find ourselves paralysed, some of our newspapers would congratulate us: 'Let foreigners go moving about,' they would say, smugly, 'but the ordinary decent British citizen has wisely decided to stay in bed.' Every possible triviality of mind has been encouraged, and anything likely to make us think and feel deeply has been discouraged. And this is not Hitler's and Mussolini's doing. It is our own. And as I see it, the rot set in when the post-war period ended in nothing, in making-do and muddling and cynical pottering as a substitute for creation. A tradition, based chiefly on a profound sense of security but containing within itself valuable seeds of growth, perished in the summer of 1914. I am not myself conservative-minded and have no respect for the past, yet I do not hesitate to declare that the England of 1914 was superior, in every important department of national life, to the England of today. But it had to go. For the next five years it was a matter of struggle and endurance, during which our loss of first-rate manhood was comparatively high and terribly damaging. But something much better, one felt, would emerge from all this . . . there should have emerged a New Britain, with much of its old leisurely charm gone for ever, robbed of many an antique grace, but alert, purposeful, courageous and richly creative both politically and culturally. And it didn't. Instead of going forward, the country halted, hesitated, wobbled, then tried to move backwards. What should have been an advance turned into a retreat. English political life, which had not been improved by the Khaki Election of 1918, slipped down to a new level in 1931, the years of the faked financial crisis, of the Labour Prime Minister who

turned Tory overnight, of the bogus National Government,
of an election swung by the nastiest lie yet, the one about the
Post-Office Savings raid. My own feeling is that English life,
political, social, cultural, took a turn for the worse about then
and has shown little improvement since. It was now we began
to see ourselves wearing that gross, vacant face of the tired rich
old man. And brightness fell from the air.[1]

That was in 1939, and typical of the kind of appeal Priestley
was constantly making, with little success, to his countrymen. A
few months later, the second and greater Great War of the century was upon us, and life was once more a matter of struggle and
endurance—and very soon, of course, Priestley's countrymen
were listening to him, on the radio, as they had never listened
before. His theme, heightened in tone by the rhetorical purpose
of encouraging an embattled nation, did not really differ from
what it had been between the wars. This new war, he said in the
Postscript of July 21st, 1940, should be regarded 'as one chapter
in a tremendous history, the history of a changing world, the
breakdown of one vast system and the building up of another and
better one.' When we had got rid of Hitler and Mussolini and all
the other creatures that had come running out of the woodwork,
we should not be going back to the old England but forward to a
new one. We ought to think in terms of community and creation
instead of property and power: and he quoted as example the
fact that a large house and garden, standing empty because their
owner had retreated to the bomb-free safety of America, should
be taken over for the communal needs of billeting and allotment-
gardening for the duration of the war.

> 'Now, the war, because it demands a huge collective effort, is
> compelling us to change not only our ordinary, social and econo-
> mic habits, but also our habits of thought. We're actually chang-
> ing over from the property view to the sense of community,
> which simply means we realize we're all in the same boat. But,
> and this is the point, that boat can serve not only as our defence

[1] *Rain upon Godshill*, pp. 222–4.

against Nazi aggression, but as an ark in which we can all finally
land in a better world. And when I say We, I don't mean only
the British and their allied peoples, but all people everywhere,
including all the Germans who haven't sold themselves body and
soul to the evil Nazi idea. I tell you, there is stirring in us now a
desire which could soon become a controlled but passionate
determination to remodel and recreate this life of ours, to make it
the glorious beginning of a new world order, so that we might
soon be so fully and happily engrossed in our great task that if
Hitler and his gang suddenly disappeared we'd hardly notice that
they'd gone. We're even now the hope of free men everywhere,
but soon we could be the hope and lovely dawn of the whole
wide world.'[1]

Caught up in a passion of determination at the same roaring
speed as he was always carried off by each successive creative idea,
the impatient idealist was at it again. But his idealism for the
quality of the life led by the English people is the one side of his
nature which has, over the years, had to learn to resist all impulses
of impatience. You can't push the English, especially if your only
weapons are your own tongue and your own pen. They will listen
to you and read you, they will make noises of appreciation and
agreement, and they will do nothing: and you too can do nothing,
except continue to write and shout and hope. And Priestley never
stopped doing all three, nor has he yet. After 1945 he not only
involved himself in far more outside activity than before, in the
cause of building a better world and particularly a better England,
but he put his hope and criticism continually into his writing.
The out-and-out appeals for a new approach to living, in essays
and articles, went on as before, though better-written than before,
blazing and crashing away in an attempt to strike sparks from the
rock-like complacency of the English. A desperate but hilarious
piece called 'The Unicorn' was published in *The New Statesman*
in 1957; we must change, Priestley was still crying, we must put
our faith not in the old worn-out magic of the English character
but in its more ancient magic that for years we have been afraid

[1] BBC 'Postscript' broadcast, 21 July 1940.

to touch—or we shall lose our character altogether. We are losing it already because we are backing the wrong beast:

Sounder and sounder men, absolutely dependable types, present at great expense our famous old Lion act, but everywhere it is a flop. 'But look, please,' they implore the audiences, 'this is our Lion. *The* Lion. The one you read about at school—the identical Lion. Give him a little pat if you like, only, of course, be careful. Stop throwing orange peel, please. No, don't go away. See—he's opening his mouth. He may roar in a moment. Yawning? Never mind—hang on, chaps. In just a minute the Member for Podbury West, already making his mark in the House, will place his head in the Lion's mouth. Or—say the word, and the chairman of the Cosy Tin Motor Company—he'll be along in a jiffy—will ride on the Lion's back. No? I must say, you people are a bit much.' It is all no use: the act is a flop. . . .

. . . It is my belief—and nearly every bulletin I read or hear adds confirmation to it—that the Lion can do no more for us, that only the Unicorn can save us now. We have reached again, as we must do at irregular intervals, the hour of the Unicorn. I am seeing it, of course, as the heraldic sign and a symbol of the imaginative, creative, boldly inventive, original, and individual side of our national character. It is such qualities and what they have contributed to our national life and culture that are so genuinely and warmly admired by the rest of the world. It is the Britain of the poets and artists and scientific discoverers and passionate reformers and bold inventors and visionaries and madmen that still dazzles the world. If we want to impress it, this is what impresses it—the Britain of the Unicorn. If as I believe, this country is in danger of decline, only the Unicorn qualities can rescue it.

. . . So—up with the Unicorn! Make way for the unsound types, all those who made such a bad impression on the committee! Forward the imaginative man, the creators and originators, even the rebels and cranks and eccentrics, all those with corners not rubbed off, bees in their bonnets, fire in their bellies, poetry in their souls! It's nearly now or never. For if we don't back the Unicorn against the Lion, if we are not a boldly imaginative, creative, inventive poeple, a world that expected more of us will

soon not even let us keep what we have now. The only future
we can have worth living in is the one we greet, bravely and
triumphantly, riding on a Unicorn.[1]

Perhaps we listened. Perhaps it made a difference. But Priestley
knew his Englishmen well enough to realize that there was no
certainty any of them would pay any more attention to such
appeals than a mumble of slightly shamefaced agreement; it was
not for nothing that he called his collected *New Statesmen* pieces
of the time *Thoughts in the Wilderness.* He knew too the dangers
of over-exposure for a writer engaged in this kind of polemic; if
he went on repeating the same kind of plea in the same kind of
essays and articles, went on bashing at the same public nerve,
people would very soon stop responding to it at all: 'O Lord,'
they would say despondently, after the first few lines, 'old Priestley's at it again,' and they would turn the page.

So he wrote such pieces only occasionally, and in the intervals
between them he let his concern for his country and countrymen
filter into that dark room in the subconscious from which all
creative ideas flash out into life. As a result, through no deliberate
intention of his own, at least half of the major creative works
which he has produced since the end of the war have been from
their conception imbued with his unending passion for stirring
the English into new life.

Festival at Farbridge was the first of these: a gigantic comic
novel which amiably satirized every aspect of post-war Britain.
It contained some 275,000 words, the longest book he had then
written; longer even than *The Good Companions*, and a good deal
more demanding, since he was writing now at the age not of
thirty-five but of fifty-five. It was a very funny book, and its
craftsmanship as usual was impeccable; the characters vivid, the
narrative complicated but always clear, the interweaving of
separate incidents and nugget-like minor characters masterly, and
the overall examination of the real major character of the book—
which was, as so often in Priestley's novels, English society—

---

[1] 'The Unicorn', reprinted in *Essays of Five Decades*, pp. 225–7.

beautifully clear. But *Festival* was more than just another good
solid novel. It was a kind of explosion of high spirits. England had
been a bleak and uncushioned place for a long time, with the five
tough years of war followed by an even tougher five years of post-
victory austerity; everyone needed some kind of relief, however
short, from the strain. The nation had it in the Festival of Britain
—'Morrison's Folly', as the Beaverbrook press unkindly christened
it—which after years of idiotic argument, farcically muddled
organization and hasty last-minute hammering, blossomed on the
South Bank of the Thames, in Battersea Pleasure Gardens and in
small and large celebrations all over the country, in 1951. 'The
great programme of poetry readings, serenade concerts, firework displays, and children's sports rolled across Britain relent-
lessly,' wrote Michael Frayn in *Age of Austerity*, 'and, though the
local Festival Rose Show may have been remote in spirit from the
pre-stressed concrete *élan* of the South Bank, it brought with it
some suggestion of national identity and consciousness.'[1]

It brought too Priestley's novel, which dealt with the organiz-
ing of one of the local Festival-year celebrations in a middle-
sized English town; in many ways the book was an intuitive
microcosm of the trials and errors and success of the larger Festival
—whose history was itself a pretty fair image of the England of
1951. Beneath its farcical satire, *Festival at Farbridge* was infused
with a real enthusiasm for the spirit, if not the organization, of
the Festival of Britain; this was after all a typically Unicorn idea.
(Indeed the Unicorn shared with the Lion the title of the most
dottily patriotic pavilion on the South Bank.) It was tailor-made
for Priestley's natural sympathy towards any scheme which
seems slightly lunatic, but which may have a chance of creating
a genuine sense of magic.

The central figure of *Festival at Farbridge* is one Commodore
Horace Tribe. He is not a figure of fun, this one, but a figure
of affection, who comes close to being Priestley's favourite
character among the tens of thousands he has created. Jung might

[1] *Age of Austerity*, p. 336. Edited by Michael Sissons and Philip French
(Hodder and Stoughton, 1963).

have had something to say about this, since if there is any kind of perennial archetype in Priestley's novels, it is the figure of Commodore Tribe; men who might be the Commodore's brother or father, or at any rate his first cousin, turn up with enough frequency to make one wonder whether some part of their creator—the actor merging with the iconoclast—has not always dreamed of a wild existence as a magnificent and successful Con Man. For the Commodore is really a con man, though of a benevolent and humane kind; his history and abilities and qualifications are as hazy as the origins of his rank. ('After serving for some years in the Royal Navy, I—er—was attached, chiefly in an advisory capacity, to the navy of one of the South American republics and had the honorary rank of Commodore. . . .')[1] He has a deep, rich voice, roughened, probably, by hundreds of thousands of whiskies drunk in hundreds of exotic foreign capitals or sleazy foreign ports; a mock-solemn voice, equally effective at captivating women or booming in deep grandeur over meetings of large pompous men. And though one somehow rapidly forgets what he looks like, once the book is under way—having been captivated, no doubt, by that voice—he has an appearance to match.

> He was an oldish fellow, somewhere between fifty-five and sixty-five probably; and he was bulky, perhaps all the bulkier because he had not taken off an enormous and rather shabby green overcoat. He was clean-shaven, florid, with a lot of white hair; and he had a piratical nose and tiny bright eyes as busy and wicked as mice. He looked something between a clever old actor and a rather raffish admiral. And whatever else he might be, he was obviously a character, a personality. . . .[2]

The Commodore comes, more or less by accident, to Farbridge: a middle-sized market town (pop. c. 50,000) somewhere in the Midlands. So does a gigantic and decorative young man named Theodore Jenks, newly arrived from the vague depths of the East, which gave him as parting presents a deeply tanned skin,

---

[1] *Festival at Farbridge*, p. 102 (1951).
[2] *Ibid.*, pp. 99–100.

a head of striking bronze, sun-bleached hair, and (from his Chinese grandmother) a pair of eyes which 'were set queerly, and of a mahogany shade, yet not hard but soft and darkly clear'.[1] A bright, pretty, dark-haired girl named Laura Casey is there in Farbridge already, and the three all meet by chance in a tea-shop called the Old Oak Nook. This piece of serendipity ends the only real parallel between *Festival at Farbridge* and *The Good Companions*, which is one of structure: each book begins by spinning three separate narrative strands out of the previous few days in the lives of each of the three main characters, and then employing coincidence to draw them together so that they can thenceforth be woven together into the texture of the story—in this case, the story of the making of a Festival in Farbridge. But even in this similarity there is a difference, for where Priestley made *The Good Companions* a deliberately picaresque romance, and sent Inigo Jollifant, Elizabeth Trant and Jess Oakroyd wandering through all kinds of unrelated adventures before leading them into their concert-party world, he draws the narrative of *Festival at Farbridge* tighter from the beginning; the early histories of the three principals are not only shorter, but are set among characters who all play other parts later in the main body of the book. For there was of course nothing picaresque about *Festival at Farbridge*; it was a work with one central theme, and the skill with which Priestley kept so huge a book constantly polarized round that theme was a measure of the way his art had developed in twenty-five years. Gradually he was growing closer to his characters, treating them less objectively; it was as if he had been at first a puppet-master, letting himself be observed manipulating the strings, but had now changed into that other, perhaps humbler, certainly more endearing, kind of story-teller who is concerned merely with the quiet recounting of a dream of life. Perhaps those years in the theatre had wrought the subtle change; perhaps it was just that he was an older, wiser and more experienced novelist. At any rate it worked.

Should Farbridge celebrate the Festival of Britain? Various

[1] *Ibid.*, p. 410.

local killjoys think not, and have voted the idea down in the Town Council. The Commodore, currently out of a job, thinks that they should, and that he should run it for them with Theodore Jenks and Laura Casey as his assistants; and there are enough disciples of the Unicorn in Farbridge to help him change the community's mind—as of course there are in Priestley's view enough in the whole of Britain to revitalize the place if given half a chance. So Farbridge is steered towards its Festival, through some magnificent parodies of English local life, until it breaks at the last into a great efflorescence of magical high spirits, much as the long-suffering Festival of Britain did itself in real life. And on the way, Priestley assembles the most engaging of all his portrait-galleries of the English, perhaps enjoying himself most, as he had ' done once before, with those who appear only for a sudden bright page or two and then vanish away, never to return again.

When he arrived at the little shelter at the cross-roads, there were no passengers waiting there and no sign of the bus. After sitting down for a minute or two and recovering his breath, he heard voices. Peering round the shelter he saw what appeared to be a pair of very dumpy centaurs, but after a moment or two these resolved themselves into two men who were each holding by the horns some kind of sheep. When he approached them he saw that these were rams, as low and broad as sofas and with huge curved horns that might have come out of Greek mythology. The men holding were alike in having brown and rather wooden faces, but one was clearly much older than the other, and presumably was a senior and superior shepherd. They were staring at their beasts, almost lost in some antique spell; and seemed to be performing a strange duet.

'Yes, Charlie, her's a proper ship.'

'Her's a proper ship indeed, Jebb.'

'Look at that back and head on ern, Charlie.'

'An' this ern too, Jebb.'

'Egad, her'll be a ram afore his mother, Charlie.'

'A proper ship, Jebb.'

'An' this un'll be a better man than his father, Charlie.'

'A better man than his father, Jebb.'

'Good morning,' said the Commodore heartily.

They came out of their duet and dream to stare at him. The massive rams protested in a sonorous bass. Then Jebb, taking charge, said Good morning, and Charlie, following his lead, said Good morning too. The rams had faces like intellectual clowns. The two shepherds, deprived of the duet, looked more wooden than ever. It seemed preposterous to enquire about a bus in this company.

'I fancy her's been an' gone,' Jebb replied.

'Ay, been an' gone,' Charlie echoed.

'For Farbridge you said?'

'That's it—the Farbridge bus,' said the Commodore, rather irritable now.

'I fancy gen'l'man has missed un, Charlie.'

'He's missed un, Jebb.'

'All right then, I've missed it,' said the Commodore. 'Now what do I do? Isn't another one for hours, eh?'

The elder shepherd brought out an enormous old silver watch and stared at it gravely. The younger one looked steadily in the direction of the watch, as if that might help. The rams attempted the opening movement of a double sonata for bass bassoons. The Commodore felt that he was marooned with this quartette in another kind of time, in which a minute of ordinary time might seem like an hour and yet the Norman Conquest be only a week or two away.

'Twenty past eleven the next bus be,' said the elder shepherd, putting away his watch. 'Or thereabouts, eh, Charlie?'

'Twenty past or thereabouts, Jebb,' said the faithful Charlie.

'I can't wait until twenty past eleven,' cried the Commodore, now in despair.

'Charlie and me's taking these two ship to Farbridge market.'

'Aye, to Farbridge market.'

'Billy Porson's van. Eh, Charlie?'

'Billy Porson's van, Jebb.'

'Well now,' cried the Commodore, seeing the light at last, 'do you think you could give me a lift?'

'Had it in mind,' replied the elder shepherd very cautiously.

This was too bold a stroke for young Charlie, who for once

had nothing to say and could only stare, with perhaps just a suggestion of a nod.

'The van's coming here is it? Good! Thanks very much. Fine animals you have here.'

He was commanded to feel their wool, to dig his fingers deep into it, and this he did with a knowing air. The broad backs looked more like sofas than ever. 'Very fine indeed! I congratulate you. Magnificent sheep.'

'Ay, her's a proper ship.'

'Her's a proper ship indeed, Jebb.'[1]

And then from one level to another, Barsetshire to Cambridge, Laura Casey, collecting lecturers for the Festival, finds herself meeting one of the most expensive on the Tanson Agency list, the distinguished critic Leonard Mortory, whose two best-known works of literary scholarship, 'Disavowals' and 'Rejections' everyone of course has read.

When Mr. Mortory finally arrived, he had Mrs. Mortory with him. He was a dusty-looking man, who stared hard through heavy tortoise-shell spectacles and kept tightening his lips as if some dreadful crisis were on hand. He had an odd trick of beginning a speech in a confident booming tone and then fading away, as if he were a faulty wireless set. Mrs. Mortory was younger than her husband; a haggard woman with untidy auburn hair and angry eyes, and badly dressed. Laura rather liked her, but did not know why. They all had tea.

'I shall give you a lecture on *The Novel*,' said Mr. Mortory.

'Good,' said Laura, 'I think people will like that.'

'Always popular,' said Miss Tanson. 'Try the cake, Mrs. Mortory.'

'I must warn you, however,' Mr. Mortory continued, 'that I take the view that life is too short for any intelligent reader to waste his time reading most so-called great novelists . . . Fielding, Sterne, Dickens, Thackeray . . .' He faded out.

Laura wondered why time that was too precious for Fielding and Dickens should be devoted to reading and listening to Mr. Mortory, and she nearly said so. As she hesitated, she hap-

[1] *Festival at Farbridge*, pp. 134–5.

pened to exchange a glance with Mrs. Mortory, who suddenly smiled. 'What's the matter with them?' she asked.

'They're no longer significant,' Mr. Mortory replied bitterly, as if all these old novelists had done him an injury. 'They don't offer us the organized co-relation of critical experience and fantasy we demand. They lack the absolute integrity we insist upon . . .' He was fading rapidly now. '. . . structural properties . . . technical insights . . . closer critical methods. . . .'

'Leonard,' said his wife, 'drink your tea. We can't hear you properly and don't know what you're talking about.'

Mr. Mortory ignored his wife's remarks, charged up his batteries, stared severely at Laura, and continued: 'We have been accused of being formalists. Very well. But some cultural tradition must be preserved in a world like this . . . decay of values . . . mass communication . . .'

'I couldn't agree with you more,' cried Miss Tanson cheerfully. 'Do have some cake.'

Mr. Mortory accepted some cake and ate it very quickly and without any sign of enjoyment. As if it were *David Copperfield* or *Vanity Fair*, Laura told herself. . . .[1]

The portraits of the English in *Festival at Farbridge* are not all a matter of cheerful irreverence. Priestley kept it light, but every now and again there comes a glimpse of the shadow, a hint of the black depths out of which he was inducing this fountain of high spirits to lead up and sparkle away. With bouncy little Captain Mobbs, the local Tory agent, Theodore goes the rounds of the County families, canvassing their support and patronage for the Farbridge Festival; among these they must visit Field-Marshal Walter Watton, ageing and distinguished warden of his country's honour during World War One. Mobbs has seen him before: 'I don't know him, but he took over our division in the First War— I was only a kid subaltern then, of course—and he was blue murder, old boy, the most blood-thirsty basket of 'em all. Started right off by saying we'd not had enough casualties. My godfathers!'[2] But when Theodore spends some time with the

[1] *Festival at Farbridge*, p. 376.
[2] *Ibid.*, pp. 285-6.

Bloody Butcher, as the Field-Marshal had been known, it is in the long dark drawing-room of his Jacobean manor-house, which is lined with glass-fronted cupboards filled not with swords and muskets, or even with books, but with pottery and porcelain.

> The Field-Marshal was a happy man. His eyes warm and alive at last, with delicate long fingers he brought out Chelsea plates and Bow mugs, Meissen cups and Chantilly figures, pointing out the beauties of texture, design and colour, absorbed and enrapt as if all the forty-ton tanks and heavy howitzers had never existed or had vanished from the world like an evil dream. The voice that had sent whole battalions to perish among the barbed wire, that had ordered artillery barrages to rip up wide farmlands and pound villages to dust, now lingered tenderly, like his long white fingers, over a Staffordshire teapot, a Sèvres nymph, a faience vase with a blue ground like an eternal June. . . .[1]

If I tend—as its author claims—to over-rate *Festival at Farbridge* among the whole array of his novels, it is probably through an accident of age. I was sixteen when it was published, one of the generation whose childhood ran through the years of war and austerity: the colour and extravagance, the splashing fountains and flashing lights of the Festival of Britain were our first astonishing sight of a nation lapsing into frivolity, a glimpse of a bright golden world, and our response to the spirit of the thing was, for different reasons, identical with Priestley's own. At the same time I lived in an area which, while not identical with Priestley's Farbridge, contained a stupendous proportion of the peculiarly English characters he had satirized. When I read the book, I fell about with laughter in the kind of total response that only one other comic novel, Kingsley Amis's *Lucky Jim*, drew from this same generation a few years later. Somehow, Priestley seemed to have held up a mirror to the whole of the England I knew, through the framework of its clumsy attempts to cheer itself up; and to this day I have only to open the book at random

[1] *Ibid.*, p. 288.

and within a very few pages I am laughing aloud again. You might say that this kind of response is a bad basis for criticism, since it makes proper analytical objectivity—Mr. Mortory's absolute integrity—impossible. On the other hand you might equally well say that it is a kind of critical response itself.

Festival at Farbridge made good-natured fun of the English; there was not much edge to it—though it was more than a 'frolic', the word which Priestley accurately applied to another novel of England which he wrote two or three years later, *Low Notes on a High Level*, which took the mickey out of the BBC, civil servants, persons with intellectual pretensions but small intellect, and other timeless English targets. *Low Notes* is combined in the Heron edition of his collected works with the cheerful little fantasy *The Thirty-First of June*, and the two belong together. On the whole, during the 'fifties and early 'sixties he went back to the pattern of keeping his affectionate exasperation with the English—which was not diminishing, since we were now slap in the middle of our never-had-it-so-good phase and growing more complacent than ever—out of his novels; not least because he was again writing quantities of didactic journalism on the subject, much of it fairly political in content, and had focused a bitter analysis of all the contemporary ills of British society into an extended topical tract called *Topside, or the Future of England*, in 1958. He also undertook in succession three large books which can only be classified together as 'non-fiction': *Literature and Western Man* in 1960, *Margin Released* in 1962, and *Man and Time* in 1964. Being still as prolific in ideas as ever, he did not of course restrict himself to these three; in the fifteen years after 1950 there were also three fantasies of varyingly sinister and prophetic nature (*The Magicians* in 1954, *Saturn Over the Water*—the best of these three—in 1961, and *The Shapes of Sleep* in 1962), several plays, a volume of short stories (most of which played ingeniously with ideas of Time), numerous essays and lectures, an excellent short biography of Dickens, and a trenchant two-sided portrait of the United States, *Journey Down a Rainbow*, which he wrote with Jacquetta Hawkes (to whom he was married in 1953. His second marriage had ended in divorce).

But in 1964 England took over his fiction again, and she has never really released her hold since. Four novels came in the next five years: *Sir Michael and Sir George*, *Lost Empires*, *It's An Old Country*, and—the longest book he has ever written—*The Image Men*; and each of them in its own way formed another kind of analysis of the life of England and the English. *Lost Empires* differs from the others not only because it is probably the best of the lot but because it is set back in the golden world; it belongs to the England of 1913, which is separated from the England of 1970 by a great many things besides the mere matter of fifty-seven years. The novel is enclosed in that England, and more especially between the walls of the old music halls. The others dealt with relatively enclosed worlds too, but each of them a world within the contemporary English scene; *Sir Michael and Sir George*, for instance, published in 1964, is the story of a rivalry between two cultural knights—very modern animals—and their respective state-supported organizations for assisting the arts. The organizations, each a kind of embryonic Arts Council, are known as the Department of Information and Cultural Services (DISCUS, run by Sir George Blake with pompous Anglo-Saxon caution) and the National Commission for Scholarship and the Arts (COMSA, run by Sir Michael Stratherrick with a certain amount of Highland dash). These two organizations, and more particularly their knights, are successively torn apart and remade by the machinations of a vaguely disreputable character named Tim Kemp, who has worked for both; 'a small chubby man in his fifties, with large round eyes, a midsummer sky blue, like a child's, and the kind of grey hair, wispy but tufty, that so many crackpots seem to have.'[1] There is a very faint hint of Commodore Tribe in Tim Kemp, who is a kind of gin-soaked, pipe-smoking leprechaun: not the least like Tribe in appearance or personality, but with the same knack of setting Establishment figures hopelessly at odds with one another, disrupting the monolithic complacency of their

[1] *Sir Michael and Sir George*, pp. 9–10 (Heinemann 1964).

lives in much the same way that Priestley has often tried, or at any rate longed, to do himself.

There is one point to be made about *Sir Michael and Sir George*, in parenthesis, which has nothing to do with Englishness—unless it too was born out of a reflection of the contemporary English scene. You can find a foreshadowing of it in the last paragraph of the novel written before this one, *The Shapes of Sleep*, in 1962.

> 'Stop working, man. And take those clothes off.'
> But when finally, a long time afterwards, Sunday morning half-gone, he found she wasn't there, he put his nose into the sitting-room and could smell breakfast. She must have brought a bag he'd never noticed, for now she was wearing a light blue dressing-gown over darker blue pyjamas. They thought of everything. They might save us all yet.[1]

J.B. Priestley, this is to say, had begun to write about women. He had rarely done it before: rather, he had written about them either as incarnations of the personality and behaviour of something called Woman, or as individuals whose sex was mentioned only in connection with their attitudes and emotions. Until now, none of them had really progressed very much beyond the deliberately lush description of the girls in his first novel *Adam in Moonshine*: 'creatures so radiant, so instantly adorable, that at the very sight of them the day turned on more lights, everything went up into a higher key, and Adam's heart gave one suffocating bound upwards to be in tune.'[2] Until now, on Priestley woman had ever caused anything about a Priestley man to bound except his heart, his pride or his hopes: and this observation does not mean only that he was not wont to follow his characters into their beds (though certainly it is difficult to imagine Inigo Jollifant taking Susie Dean to bed, which may be an irrelevant 1970 criticism of a 1929 novel or may embody one of the things that is wrong with Susie Dean and Inigo Jollifant). The change which had been gradually creeping into his novels after the Second

[1] *The Shapes of Sleep*, p. 229 (Heinemann, 1962).
[2] *Ibid.*, p.5 1952 (Heinemann edition).

World War, and which was fully accomplished by the appearance
of *Sir Michael and Sir George*, was really a matter of analysing
relationships in several different ways at once. Partly this involved
a more deliberate treatment of sexual love—as, for instance, in the
first appearance of Sir Michael Stratherrick, written for a mis-
chievous effect which Priestley would probably not have thought
worth aiming at ten years earlier.

> At the very moment when Sir George was asking that question
> in Russell Square, Sir Michael, in Hampstead, was sitting on Sir
> George's bed, his tie in one hand and a cigarette in the other,
> wondering if a whisky-and-soda would be worth the trouble
> of going down to the dining room for it. Alison, wife to Sir
> George, was lying naked beneath a bedspread, its pink several
> shades lighter than her face, flushed from the act of love. She
> was a handsome woman, generously designed, who could
> assume a formidable manner in company, where most men
> imagined her to be sexually cold, when in fact she was sensual
> and ardent. This was one reason why Sir Michael was here; he
> liked his affairs to be spiced with such contrasts and contradictions,
> to pluck fruit where most men only saw a fortress in a desert.
> Loitering like this, tie in hand, he realized he was not being
> very clever. He had escaped from her embrace, no more than
> her body's gratitude, her wits not working yet, by muttering
> something about COMSA and an engagement, and he had
> begun dressing with a fair show of briskness; but now here he
> was, unable to keep up the pretence, inviting the kind of com-
> ment that could cut and wound a man when he was feeling
> drained out, empty and melancholy, vulnerable. They were all
> the same, except the real sillies; feeling vulnerable themselves,
> let down, insecure, because no protestations of devotion, no
> emotional and spiritual guarantees, followed the excitement,
> which, now they no longer needed it, began to seem a cheating
> male trick, they lashed out angrily—but not blindly, being
> guided by intuition to the gaps between joints in a man's self-
> esteem. Well, once again, he was asking for it.
> 'I must be mad,' she began.[1]

[1] *Sir Michael and Sir George*, pp. 14-15.

He is still writing about Woman, but now the frame of reference is broader; to write, in a permissive society, about the relationships between men and women without ever referring directly to their sexual behaviour is to risk appearing to ignore an entire dimension of your characters. At any rate Priestley's women seem to me a great deal more convincing in his later novels than in those written before 1950, and so do the ways in which his men react to them. Sir Michael's total and devastating infatuation with a shorthand-typist in his office is a shrewd, compassionate portrait of an attractive and sophisticated middle-aged man, who has strolled through life collecting and discarding women as easily as a small boy picking up pebbles, suddenly overwhelmed by passion for a dim and highly respectable little bird from the suburbs, who is also by a happy genetic accident quite shattering in appearance, 'more beautiful and more terrible than an army with banners'. There is another of these obsession-firing *anima* figures in Priestley's 1967 novel *It's An Old Country*, where the hero escapes enthralment by having a brief affair with the object of his infatuation which turns her into just another woman. But for Sir Michael there is no such escape, since he is not only helplessly bewitched by his little-Shirley-from-the-suburbs but genuinely in love, and he ends by marrying her. Both Shirley Essex and Alison Drake, in this book, are more convincing characters than any woman in a Priestley novel since the unpleasant Lena Golspie of Angel Pavement. From this point on the women are seen whole. They had always been feminine, but now they are female. And as a result—particularly in *Lost Empires*, which is more about the relationships between the sexes than it is about anything else—they enrich the novels as they had somehow failed to do before.

This was a matter of gradual subconscious development rather than a long-time novelist's decision to Add Sex, like a cook who has suddenly learned the knack of adding a pinch of salt when whipping up meringue. Priestley remained, as usual, his own man, and made no attempt to veer towards the now established convention of describing sexual encounters in as much clinical and athletic detail as if they involved no more of the personality than a wrestling match. He altered his approach in his own way, travelling as before the central mainstream of the English novel in which, by this time, he has become a large wave rather than a boat; and in the last ten years or so a great many readers who had unthinkingly accepted the old image of the genial family entertainer may have been agreeably surprised to find that this cosy-looking chap with the pipe was capable, among a great many other things, of writing about sex with as much insight as any other novelist alive—and a great deal more than most.

But the real difference, not only between the pre-war and post-war Priestleys but between Priestley and most of his contemporaries, lay in the distinction he was making between eroticism, sex and love—and, within the last, between loving and being 'in love'. He was, as always, using his novels to reflect his own feelings about the changing nature of contemporary society, and he was in doing so being both wiser and more avant-garde than many of his fellows. A great many no-holds-barred novelists today are not really engaged in analysing sexual relationships at all. Instead they are following the over-simplified, old-fashioned path of assuming that there are only two elements in the whole business, and that these are sex and love: the one an enjoyable sport, and the other a kind of anguished neurosis. They have forgotten, I think, that this is exactly the kind of division the Victorians made. If they think about the nineteenth-century novelists at all in this contest, it is with pitying derision for the way their society restrained them from telling it like it is. Yet many of them are caught in an inversion of this same situation themselves. The young novelist of 1870 made this simple distinction between sex and love; love was the thing you wrote about, and sex was the thing you put behind a curtain and ignored—if you wanted to write about it at all, you retreated behind the curtain and produced a pornographic book for private circulation, in as much polite secrecy as you would retire to the bathroom to use the lavatory. The young novelist of 1970, freed of the demand for secrecy or politeness, has pulled down the curtain but has not got rid of the one-two division. Instead of writing about sex and love as two halves of the same coin, he is trapped over and over again by the new convention—(the mirror-image of the old, based both on the need for selling books and the need for being what Dickens called 'in the swim' and what we call 'with it')—which demands that he ignore the castrated Victorian image of love and instead write almost exclusively about everything that lay behind that curtain—all of which is lumped together as 'sex'. And he is deceived, just as the young Victorian was deceived, for he is not really writing about sex at all; contrary to both conventions, there are not two divisions to be made in the analysing of sexual relationships, but three. Eroticism, sex, and love: you can find an understanding of the distinction between these three in the work of a number of our more perceptive modern novelists, including Priestley; and you can also find it set out in an essay of that name which he wrote in 1966. One of the things that is wrong not only with our literature but with our society, he points out, is the way we tend to confuse sex with the kind of solitary, self-regarding excitement that is really eroticism, which 'flourishes in our society on a scale never known before, not even during the decadence of Imperial Rome'.[1] The Soho strip-clubs, the two-inch-thick American paperback novels, the deliberately 'outspoken' films— all these are eroticism.

> Now to my mind it is a great mistake to condemn all this eroti-cism as 'sex'. I disagree entirely with all those moralists who are always telling us there is 'too much sex' in movies, stage shows, fiction. They are confusing two very different things. And it is this confusion that has in fact encouraged eroticism. In other words, eroticism has got away with it just because so many moralists and social reformers have mistakenly condemned it simply as sex. Ordinary people very sensibly feel that there cannot be all that wrong with sex, that while there may be a lot of sex in movies, shows, fiction, after all there is just as much

[1] 'Eroticism, Sex and Love', in *The Moments and Other Pieces* (Heinemann 1966).

sex, if not more, down the nearest street. And of course they are right.

Sex is not something wickedly thought up since grandma was a girl and the preacher was at college. It is a natural hunger and need, built into us from the beginning and unconsciously felt as an urge from the age of puberty onwards. Of course we can fight it and starve it, just as we can turn ourselves into living skeletons by eating the merest scraps of food, or dangerously dehydrate ourselves by drinking the barest minimum of fluids. But it is as natural for young people to be deeply concerned with sex as it is for them to use their lungs, arms and legs. To blame them for it is idiotic. They would not have come into existence if it were not for sex.

I am not going to pretend that there is no difference in our civilization between eating, drinking and making love. We have inherited some very complicated feelings about sex, including some that suggest a strange sort of guilt. As if we ought to know some other and nicer way of producing children! The truth is, the roots of our civilization—together with all these feelings we have inherited—go back about 2,500 years to a time of transition from matirarchal to patriarchal religious and social systems, when men came to believe that Woman was the enemy of Man's conscious development, that unchecked sexual indulgence robbed men of the energy, will, purpose, necessary for civilization. To this day, I believe, it is largely men not women who feel guilty about sex. And there have been many people, not necessarily savages but outside our particular civilization, who have never known these feelings of guilt.

Each sex wants and needs something from the other sex. (I have already shown that this is not true of eroticism, which is entirely self-regarding and does not go out to the other sex.) But it is a mistake, made far more often by men than by women, to imagine there is nothing but physical desire here. Indeed, the older I get the more I am convinced that sexual intercourse itself is far more a *psychological* than a physical act, and that this— really the psychological relationship—explains the seemingly mysterious successes or failures. We are not bulls and cows, so there are innumerable decent couples who are simply not right for each other and do not discover this until they have been married for some time. This is why divorce should be by mutual consent, without any faking of bogus evidence about adultery or cruelty. In Britain you have to make up a dirty story to convince the judge he should grant you a divorce, and then all too often he abuses you as a dirty low fellow because he believes this story, forgetting that he asked for it.

Now men often persuade themselves that they 'want a woman' as they might want a meal or a smoke, but nearly always this is so much cynical self-deception. In fact they need a great deal more than that—unless they have been completely perverted by eroticism—and what they really need is the psychological relationship with Woman herself, the other and complementary sex. Even the sailor hurrying to the nearest brothel is unconsciously in search of this relationship, though he may imagine that all he wants is perfunctory and brutal copulation. But it must be clearly understood that on this level we are discussing, there is no relationship of *persons* but simply a relationship between the sexes, as sexes, not this man and that woman but Man and Woman. When we come to persons, we arrive at love.

Eroticism, closing in on itself, wanting a sensation and not another person, bars love out. Indeed, too much eroticism probably makes real sexual love impossible. Not that this love is easy and effortless, as ten thousand pieces of sentimental claptrap assure us it is. Here it is worth pointing out that as our own age has become more and more insecure, less and less certain of itself, as more and more people have felt bewildered and fearful, there has been an increasing emphasis, not only in fiction and drama and the movies but also even in advertising, upon the value and joy, the magical saving grace, of sexual love. This is not necessarily wrong, but it can be argued that we may now be asking sexual love to shoulder too many burdens, overloading it to the breaking point. . . .

. . . I am myself suspicious of sexual love that appears to rest on no foundation of respect, admiration and *genuine liking*. This may seem odd because love is greater than these. Yet I have known a good many married couples who would have been indignant if they had been told they did not love each other, who would have declared at once and in all sincerity that they did, and yet obviously *did not like each other*. And though sexual love, in all its delight, tenderness and truth, is more than liking, I feel it ought to contain an immense amount of liking. We ought to be married to the kind of person we like enormously—a wonderful magical man—a glowing gem of a woman, a sweetheart and a honey. And if we are, then we can go down the years, not just feeling or accepting love, but consciously creating it, turning a relationship into a glorious work of art.[1]

And it was at this point, by whatever route, that the relationships in his novels had now arrived. Perhaps he was preparing himself to take up, at the age of eighty or so, the role of Wise Old Man—there was one such in *It's An Old Country*, a Dr. Firmius, living quietly in a London basement and writing a book about his private dream of setting up a special kind of university which would offer a year's teaching to certain men and women entering their perilous fourth decade (this, you may recall, was the age at which Priestley himself discovered Jung). 'It will be concerned entirely with culture and wisdom. It will try to rescue men and women in their forties—often a desperate age—from emptiness and despair. . . .'

With this novel, Priestley was back in his concern for England, and various kinds of emptiness play a large part in the portrait of England which he shows through the eyes of one Tom Adamson, newly arrived for the first time, at the age of thirty-three, from Australia. In pubs and hotels and cocktail parties and offices, the English are shown very often as machines no more bright or creative than the machines which they themselves drive: cars, those symbols of the industrial urbanization which was becoming Priestley's prime target now:

> . . . cars apparently filled with noisy lunatics, the daftest of them at the wheel, men who could hardly have been more dangerous if they had been given machine-guns and hand grenades. They were all half-stoned and had probably been celebrating the end of another meaningless week in a meaningless society. Perhaps

[1] *Ibid.,* pp. 106–10.

in another twenty years, machine-guns and hand grenades would be allowed on Saturday nights, just to add a once-a-week spice to the lives of London's twenty million citizens.[1]

It takes more than the introduction of a breathalyzer test to change Priestley's views on this sort of thing; he is attacking not so much the people, half-stoned or not half-stoned, as their habit of life. Tom's arrival in the Cotswolds, now Priestley's own countryside, is neatly symbolic of the whole thing.

> ... He drove at ease into an enchantment. The green hills and the old stone walls belonged to some dream of England. It was a tiny world, which no doubt at any moment might be taken to pieces and exported in plastic containers, that seemed to have been created by and for shepherds and craftsmen, pilgrims and lyric poets. The slumbering rows of houses looked as if they were turning centuries of pale sunlight into walls of honey. They had doorways waiting for Piers Plowman to return. ...
> ... Littlewold, when at last he found it, seemed one of the smallest and sleepiest of the villages. When he got out of the car, in front of the inn in the little square, not for the first time but with more force than ever before he realized what is wrong with motoring, which keeps us in the atmosphere of the cities we have left behind, boxed in with the fume and fret of them, still unable to breathe untroubled air. Now, out of the car at last, he could smell, taste, savour Littlewold and all its ancient, pale-gold companions. ...[2]

When Tom Adamson is done with his quest through England—looking for, and eventually finding, a father he has never seen—he does not want to go back to Australia; but neither does he want to stay in England. He wants to become a kind of global man, working perhaps with the United Nations: 'I'd rather be in a dam' awful place with a sensible purpose than in some pleasant place not knowing what I was supposed to be doing there.'[3] To

[1] *It's an Old Country*, p. 186 (Heinemann 1967).
[2] *Ibid.*, pp. 76-7.
[3] *Ibid.*, p. 228.

Tom, England is a country in which he could live only if he chose the right place, were thirty years older and had an assured income (one hears the echo: 'In spite of everything, this is still the most civilized place in the world to live . . .'). In the absence of these factors, he is not keen. He sees English life as something which, before the Second World War, was like a jigsaw neatly fitted together on a table. 'Then somebody booted the table. The pieces are still there but now they aren't joined up, any of 'em. . . .'

And Tom Adamson, Australian, feels no obligation to help put the pieces together. But of course J. B. Priestley, Englishman, does. His most recent attempt at doing this, by focusing a small satirical spotlight on a considerable number of the jigsaw pieces, has also been his largest: *The Image Men* is a gigantic work divided into two volumes of some 150,000 words each. It is basically a big double portrait of its two heroes, tall lean Cosmo Saltana and short tubby Owen Tuby, happy iconoclasts of the kind Priestley most enjoys inventing. Saltana and Tuby are Con Men with a vengeance; they con the entire nation, right up to the Prime Minister and the Leader of the Opposition, with their development of an Institute of Social Imagistics which is no more than a kind of skilful public relations operation wrapped up in academic jargon. Priestley's targets this time are legion: in *Out of Town*, the first volume of the book, his arrows are directed chiefly at that very vulnerable neo-scientific subject, sociology; in *London End*, the second, at every conceivable aspect of life in the capital, particularly those connected with some variety of success.

With *The Image Men*, Priestley is back in his affectionate exasperation with England, but the exasperation is not really very serious. Iris Murdoch called this 'a very clever and funny book with real people in it', and that is precisely what it is; no more, no less. The principals, and their relationships with one another, are real, but the world they inhabit is fantasy; if you are going to show the entire Establishment really being taken for a ride, then your riders-in-chief must be cold and unprincipled persons driven solely by self-interest, not a pair of old sweeties, however crafty.

There are too many cold and unprincipled opponents up there, and too many agreeably shrewd ones as well; our masters are no longer all bumbling pompous asses. Saltana and Tuby would never have been able to put one over on Seth Hull, of *Festival at Farbridge*—nor on Sir Michael, though they might have done pretty well with Sir George. Their history is not a satire, nor really intended as one; it is a long leisurely joke, with the Englishman making fun of England, and no cutting edge in the laughter.

But when Priestley is not writing fantasy, you cannot say the same.

> Politicians should take time off from the smoking rooms, and committee rooms, statistics and Trollope, to read a few novels and visit theatres not occupied by whodunits and lounge-hall farces. Then they could ask themselves why the more sensitive and articulate young English express so much contempt and disgust, appealing at once to a kind of unfocused rebelliousness among younger readers and playgoers. No matter how hastily contrived, how wilful and wild, this strictly contemporary fiction and drama is important, especially to the politicians, because it is news from the hidden centre, dispatches from the invisible front, telegrams of warning from tomorrow.
>
> Even now, in spite of all the pressures and mass-persuasion techniques, youth arrives among us with certain expectations, and some of these cannot be satisfied with money, food, clothes, sex, table tennis and records of pop singers. They want to reach maturity integrated into a society that has a common purpose and noble aims and is not a slobbering mess of irresponsibility, mean devices, and self-deception, where privilege and money can buy honour and once-great names, and parsons preach the H-bomb. There is something in them, through what inheritance we do not know, that recoils from corruption. And this is the most corrupting society that England has known in my lifetime.[1]

This is the other Priestley. He is not really a satirist. When he

[1] 'Fifty Years of the English', essay in *The Moments and Other Pieces*, p. 216.

uses fiction as a weapon of social criticism, he ridicules rather than savages, and his prime weapon is an amiable mockery rather than an avenging sword. Savagery has never been part of his equipment, either as man or as writer. 'My hobby,' he once said, 'is the search for wisdom. I look for it as other men look for rare birds.'[1] And men who search for wisdom do not make satirists; your true satirist is a fanatic, a man who knows how to hate and—all in a good cause—how to be cruel. Priestley doesn't. His fiercest emotion is rage. And he is most effective as a social critic when he is angry with some aspect of English behaviour, and the mockery turns to irony. 'These places left to rot have people in them,' he wrote bitterly of the depressed areas in *English Journey*. 'Some of these people are rotting too. Such people appear to have been overlooked; or perhaps they were mistaken for bits of old apparatus, left to rust and crumble away.'[2] And the irony was set out in clearer detail in *Wonder Hero*, the novel written to match.

> They looked again at the melancholy river, which had been robbed of its trade, but not of its filth, like Slakeby itself, which still looked as dirty as it did when every big chimney was spouting black fumes. . . . Perhaps it was the dirt of neglect now and not that of the blacker industries. Some of the men hanging about the streets had something of the same appearance, a look of being uncared-for; greasy hair and greyish skins. Slakeby reminded Charlie of towns he had seen towards the end of long strikes. There were plenty of fellows out of work in Bendworth and Utterton, but in Slakeby there were more fellows unemployed than working. A few of them had got allotments—Tom Anderson had applied for one—and some of the others attended classes, but most of them did nothing beyond attend at the Labour Exchange, the commissioner's office, and such places. The streets were filled with them, just hanging about, no money in their pockets, not enough food in their bellies or blood in their veins, seeing little hope anywhere.

[1] *Rain upon Godshill*, p. 8.
[2] *English Journey*, p. 345.

'And you see, Charlie,' said his uncle, as they entered Church-gate, the main street, 'when once a town goes slithering down like this, everybody goes with it. It's not just engineering and shipbuilding trades that's gone here. There's dozens o' shops closed, and a lot o' them that's open is only just scratching for a living. And there's cashiers and clerks and suchlike—all out o' work. This street's best we have, as you know yourself, and it mightn't look so bad is you look at it very sharp, but take a good look and you'll see it's gone down the hill, like the rest of us. It's only those Woolworth sort o' places that's busy. Rest of it's got a ragged look, hasn't it?'

Charlie admitted that it had. Then he noticed two very imposing new corner buildings a little further down. They were both in sharp contrast to anything in their neighbourhood. He enquired what they were.

His uncle chuckled. 'Let's go and have a look at one,' he said, and they crossed the road.

'A bank,' said Charlie.

'Ay, they're both banks. . . .'[1]

It is as inevitable that Priestley should be a socialist as that he should speak with a Yorkshire accent; but just as the accent is not as pronounced and self-conscious as many people expect, nor is the socialism. He never became a socialist, he was born and brought up as one, and his belief was 'almost something belonging to tradition and filial piety'. The Bradford of Priestley's youth was a place in which radical and Labour sympathies were strong; he may have grown up there in a golden Edwardian world, but he grew up too in a world of strikes and desperately low wages, visiting his grandparents and uncles and aunts in 'the wretched little back-to-back houses in the long, dark streets behind the mills'. He knew older men and women who had spent their childhood going out in the dark chill of early morning to work in the factories, and working there all day until they came home once more in the dark. His father, being both schoolmaster and humane citizen, fought for years to end the 'half-time' system

[1] *Wonder Hero*, pp. 222–4 (Heinemann 1950 edition).

which still had children of twelve and thirteen in their schools for half the day and in the factories for the other half. Young Jack was fortunate in the security of his own home, but this made him more, not less, sensitive to the great gulf that existed between the thousands of ordinary people working endlessly in the mills and the distant mill-owners who had bought themselves great houses and great names out of the labour whose reward just about kept their employees in boots. Nobody starved to death in Bradford, but injustice was clearly visible all round. 'If you wanted to over-simplify,' he said once, 'and say just one thing about my political beliefs, it would be that I am a radical in the sense of being for the poor against the rich.' And this he absorbed by a kind of intellectual osmosis; from his surroundings and above all from his home. You can learn a great deal about Priestley, and about the origins of his shadowy ideal world, from his description of his father in *Midnight on the Desert*.

> My father was a schoolmaster, and a very good one, with an almost ludicrous passion for acquiring and importing knowledge. He was not a born scholar, but he was a born teacher. Outside his school, he did a great deal of useful public service—speaking, helping to organize, working on committees, and so on—not because he was a busybody or was socially ambitious, but because he was essentially public-spirited, the type of citizen that democratic theorists have in mind but rarely in actual view. But there was nothing of the smooth committee humbug about him. He was very brisk, humorous, stout-hearted, not to be patronized or bullied... He was not a romantic figure, did not pretend to be. His world lacked glitter and glamour. I never remember seeing him either in ecstasies nor yet defeated by despair. But he never failed a duty, left the world better than he found it, was loved by his friends and respected by his army of acquaintances, and had a lot of fun. Beneath the rather droll surface peculiarities—his love of making acquaintances, of asking questions, of imparting information; his fear of minor social criticism; his distrust of the picturesque, romantic, grandiose things of this life; his odd mixture of impatience and explosive hot temper—he was a living rock of

good solid human nature. If I was picking a team to go and colonize another planet, I would choose his kind first. Years ago, when my first scribblings were achieving print, he was proud of me; and now, too long after we exchanged our last words, I think I am prouder still of him. Because he did not want too much himself and hated to see others have too little, because he knew that life now has something better to offer than a universal all-in wrestling match for money, because he knew that there were more and more people like himself coming into the world, people who could be trusted to do their duty by the public that employed him, who did not need to be threatened with starvation nor inspired by greed, he believed not only in government for the people by the people but also in production, which touches us more than government does, by the people for the people, and so was a socialist. And he remains in my memory as the ideal socialist citizen. Of such could be made the best kingdom yet on this earth.[1]

It was this kind of liberal socialism that Priestley absorbed. He is not a left-wing Labour man, and never has been. 'I am a pink,' he says, 'and a pleasant healthy colour it is too.'[2] In the socialist tradition of English literature, he belongs with Dickens and Wells; angered by injustice, fired by dreams of an ideal democracy, but not driven by bitterness and resentment to the point of demanding revolution, off with the head of the old system and on with the new. Priestley doesn't like systems; they are all too inflexible to suit him. He is too rational to think of life in terms of a battle between the Boss Class and the Workers, and he is as unsuited to a party based on trades unions as on one based on landed gentlemen. And he could no more be a Marxist than he could be a Fascist. It is a fair measure of his political beliefs that while he has always supported the socialist cause, he has never been a member of the Labour Party.

'In a way it's misleading to describe me as a socialist. The most important thing for me is not the economic aspect. I believe

[1] *Midnight on the Desert*, pp. 133–5.
[2] *Margin Released*, p. 227.

basically that power must be divided; that this is the only chance
for the individual to enjoy a reasonable amount of freedom.
Liberty is more important than efficiency. There's a common
idea that a country is a kind of firm. But the first consideration
is not efficiency, it's having a certain flexibility—and you get
that only by dividing power. Communism concentrates power.
The terrible thing about it is not the economics—though they're
dreadful, from a practical point of view—but the fact of limiting
the freedom to think. And if capitalism is given its head, without
checks, it becomes the same kind of tyranny. You could have a
tyranny like any other in America if the businessmen had everything all boxed up—there's too much emphasis on business
there already. Coolidge said, the U.S.A. is about business; but
he was wrong, it's only a means to an end. . . .

'Labour in England is coming up to the kind of situation that's
essential: allowing a certain amount of private enterprise, but
with a government in control to protect the individual. After
all, the important thing isn't who owns the gas-works in a town,
it's having some kind of control over it on behalf of the towns-
people. Our kind of system makes for a good deal of muddle
and argument, and slows things up, but it's the only thing that
makes personal freedom properly possible. It accounts of course
for our inefficiencies; like, for instance, the way we're so slow
building motorways, because we take so long to acquire all the
rights instead of just bulldozing through. . . .'

A professional politician on either side of the House might,
after listening to this, comment wryly that it is a great deal easier
to talk largely about personal freedom and government control
than it is to find the practical balancing-point between the two
on which the country can support itself. Priestley would no
doubt agree—but add that it is the politician's job to work out
the means of support, not his. And he would be right. Priestley
has seldom been actively involved in politics, but he is the kind
of man whom professional politicians need: as both a bulwark and
an irritant; a voice of conscience; a reminder of what politics
and government are for. His only real involvement in politics
outside his writing came at the end of the Second World War,

when he campaigned with enormous energy and devotion for the Labour Party before the General Election of 1945. His popular reputation, from his pre-war books and particularly from his wartime broadcasts, made him an exceedingly useful public figure, and throughout that summer he worked very hard, sometimes making four speeches in a day. 'What had happened, of course, was that with the chief Labour men all in the wartime coalition, the Labour organization as such had gone to bits, and the election was fought by a very hastily organized group— young people giving up their holidays to campaign, that sort of thing. And with them what you might I suppose call the intellectuals; Kingsley Martin, Harold Laski, Percy Cudlipp on the *Daily Herald*, and me.'

It was at this point in his life—and one other, a few years later —that the man of action lurking in Priestley's personality briefly took over control. He was so caught up in his conviction of the country's need for a Labour government that at a weak moment he even agreed to stand for Parliament himself—as an Independent, for the Cambridge University seat which still existed then. By the time the University results came in—they were necessarily always late—Labour's huge majority was well established, killing their putative need for sympathetic Independents which had bewitched Priestley into appearing on the ballot sheet. But he won more votes than a progressive candidate had ever received for the seat, and for a few horrified hours before the final result he had to face the idea that he might have got in. Mercifully for all concerned, he didn't. He would not, to say the very least, have enjoyed being an M.P. ('To sit there,' he says softly, appalled even in reminiscence, 'to sit day after day, listening to all that *rubbish* . . .') Nor, unless all his talent as a man of letters had suddenly disappeared, would he have made a very good one. Priestley is not one of Nature's politicians; he is too easily bored, too impatient with pomposity, convention, platitude, complacency, and all the other things that men have to endure if they cherish political ambitions. He would make a statesman in a very large arena, but not in a small one. It is typical of his kind of belligerent self-respect that he is one of the very few public figures who have not only attacked successive governments' use of the Honours list as a means of dishing out political rewards, but have on that ground consistently refused all offers of Honours for themselves. (In this respect plain J. B. Priestley is in the fairly good company of plain H. G. Wells, plain Rudyard Kipling and plain G. B. Shaw.) It may also be typical that none of his close friends is a politician.

After the election and his campaigning were over, the Labour members gave a dinner for Priestley in the House of Commons. The public was less grateful, and the popularity which had both warmed and maddened him before and during the war tended in some respects to droop after it. Popularity, that is to say, as reflected through the mass media—it had never had much connection with the reputation of Priestley the author, except possibly in the subconscious minds of some of the critics, and it had no connection now; playgoers flocked to *An Inspector Calls* and *The Linden Tree*, and quantities of readers bought *Bright Day*. But some sections of the Press which had attacked him for his support of Labour campaigning managed in various rather shadowy ways —it's easily done—to project a rather disagreeable image of J. B. Priestley, especially when he was found to be writing a large novel celebrating the idea of a Festival which they were busily ridiculing; and when his second marriage ended in divorce there was some undeserved mud-slinging. If the mistaken image of his work dates from *The Good Companions* and the wartime *Postscripts*, the mistaken image of his personality—dour, cantankerous, intolerant, Leftist Yorkshireman, of which bunch the only accurate word is Yorkshireman—dates from this period of ten years or so after the war. England is an odd place. For an essentially good-natured race, we have a remarkable propensity for believing what it is suggested that we should believe—which is, of course, one reason why Priestley had such an enjoyable time writing *The Image Men*. Still, being as English as the next man, and probably more so than most, he is essentially good-natured himself, and though he will grumble a bit if shown those old and rather smeared images, they will generate no heat. Priestley isn't the type; he reserves his heat for other things.

> 'I express dogmatic opinions, but I don't really hold anything against anyone. What's the point? Better to say someone's an imbecile and that's an end of it. After all, novelists and dramatists should *like* a lot of people. Shakespeare obviously did. The great fault now with novelists is that they hate everybody—sometimes I think there's a lot written out of resentment. I don't dislike people, I laugh at them. I don't think I've ever written anything you could describe as savage—some of the *New Statesman* pieces have been fairly fierce, but that's not fiction, they're polemical. I differ from so many people on the Left who seem to want to go on disliking, disliking—it must give them a cosy feeling of solidarity. But it bores the hell out of me. . . .'

One of his fiercer post-war *New Statesman* articles generated a good deal more than heat; it sparked off the entire Campaign for Nuclear Disarmament. This led to his last real excursion into active public life. (Like Ritchie Calder and a number of other well-known British idealists, he had done some work for UNESCO after the war, but this had not lasted long. He had put in a report pointing out that the organization would function best if it were to keep its headquarters staff down to a minimum and appoint teams of top-ranking specialists for specific short-term projects; UNESCO did precisely the opposite; Priestley resigned.) CND, at any rate in its early days, had a close and obvious connection with Priestley's humanitarian concern for the future not only of English society but of Western civilization; he attended its founding meeting, made scores of speeches all over the country in its support, and severed his official connection with it later on not over policy but because he disagreed with certain organizational changes. (Jacquetta Hawkes remained an active member of the executive, and was a familiar figure at CND protest marches in a fetching red gondolier-type hat.)

Since then, the long love affair—or more accurately, the long marriage—between J. B. Priestley and his native land has been confined to his essays. Confined, though, is a misleading word;

these essays, most of them in the *New Statesman*, are not only superb bits of writing but contain some of the best social and political commentary Priestley or anybody else has written in the last twenty-five years. *Thoughts in the Wilderness* (1957), *The Moments* (1966) and all the pieces written since and not yet published in book form, should all be put together in the year 2050 or so, when they would be found to give an excellent and vivid portrait of mid-twentieth-century England as seen through the eyes of an astonishingly modern writer, 'who might', someone will say, 'have been born in 1994, not 1894'. For in most of his insights Priestley is, as always, ahead of his time. He was writing dark and fervent warnings against the stultifying effect of Block Thinking—blocks of attitudes, blocks of characteristics, blocks of ideas, each available in a complete set, cowboy or Indian, choose your own—shortly before most of our more enervated politicians retreated into it, apparently for all time. When he coined the word *Admass* it was not as a warning, since *Admass* was already sweeping over us. But we might have done well to listen to the way he ended his coining paragraph (in *Journey Down a Rainbow*, in 1955), or to consider one or two of the offshoots of *Admass*, like *Nomadmass*, 'the long thin empire of the internal combustion engine'.

> *Admass.* This is my name for the whole system of an increasing productivity, plus inflation, plus a rising standard of material living, plus high-pressure advertising and salesmanship, plus mass communication, plus cultural democracy and the creation of the mass mind, the mass man. (Behind the Iron Curtain they have *Propmass*, official propaganda taking the place of advertising, but all with the same aims and objects.) The people firmly fixed in *Admass* are *Admassians*. Most Americans (though not all; they have some fine rebels) have been *Admassians* for the last thirty years; the English, and probably most West Europeans, only since the War. It is better to live in *Admass* than to have no job, no prospect of one, and see your wife and children getting hungrier and hungrier. But that is about all that can be said in favour of it. All the rest is a swindle. You think everything is opening out when in fact it is narrowing and

closing in on you. Finally you have to be half-witted or half-drunk all the time to endure it. . . .[1]

Priestley often, and accurately, sees a gloomy similarity between the towering societies of America and the Soviet Union: 'The management is different,' he wrote in an essay on 'Eros and Logos', 'but the enterprise is broadly the same.'[2] Perhaps this is one reason for the curiously antagonistic manner in which he has been treated over the years by the American Press, who tend even more than most other Americans to fret and sulk if someone gives their country anything less than extravagant praise. They know—or ought to—that he has done quantities of perceptive and sympathetic writing about the U.S.A.: but to equate them in any way at all with the Communists—well—jeeze.

'If I must choose,' wrote Priestley, 'I would prefer an American victory to a Russian one, just as I would prefer writing TV advertisements for cornflakes to lumbering on thin cabbage soup in Siberia.'[3] But he does not really want either of them; he wants England, and preferably an England of a character strong enough to resist being culturally or politically swallowed up by either giant. He did what he could, at the time when he felt it most vital, to strengthen the political side of things: 'It was very important indeed,' he said recently, 'that we didn't have the Tories in 1945 and did have the Labour Party—because it changed the whole outlook of Western Europe on Communism by showing that it was possible to have another kind of Socialist government. Where else could they have found such a comparison?' But there is not much to be done about the cultural side—except to go on shouting a warning. While the Tories were back in power in the 'fifties, Priestley was attacking both cultural and political aspects simultaneously: 'It is these bogus Yeomen of the Guard,' he wrote wrathfully, 'who have opened the gates to Admass.'[4] But

[1] J. B. Priestley and Jacquetta Hawkes: *Journey Down a Rainbow*, pp. 51-2 (Heinemann, 1955).

[2] Essay reprinted in *Essays of Five Decades*, p. 210.

[3] *Ibid.*, p. 210-11.

[4] 'The Blue Yonder Boys', essay in *The Moments and Other Pieces*, p. 54.

now? In the *New Statesman* in 1967, while making a case against joining the Common Market, he wrote:

> A few years ago, in a piece here called 'Ambience or Agenda', I argued that a change of atmosphere, a different climate of values, ideas, opinions, was even more important than the most elaborate party programme. The ambience would produce the agenda, not the agenda the ambience. But it seems to me that Labour, though meaning well, has so far been all agenda and no ambience. Instead of being made to feel we must make sacrifices out of love of our country, we have been encouraged to suspect that we are being punished for something. Again, while we can live more frugally, we would do it with a better heart under an obviously frugal government. Finally, we don't feel we are living in an audaciously creative country, but in a rather stiff and disagreeable one.[1]

'An audaciously creative country'—there you have it again. Irony pursues Priestley as it has always done, for a year or two earlier, at about the same time as the earlier piece he referred to, he had also been writing, in 'Fifty Years of the English', that he had some confidence in the Labour Party now that it was under the leadership of Harold Wilson, not only because Wilson appeared to be uniting it more successfully than Gaitskell had done, 'but also because he frequently mentions, often as a first objective, "a release of energy". For the energy is still here, waiting to be released by politicians with courage and imagination.'[2]

Well: it is here still, and still waiting; and so—still shouting—is Priestley the Englishman. You can only properly understand him through an understanding of England; he is a living continuance of its central literary tradition, an archetype of its stubborn individualists, and above all an idealist in the line of Morris and Owen and Wells hoping for a new and better Camelot. If this ever arrives, he will have had a lot to do with it. In the meantime, it is agreeable to reflect on one small additional fact which makes it impossible to think of the whole Priestley without also thinking

[1] '*Off-Shore Island Man*', reprinted in *Essays of Five Decades*, p. 307.
[2] *The Moments and Other Pieces*, p. 217.

of England, and vice versa. Most professional authors have certain pet devices for finding suitable names for the characters they invent. Priestley does too; he takes them from the A.A. book. 'Going through Britain,' he said once, 'I pass hundreds of my minor characters.' It struck me as the neatest bit of accidental symbolism I had ever heard.

V

BE CHEERFUL, SIR

The coming of the *Idea*. There is nothing piecemeal about its arrival. It comes as the ancient gods and goddesses must have manifested themselves to their more fortunate worshippers. (And indeed it comes from the same place.) At one moment the mind knows it not. The next moment it is there, taking full possession of the mind, which quivers in ecstatic surrender. I have been accused—and not unjustly—of having too many ideas. 'More hard work, more patience,' they tell me, 'and not so many ideas, my boy.' But although hard work and patience may bring rewards I shall never know, where is the ravishing delight in them? Lord, let me live to welcome again with all the old abandon, not knowing whether I am dressing or undressing, whether it is Tuesday morning or Friday evening, the sunburst of the Idea![1]

There it was in *Delight*, among celebrations of fountains and conductors, lawn tennis and wood, making stew and answering back: the one central point of Priestley's existence. Sometimes when writing a caricature self-portrait he has described himself as self-indulgent; he is no voluptuary, but no puritan either, and perhaps indeed there is a kind of self-indulgence in the way he has always surrendered in delight to the glorious, mind-blowing explosion that is the creative idea. But no one who is any kind of creative artist would blame him. For the makers, these sudden bolts of lightning are the focal points of existence; they are what life is all about. To nudge one of them aside—go away, I'm busy, I haven't time for you now—is unthinkable, except in those cases where the bolt of lightning is seen, after the first dazzle, to be no

[1] *Delight*, p. 109.

more after all than a blazing firework which will shortly sputter out. To fail to seize and develop a genuine creative idea goes totally against the artist's central superstition: the feeling that if you do not dance when the Muse plays a tune, you may never hear the music again. So although Priestley is a restless and impatient man, the sort who can never stay in one place for very long without becoming involved in plans for visiting another, and who is shortly thereafter fidgeting to get home again; who rushes to the railway station in order to be there half an hour before the train pulls out; who writes rapidly, paints only in a medium which demands speed, plunges head-deep into plans as soon as some new project is discussed—in spite of all this, his constant reaching out towards the next idea does not prevent him from giving his full attention to the one that goes before. The solidity of his talent and the sensitivity of his literary conscience together see to that. There can certainly be great peril in a rapid flow of ideas, if they shower themselves into the mind of a writer who has the wrong kind of character to keep up with them; he, whether the ideas themselves are good or bad—generally nobody ever has a chance to find out—tends to end up as the would-be writer, the ideas-man without staying power; the chap who is only too ready to pour out with his third drink the entire plot of his next short story, but who will somehow never get it written. He is unfortunate, this one; if he has a genuine literary conscience he will end up embittered, envious, disappointed in himself; if he has not, he will do very well in advertising. He has hardly anything in common with Priestley, who may occasionally get a little bored with a project when he is four-fifths of the way through, and have a part of his subconscious mind open and ready for the next idea—but who always gives his full attention to something once he has begun it, and always finishes it once he is fully embarked. Indeed occasionally, in the case of a few unproduced and unpublished plays, he has returned to it again and again like a dog worrying a bone, feeling that he had served the original idea poorly and there was still some improvement that could be made.

Too many ideas? Too much work? Or simply a gigantic reservoir of creative energy, to whose like we are not accustomed among the other major writers of this century? I remember once hearing Priestley say in passing about one of his books: 'Of course, I never intended that to be a major novel'—and feeling a new variant of the old question twitch in my mind. If you know from the beginning which book is likely to be a major piece of work, and which one minor, wouldn't it be better sometimes to dismiss one or two of the minor ideas, so as to concentrate better on the major books? But even as I wondered, I knew that the question was nonsense: for there is no scrap of evidence that his small works have ever taken anything away from his large ones. On the contrary, you have only to hear him talk about one of the major books while it is in progress, or recently finished, to realize that his relationship with it while it is in the making is total, not capable of being damaged or improved by any kind of influence from outside. As with those arroyos in the Arizona desert, beside one of which his writing-hut was built during the pre-war winter sojourns, either the river comes rushing down in flash-flood torrents, or it does not come at all.

'These factual things,' he said gloomily one day when he was working on *The Prince of Pleasure*, his study of the Regency, 'I don't really enjoy them. Stopping every moment to look up a reference—it's like walking across a ploughed field in boots too big for you. And as you get older, you lose your original drive and energy—two hours of close attention now and I've had it for the morning. I remember Desmond MacCarthy reviewing *Midnight on the Desert*, or one of those, and praising what he called the flow and freshness of the style—well, I haven't got that any more.'

If I hadn't found it too demoralizing, I should have retorted that after two hours of close attention I had generally had it for the morning too, and I was forty years younger; and that as for drive and energy, he had so far published more in his seventies alone than I or any of my contemporaries had in our lifetime—eight books, two plays, and several dozen essays. Instead, I observed mildly that I recalled one of the major reviews of *The Image Men*, which had recently been published, praising precisely the flow and freshness of its style. But it wasn't the quoted praise which made Priestley instantly brighten; it was the mention of the novel.

'*Image Men*—well, that just flowed out. I loved those two characters, Tuby and Saltana; I'd gone on for three hundred thousand words and yet it was a wrench to leave them. I could have written a novel of two million words about those two. But I had to say good-bye to them, and I've been a little sadder since. Perhaps they take away a part of you. There isn't much in writing, you know, that I enjoy so much as the feeling of a novel going well, when I can come down to the study and there are Tuby and Saltana sitting over there in the corner, and I'm about to join them . . .'—he grinned, like an over-sized imp, and rubbed his hands—'. . . and it's: "Well, boys, what's for today?" '

And there you have J. B. Priestley; in that deep delight, and the communication of it, the giants among enchanters have their real rare power. Once that kind of creative energy is under way, it makes no difference whether the writer in question turns out an *œuvre* of fifteen hundred books or a hundred and fifty: talent is not like a butter ration, which can be spread in thick dollops only if you use very few pieces of bread. If Priestley had worked only in one field, would the narrowing of focus have turned him into the unalloyed, hundred-per-cent artist that he has not in fact become? Unlikely—for the nature and range of any artist's work must always depend upon his personality, and in the last analysis Priestley is probably more concerned with the condition of man than with the condition of literature. Though his basic attitude to life is that of the artist, it is not that of the Louis Dubedat brand: 'I wouldn't sacrifice a wife or a child for my art. That kind of thing could be more forgivable in a musician or a painter, perhaps—but a writer, after all, is supposed to understand what people suffer. And if he doesn't *care* . . .'

The caring, for him, is everything. Where Priestley is concerned, it is in fact a mistake to make this distinction between care for the condition of literature and for the condition of man, for an essential part of his vision is his ability to see the two inter-twined. This was the driving force behind his decision to undertake, at the age of sixty-five, the huge critical book *Literature and Western Man*, of which he observed: 'A young man couldn't write it, because he wouldn't have the necessary reading; and an elderly man, who might have the reading, would have more sense than to attempt such a book.'

> And if I have not had more sense, undertaking, at a time when most men begin to slacken off, to sit in the sun, a most formid-able task, often both laborious and irritating (I possess about 10,000 books and can hardly find any of them without a search), this was not because I was tempted to make some use of nearly half a century of wide if desultory reading, together with much experience, not to be despised for this task, of the writing and publishing and criticism of books and the writing of plays and the managing of theatrical enterprises, experience that has taken me, so to speak, out of the dining-room, where many critics and most literary historians may be found, into the kitchen where the dinners are cooked. What really tempted me, so that I fell, was my conviction that ours is an age of supreme crisis, when the most desperate decisions have to be made, and that some account of Western Man, in terms of the litera-ture he had created and enjoyed, might help us to understand ourselves (and doing the work has certainly helped *me*), and to realize where we are and how we have arrived here.[1]

'It's not really a work of literary criticism,' he says, looking back at it. 'It's the product of a full mind.' One might add, of one particular full mind, for it is doubtful whether anyone other than Priestley could have written *Literature and Western Man*, with its magnificent grasp of the relationship of the arts to their respective ages, its sense of time, its intuitive understanding of the giants. Nobody else has ever written with quite the same understanding of one giant in particular; nobody else has been so curiously well qualified.

[1] From the Introduction to *Literature and Western Man*, p. x (Heinemann, 1960).

He loved the England of his boyhood, which still belonged
to the eighteenth rather than the nineteenth century, but the
very different England of the 'fifties and 'sixties, with its booming industry and new, hard, narrow middle class, he regarded
with a mixture of fear, contempt and horror. He saw its affairs
conducted in a fog, its expectations originating in a convict
hulk, its society a series of prisons as in *Little Dorrit*, its pursuit
of wealth the scramble round the dust-heap of *Our Mutual
Friend*. On a long and wide view of the nation, he was very
English; but, unlike Thackeray and Trollope, at ease in their
clubs, he was not at all a Victorian middle-class Englishman,
was indeed the very opposite of one. His outlook and sympathies are very close to those of the traditional working-classes,
whose mistrust and dislike of institutions, bureaucracy, the
official machinery of government, legal hocus-pocus, solemn
political humbug and jobbery, he shares and expresses with
comic genius. It is easy enough to dismiss his account of politics
as a game between Coodle, Foodle and Cuffy, Duffy, Fuffy, his
foggy Chancery, his Circumlocution Office and its Barnacles,
as the wild exaggerations of a comedian; but he is often nearer
the essential truth about Victorian England than Macaulay and
his pooh-poohing critics ever were. His standpoint was the one
that politicians, important officials, all persons in power or
seeking to be, always claim to have but somehow never act from
and contrive to forget, that of ordinary human happiness, the
life-enhancing quality, innocence of mind and heart. And it
is useless here to accuse him, as some critics have solemnly
done, of inconsistencies, as if he were a social and political
theorist and not, as he was from first to last no matter how his
work changed and developed, a dramatic artist, one of the
world's supreme story-tellers. From his first comic and melodramatic improvisations to his last symbolic narratives of what
seemed to him a detestable society, an age profoundly corrupt,
he was never an immaculate artist, never free from dubious
tricks to keep the crowd amused, always vulnerable to the
stupidest criticism; but his positive qualities (not excluding
subtleties that have largely passed unnoticed) are gigantic and
rare, those of a great creator, equally capable of enthralling a
child and winning the admiration of a philosopher. We began

with Santayana, deliberately choosing a man very different from Dickens in all essentials; so let us now end with him. He wrote: 'I think Dickens is one of the best friends mankind has ever had.'[1]

One hears not echoes but harmonics, sympathetic vibrations; though Priestley has sometimes been driven wild with irritation by superficial comparisons between his long novels and Dickens' long novels, his humour and Dickens' humour, his characters and Dickens' characters, and so on, he could hardly deny that in certain deeper respects he and Charles Dickens belong to the same family; in each of them a certain background has combined with a certain character—different in each case—to produce the same fundamental scale of values. If Priestley could be said to have a particular fellow-feeling for any aspect of a particular English novelist, it is probably not any part of Dickens but the instinctive grave irony of Henry Fielding; there is a certain familiar tartness in one of his comments on Fielding and *Tom Jones*: 'He and his masterpiece are big enough and strong enough to endure neglect, to await the time when fashion will swing from introverted to extroverted novels and novelists, when comic characters and a general liveliness and bustle (together with occasional horseplay) no longer alienate critics, when readers with pretensions to intellect will not object to a certain masculine weight and thrust of intellect in their fiction.'[2] But his peculiar feeling for the twin traditions of thought and literature in England, which shows itself in the nature of his own fiction as well as in his understanding of the work of others, gives Priestley a huge advantage over many others in discussing the great humane English writers like Dickens and Shakespeare. *Literature and Western Man* has the range of a hundred generalized academic literary histories, but its warmth of understanding is uncommon. It would make good prescribed reading for all undergraduates, entering institutions intended to teach them to think. It might equally be prescribed for every literate human being who has reached the age of forty or so—an

[1] *Literature and Western Man*, pp. 233–4.
[2] *Ibid.*, p. 92.

age by which, taught or self-taught, he may be presumed to have learned to think, but may be wondering what he should be thinking about. For this, I sometimes feel, is the kind of reader whom Priestley had always been aiming at, not only in this book but in all the rest. And the final passage of *Literature and Western Man* is in a way a microcosm of all that he has to offer them. It is a long passage for a quotation, but it puts a great deal of J. B. Priestley into a short space.

> The modern age shows us how helpless the individual is when he is at the mercy of his unconscious drives and, at the same time, is beginning to lose individuality because he is in the grip of huge political and social collectives. It is an age of deepening inner despair and of appalling catastrophes, an age when society says one thing and then does something entirely different, when everybody talks about peace and prepares for more and worse wars. Western Man is now schizophrenic. Literature, which is further removed from the centre than ever before, does what it can. The writer of genius cannot help responding to the innermost need of his age; he sees and reports what in its depths it asks him to see and report. He cannot help becoming, through his own relation to his unconscious (and without this relation no creative work of value is possible), an instrument of whatever there is in the general deep unconscious, the inner world of the whole age, that is trying to compensate for some failure in consciousness, to restore a balance destroyed by one-sidedness, to reconcile the glaring opposites, to bring to our outer and inner worlds a life-enhancing unity. But literature itself now becomes one-sided, inevitably because it is over-introverted, often so deeply concerned with the inner world, with the most mysterious recesses of the personality, and so little concerned with the outer world. It now becomes a literature largely for specialists, themselves nearly always equally introverted; and people in general, for whom it is really intended, find it either too 'difficult' or too 'neurotic' and 'unhealthy'. (It is a mistake, all too common, to imagine that the new depth psychology created this literature. They are in fact parallel developments, and on the whole we can say that depth psychology owes more to modern literature than literature does to

depth psychology.) And in a sense these people who do not want modern literature, because they feel it is too entirely attentive to the inner world, that it lacks a life-enhancing quality, are quite right. The men who have created this literature have obeyed their daemon, have fulfilled their genius, and we should be grateful to them. But we should also realize that this modern literature means little or nothing to the mass of the people, the very people in danger of losing true individuality, personality, to the collectives of our time; and that even for the minority of persons capable of understanding and enjoying this literature, it cannot carry the load. Nothing we have can carry it. Since the Second World War, in this atomic age, sure of nothing but sex—and, to take two successful English examples, what is there left at the end of *Lucky Jim* or *Look Back in Anger* but sex?—we are now piling on to sex the whole gigantic load of our increasing dissatisfactions, our despair, a burden far greater than it can safely take.

Religion alone can carry the load, defend us against the dehumanizing collectives, restore true personality. And it is doubtful if our society can last much longer without religion, for either it will destroy itself by some final idiot war or, at peace but hurrying in the wrong direction, it will soon largely cease to be composed of persons. All of this, of course, has often been said, but generally it has been said by men who imagine that the particular religion they profess, their Church greatly magnified, could save the situation. I think they are wrong, though I would not for a moment attempt to argue them out of their private faith. If such a faith, such a Church, a religion, works for them, well and good. But I have no religion, most of my friends have no religion, very few of the major modern writers we have been considering have had any religion; and what is certain is that our society has none. No matter what it professes, it is now not merely irreligious but profoundly anti-religious. And if we all joined a Christian Church tomorrow, the fundamental situation would be unchanged, because no Church existing today has the power—and we could not give it this power by joining it—to undo what has been done. We should be acting on a conscious and not an unconscious level, and the forces from the unknown depths that religion, if its

symbols have the right magical potency, can guide and control
would still be without guidance and beyond control. For the
symbols no longer work, and they cannot be made to work by
efforts on a conscious level. (The stammering helplessness of the
Churches during this age of war and more war and now, the
final horror, a nuclear arms race is proof that whatever they
may do for this man or that woman, they are now among the
institutions contained by our society, compelled to follow
every lunatic course it takes.) No matter what is willed by
consciousness, that which belongs to the depths can only be
restored in the depths: the *numinous* lies outside the power of
the collectives, cannot be subject to state decree, created by a
final resolution at an international conference, offered to all
shareholders and employees by the board of Standard Oil or
General Motors. So we have no religion and, inside or outside
literature, man feels homeless, helpless, and in despair.

We must wait. Even if we believe that the time of our civilization is running out fast, like sugar spilled from a torn bag,
we must wait. But while we are waiting we can try to feel and
think and behave, to some extent, *as if* our society were already
beginning to be contained by religion, as if we were certain
that Man cannot even remain Man unless he looks beyond
himself, as if we were finding our way home again in the universe. We can stop disinheriting ourselves.

We can avoid both the *hubris* and the secret desperation of
our scientific 'wizards that peep and mutter'. We can challenge
the whole de-humanizing, de-personalizing process, under
whatever name it may operate, that is taking the symbolic
richness, the dimension in depth, out of men's lives, gradually
inducing the anaesthesia that demands violence, crudely hor-
rible effects, to feel anything at all. Instead of wanting to look
at the back of the moon, remote from our lives, we can try to
look at the back of our own minds. Even this *As If* will do
something to bring our outer and inner worlds, now tearing us
in two, closer together, more in harmony. We may need much
more to establish order, justice, real community, in the outer
world, and may not ourselves find the right healing symbols
for the inner world but, just as a first step, we can at least believe that Man lives, under God, in a great mystery, which is

what we found the original masters of our literature, Shakespeare and Rabelais, Cervantes and Montaigne, proclaiming at the very start of this journey of Western Man. And if we openly declare what is wrong with us, what is our deepest need, then perhaps the despair and death will by degrees disappear from our modern arts. Literature, where the whole man should find himself totally and touchingly reflected, might then look both outward and inward, as it should; and so bring with it a new rich life, a life sometimes tragic, at other times careless and gay: as different and as satisfying as Shakespeare's midnight heaths, where good and evil battle in thunder-and-lightning, and his Forest of Arden, where, the West meeting the Ancient East for a moment, the young voices pipe up in an eternal spring:

> *This carol they began that hour,*
> *With a hey, and a ho, and a hey nonino,*
> *How that life was but a flower . . .*[1]

Priestley offers a good pair of eyes through which to look at civilization and at the world, because in spite of his place in its tradition, and his deep emotional involvement with the fate of its people, he is really not very firmly attached to it. He preaches no dogma, subscribes to no creed; just as he belongs to no school of writers, hates sitting on committees and joining groups or societies or clubs, so he will not let his mind sit inside the structure of any set of beliefs, religious or social or political. He has been committed to certain causes; he has always cared for the general state of society; but at the same time he is curiously detached. Time-haunted, always brooding over the nature of reality, he will produce large prejudiced opinions about this or that, but always with a glint of humour; for these sit lightly on the surface of a mind that knows, perhaps better than the rest of us, quite how little about anything anybody knows. Like every other writer of this century, he shares the general assumptions that have been absorbed into contemporary thought from the ideas of Freud, Adler and Jung.

---

[1] *Literature and Western Man,* pp. 443–6.

But Jung more than anyone else has coloured Priestley's view of human personality. The two had a natural affinity of outlook, much as Priestley and Richardson had an affinity of intuitive talent when working together in the theatre, and they met several times after Jung's seventieth birthday in 1945, when Priestley went to Zürich to meet him in order to write about him for the BBC. ('A curious thing happened later—in the last two years of Jung's life, when he was past eighty, I was told at intervals by several different people who'd visited him that he wanted to see me again. I didn't really believe them—after all he was an old man, with people crowding around him—I felt it was just being said to flatter me. But now I have a strong feeling that it was true; that knowing I was one of the people outside the Jungian circle who understood what it was all about, he felt I might as a well-known author have been able to do something to explain things. . . .')

To some extent, Priestley might be said to have been 'explaining things' ever since he first read Jung in the 'thirties. Though Jung, like Ouspensky, has probably had most influence on him in a kind of private intellectual sense—the development of self-knowledge, of a personal vision of life—the sympathy with Jungian ideas is clear in that last passage from *Literature and Western Man*. It combines naturally with Priestley's constant interest in the fringes of consciousness: dreams, intuition, the nature of the imagination, the need for and function of religion, and above all, of course, the constant battle for an understanding of the enigma of Time.

Man and Time was published in 1964: a large, expensive and lavishly illustrated 'coffee-table' book that presents the sum of Priestley's five decades of wondering, reading, brooding about Time. None of the theories that he examines will do for him; he arrives, at the end, in a kind of open-ended pattern of belief which owes something to each of them but is not identifiable with any. It is his substitute for a ready-made religion, perhaps; but Priestley is not like Blake, with his fierce cry: 'I must create a System, or be enslav'd by another man's.' What he has put together for himself

is not a religion nor even a system, but a vaguely-outlined hypo-
thetical portrait of those things which can never be anything but
vague: seen through a glass, darkly.

Like most writers, he had always thought about Time; not
only through the obvious fact that anyone who writes a novel or
a play is automatically creating a different time-scale from the
one in which he and his readers actually exist, but through the
strange quirks and changes that can often seem to take place in
that 'actual' time-scale itself—the strange dream-like sense of
slowing down, for instance, which can take over the mind in a
moment of mortal danger, and which is what is really meant by
the old tag about 'seeing your whole life pass before your eyes'.
He was caught for good in the Time web when he came to read
Dunne's book *An Experiment with Time* in 1927; concentrating—
since he had a review to write—not only on all the enjoyable
stuff about dreams but on the very much tougher development
of Dunne's theory of a serialistic Time. The Time theory slid into
the back of his mind, probably because he was busy with novels
already conceived, and did not emerge until some years later
when he began thinking in terms that led to the Time plays. But
the book had one immediate effect on him as it has had on almost
all its readers: without actually following Dunne's method of
keeping a notebook beside the bed and writing down every detail
of a dream as soon as one wakes from it, he did find himself remembering more and more of his dreams. For a man who considered Jung's theory of the collective unconscious, 'one of the
great liberating ideas of this age', and who some years later went
through a period during which he happened to have some re-
markably powerful dreams, this was not without its effect. By
the time he was at the height of his involvement with the theatre,
Priestley was thinking both about Jung and the Time problem
whenever he was not thinking about his work. Even the making
of the work seemed relevant, because of the curious dual manner
in which his plays seemed to emerge. With Jung's ideas in his
head, he could come up only with the theory that the rapidly-
written plays were the result of the unconscious somehow vol-

canically breaking through into the conscious mind and driving it with a force it could not normally possess.

> But now I see that we cannot rule out Time, which has its own relation to the unconscious. We know that on one level the unconscious is capable of keeping an eye on chronological time for us, waking us if necessary at any hour we choose. But this is not its own time. It refuses to accept, when it is about its business and not acting as an alarm clock, our whole idea of temporal succession. Its time order is not ours. . . . [1]

Now he was brooding about two kinds of experience: the one, at moments of great danger and others of aesthetic contemplation, seeming to detach the mind from any sphere of action; the other not withdrawing it from action but throwing it into a fury of creative energy. The two belong to different states of consciousness, but they are alike in appearance to be outside passing time, and for Priestley ('and after all they were *my* experiences, and any critical Dr. Brown or dubious Professor Smith may never have known them'), this second quality could not be explained away.

> Time seems to divide itself into times here. There is one for passing time; there is another for the first kind of experience, the contemplative slower-up; there is another for the second kind of experience, the purposeful, imaginative, speeder-up: three times. So can it be true to say that nothing in our actual experience suggests—if we want to be geometrical about it— that there might be three dimensions of Time? I say it cannot be true. I will agree that no exact analysis may be possible, that no sharp lines can be drawn, that all except one's innermost feeling is blurred and shadowy, that the relation between consciousness and the unconscious may complicate the issue; but I cannot escape the feeling that Time, itself so blurred and vague and elusive, divides itself into three to match these different modes of consciousness. We are at least entitled to say that it is *as if* there are three kinds of time.[2]

[1] *Man and Time*, p. 290 (Aldus, 1964).
[2] *Ibid.*, p. 291.

So risking a confusion with Dunne's numbering of his serial
Time, he developed a concept of Time divided into time One,
time Two and time Three, pointing out that 'we live in all three
of them at once, though we may not enjoy, so to speak, equal
portions of them'. Time One is the passing time in which we live,
and to which we are precisely related by our brains (except when
illness or drugs interfere, altering the chemistry of the brain and
giving the delirious patient or the nodding heroin addict a different apprehension of time). This is the line of history. Outside
time One, in a state unrelated to our time One journey from the
cradle to the grave, we exist also in time Two, the time of dreams,
of precognition, of all experiences inexplicable in terms of time
One. But it will not do to think of time Two, as Dunne seems to
through his concept of Observers, in terms of an endless railway
line running alongside a very short one, making possible a simul-
taneous contemplation of every part—beginning, middle and
end—of the shorter line. From the dream-state, and all other
'outside Time' experiences, which compose time Two, we may
sometimes seem to see the future as if the whole pattern of time
One were fixed and inevitable. But it is not fixed, 'for it can be
changed even after it has seemed to reveal itself in dreams and
time Two'. It is more like the view of the future that comes into
your head if somebody says, not talking about time theory at all,
'What is going to happen next year?'—a series of large predictable events set among a great mass of unpredictable events which,
looking forward from the present moment, we can see only as
alternative possibilities without knowing which possibility will
actually happen. 'The alternative possibilities,' Priestley wrote,
'together with the choice between them, cannot exist in time
One. Nor did they exist in time Two. Therefore another Time
in time is necessary, time Three.'

> Because imagination appears to be free of the limitations we
> know in time One, we think of it as being outside Time. It is
> there, however, that the nothings begin. We might do better
> if we thought of it as belonging to a different Time order, to
> another time. And I have already suggested, after remembering

my own experience, that imaginative creation seems to imply not a second time order, contemplative and detached from action, but a third, in which purpose and action are joined together and there seems to be an almost magical release of creative power. . . .

I have lately received, from Italy, some material based on the findings and theorizing of a small newish international group of medical psychologists. This restored to me a term much used before the First War . . . the 'superconscious'. On this theory the ego and its field of consciousness occupies a middle place between the unconscious, personal or collective, and the superconscious, the source of our nobler feelings, intuitions and inspiration, genius, illumination, and ecstasy.

And if we relate this division to our temporal system here, we could say that the ego and its field of consciousness belong to time One, the unconscious to time Two, the superconscious to time Three. But we must remember that there are no separate compartments and exact divisions, and that we live, even here and now, in all three times.[1]

Priestley naturally shares with Dunne the belief that the end of our allotment of time One is not also the end of us. If we have been existing simultaneously in times Two and Three, which are not confined between birth and death, how could it be? Instead: 'When we have come to an end in time One, we go forward— spatially and geometrically, we may say, at a right angle—in time Two, no longer concentrating our attention on the physical world, but now having in place of it all that accumulation of mental events, all the sensations, feelings, thoughts, left to us from our time One lives.'[2] *And Death shall have no dominion* . . . but nor will he provide an easy obliteration of everything that we have been or done. 'Anybody who can find wishfulfilment here,' adds Priestley sardonically, 'must feel a great deal more complacent about his time One life than I do about mine. I can see this time Two existence, with time Three and its fiery creative

---

[1] *Ibid.,* pp. 298–300.
[2] *Ibid.,* p. 302.

energies now a new time Two, offering us some very rough going.'[1]

But to what he has derived from Dunne, he adds what he has made out of Ouspensky. His time pattern is not a matter of spiral recurrence, with its possibilities of improvement or degeneration; he had never accepted that idea even when he was writing *I Have Been Here Before* (possibly another reason why the play gave him so much trouble). But he does envision the chance, when one hovers in time Two glumly contemplating all the mistakes made in time One, 'the chance not of simply re-living them, though that may have to be done, but of *beginning to put them right*'—a chance within reach only 'if we can work with others, whose lines cross ours in this time Two world, in trust and love'.[2] Thus, on the other side of the line of history, we could create a new and more rewarding life. We are already, after all, even in time One given strange hints and echoes of an indefinable experience that has to do not with dreams of intuition, contemplation or creativity, but with something else.

> This something else is impossible to prove and hard to capture in words. It can come at high moments of love and, though rarely, at a meeting of friends; it can transform some sudden glimpse of a landscape into an irradiated sign; it haunts some music for us; its light and its strange shadows fall on certain scenes in drama and fiction. Always it adds depth to life, suggests an ampler Time, opens a new dimension.
>
> It never stays long, at least for most of us, but if, fixed in our attention to time One, we cease to be conscious of this something else, this bonus from the unknown, really arriving from another mode of Time, we begin to feel stale and weary. We are not only not preparing ourselves for existence in the next world, we are beginning to lose interest even in this one, for the scene is flat and its colours are fading. To die is not to close our eyes when we come to the end of our time One: it is to choose to live in too few dimensions.
>
> My personal belief, then, is that our lives are not contained within passing time, a single track along which we hurry to

[1] *Ibid.*, p. 304.
[2] *Ibid.*, p. 305.

oblivion. We exist in more than one dimension of Time. Ourselves in times Two and Three cannot vanish into the grave; they are already beyond it even now. We may not be immortal beings—I do think we are or should want to be—but we are something better than creatures carried on that single track to the slaughter-house. We have a larger portion of Time—and more and stranger adventures with it—than conventional or positivist thought allows.

But it is still a portion; we have not unlimited Time, though what the limits will be in time Two and time Three, I do not know. Nor of course do I know what happens. I suspect, however, that in time Two we begin by being more essentially ourselves than in time One but end by being less ourselves, personality as we know it vanishing altogether in time Three.[1]

Now you can, if you enjoy that kind of thing, have a high old game with this Time-pattern of Priestley's. You can poke holes in it, deride it for owing this to ancient Chinese thought or that to Christianity: you can rip it into small pieces and jump up and down on it, but there is one thing you cannot do with absolute conviction and that is deny it. Priestley is the archetypal agnostic. His cosmos is a great glowing blur, in which he claims no certainty about anything except his own emotions and values. In Jungian terms, intuition is his primary function. He will neither subscribe to any ready-built system nor build one of his own; at the centre of him there is humility, *nescio*, and if pushed against the wall he will calmly produce only a quotation used by John Cowper Powys in his *Autobiography*, about the necessity for being credulous of everything and sceptical of everything. At the same time he is likely to issue the kind of commentary on life which drives scientists and other rational persons to distraction.

'I think all the evidence is that in ten or fifteen years' time there'll be some great breakthrough, probably through science, and we'll all end up believing in a completely different kind of universe. Whether it's through sub-atomic work or astrophysics—a great breakthrough, so that suddenly we'll all be out of this intellectual prison. . . .

[1] *Ibid.,* p. 306.

'Of course we may all destroy ourselves. But if we avoid nuclear war—and touch wood I think we shall—then the next real danger is in the scientists and technologists themselves. They suffer from *hubris*, they're ruthlessly opposed to anything that contradicts their idea of the universe, like ESP. As H. H. Price said, if logical positivism had existed in the seventeenth century, physics would never have got started. What's wrong with science is that although it's very beneficial as a way of finding out, it's not about life at all. It gives you *real* knowledge of nothing. The great scientists are really imaginative men, who have never taken the limited view. . . .

'Believing that life and the universe are a mystery quite beyond our grasp keeps you humble. Either there's an order of being in the universe, of which we're a very low order, or else it's all an accident. And really, the arrogance of thinking it's an accident, the conceit of thinking we know everything . . . As Fred Hoyle once said, the distances between the planets could be said to be part of a divine plan, because otherwise it would be possible for one to get control of the rest, and there'd be no experiment. Too many of these boys are conquerors. They have to conquer mountains, conquer space, conquer everything. . . .

'I believe in being woolly-minded, in leaving a lot of loose edges. Whatever this universe is, it's very large and very complicated, and it's very unlikely we can contain even a fair-sized part of it in our intellects. So you have to have loose edges. The size of the universe depresses many people, but not me, I'm delighted at it. Every time someone finds new immensity, I think: *what a place to be . . . !*'

To leave loose edges, by our common standard, tends to imply weakness. You could call it a weakness in J. B. Priestley that he has never committed himself to any one system or belief, never aimed his entire life at one single point; never burned his boats, never been an all-or-nothing man, never—as an artist—based his reputation on his achievement in any one form. But it is difficult to make any kind of indictment of a man as paradoxical as Priestley, since for all his care for the function of literature and the state of humanity, a fair-sized chunk of him is not, so to speak, here at all. It is away somewhere, not surveying from a great melancholy height the mess we have made of Western civilization, but caught up in a philosophy of undiminishing wonder, the only kind of quality which, if enough of it filters through the cracks, can ever set that civilization to rights again. 'Much of the evil of our age,' Priestley wrote in *Thoughts in the Wilderness*, 'comes from the notion that we have merely so much time before oblivion overtakes us.'[1] Perhaps no man who spends so much of his life trying to look out beyond Time can be expected ever to plant himself firmly within it.

On the Isle of Wight once, thirty years ago, with a vague ornithological image left in his mind by some bird-ringing done from a lighthouse, Priestley went to bed and dreamed a dream that he recorded, later, in *Rain upon Godshill*.

I dreamt I was standing at the top of a very high tower, alone, looking down upon myriads of birds all flying in one direction; every kind of bird was there, all the birds in the world. It was a noble sight, this vast aerial river of birds. But now in some mysterious fashion the gear was changed, and time speeded up, so that I saw generations of birds, watched them break their shells, flutter into life, mate, weaken, falter, and die. Wings grew only to crumble; bodies were sleek and then, in a flash, bled and shrivelled; and death struck everywhere at every second. What was the use of all this blind struggle towards life, this eager trying of wings, this hurried mating, this flight and surge, all this gigantic meaningless biological effort? As I stared down, seeming to see every creature's ignoble little history almost at a glance, I felt sick at heart. It would be better if not one of them, if not one of us all, had been born, if the struggle ceased for ever. I stood on my tower, still alone, desperately unhappy. But now the gear was changed again, and time went faster still, and it was rushing by at such a rate, that the birds could not show any movement, but were like an enormous plain sown with feathers. But along this plain, flickering through the bodies themselves, there now passed a sort of white flame, trembling, dancing, then hurrying on;

[1] 'Time Please', p. 44 in *Thoughts in the Wilderness*.

and as soon as I saw it I knew that this white flame was life itself, the very quintessence of being; and then it came to me,
in a rocket-burst of ecstasy, that nothing mattered, nothing
could ever matter, because nothing else was real, but this
quivering and hurrying lambency of being. Birds, men or
creatures not yet shaped and coloured, all were of no account
except so far as this flame of life travelled through them. It left
nothing to mourn over behind it; what I had thought was
tragedy was mere emptiness or a shadow show; for now all
real feeling was caught and purified and danced on ecstatically
with the white flame of life. I had never before felt such deep
happiness as I knew at the end of my dream of the tower and
the birds, and if I have not kept that happiness with me, as an
inner atmosphere and a sanctuary for the heart, that is it because I am a weak and foolish man who allows the mad world
to come trampling in, destroying every green shoot of wisdom. Nevertheless, I have not been quite the same man since. . . .[1]

It sounds a light remark, but it was literally true. That dream
held images so powerful that they had a genuine influence on the
current of his thought. Twenty-five years later, writing about it
again in *Man and Time*, he used the dream as a pattern of his
triple vision of Time, seeing time Two as 'a move from personality to the essential self, never realized in time One', and time
Three as a matter of 'dissolving into selfless consciousness, as I
appeared to do when ecstatically aware only of that white flame.'[2]

> A condition of complete simplicity
> (Costing not less than everything)

—Priestley and Eliot are about as dissimilar as it is possible for
two writers to be, but perhaps in the end they arrive at very much
the same point of focus. The difference lies in what they make of
it. For Priestley, the hurrying white flame is numinous, but it is
not God. 'We might say it was moving to and from unimaginable
creative Being, both away from and towards a blinding Absolute,
possibly through the history of a thousand million planets. . . .

[1] *Rain upon Godshill*, pp. 304–6.
[2] *Man and Time*, p. 308.

We men on earth are probably on a very low level, but we have our task like other and higher orders of beings. As far as I can see —and I claim no prophetic insight—that task is to bring consciousness to the life of earth—or, as Jung wrote in his old age, 'to kindle a light in the darkness of mere being'.[1]

And as in the life of earth—in time One—Priestley has used the work of Gurdjieff and Ouspensky to expand his own consciousness, so he has always tried through all the different varieties of his own work to awaken and expand the consciousness of others. From this come the roars of rebellion against all totalitarian systems, the pleas for an end to Block Thinking and a resistance to the creeping anaesthesia of Admass; the humanitarian care for the condition of man and the urgent appeal to the latent brilliance of the Unicorn in his own nation; above all, perhaps, the echoing image of his ideal world, which may in the end turn out to have been the lost world of his youth translated into terms of time Two. 'To bring consciousness to the life of earth': it is a fearsome undertaking. We shouldn't be disconcerted that Priestley has written so many books; we should marvel that he has been able, as few others have done, to encompass so much of this brave ideal without writing twice as much.

EPILOGUE

While a major writer is not only very much alive but energetically producing work as good as anything he has ever done before, it is impossible to sew up his overall achievement in a neat little verbal box. His true worth is not likely to emerge until a very considerable time, perhaps fifty years, after he is dead; by then, all irrelevancies of fashion and contemporary significance have faded away, and the man or woman in question can be seen to have settled down into his proper permanent place in the landscape of literary history. To borrow an image which Priestley once used in another context: a literary reputation is like a tree, not a telegraph pole. If it pops up at its full height overnight, it will very soon fall down again with equal despatch; but if it is of the kind that is likely to endure like a Sherwood oak or a Chiltern beech, it will be a long long time a-growing. So who can sum up J. B. Priestley now?

No one. But during the weekend last year which contained various celebrations of Priestley's seventy-fifth birthday, a great many people tried, in newspapers and magazines, on television and on radio. Comments of varying length came from Sir Ralph Richardson, Iris Murdoch, C. P. Snow, Pamela Hansford Johnson, Malcolm Muggeridge, Paul Johnson, Raymond Mortimer, Irene Worth, Michael Foot, Neville Cardus, and a number of others. Not everyone tried to sum Priestley up; many were simply paying tribute or recounting friendship; but inevitably those who wrote or spoke at any length made some attempt to place him and his work, in relation both to our own time and to literature, and found themselves sooner or later commenting rather irritably on the ironic gulf between the real writer and his popular image. Priestley, though determined as ever not to appear a 'smiling enjoyer of it all', was I think pleased with the Press his birthday brought him, and for once read it all; but he cocked a sardonic eyebrow at some of these comments. 'You know,' he said, between small reflective puffs of smoke, 'my friends all have a tendency to be defensive about me, as if I were being attacked by strings of enemies. Yet I've never minded attacks, I've even enjoyed them. Neglect is the only thing worth being defensive about. I'm grateful—but really, it's time you all stopped.'

I went away and thought about the articles and reviews and talks, and about what he had said. He was right, in a way; a note of reproof did creep into these pieces here or there, aiming itself at critics or public or both, and implying that they had failed sometimes to give Priestley the full credit due to him. And the reproof was pointless, for nobody had ever really misjudged Priestley; they had simply not known what to make of him. We are not accustomed to men of letters in this hasty century of ours; we don't know how to cope with them, they bewilder us. We like our novelists to be novelists, our philosophers to be philosophers; our chemists to stay inside their laboratories, and our plumbers to be prevented by strict rules from picking up a carpenter's hammer and hitting a nail. The world has become too complicated; specialization, once a word spoken with lofty contempt, has become now the only kind of concept we can understand or respect. Where our writers are concerned, we will grudgingly accept the idea of a novelist writing a television play or the screenplay of a film, but nine times out of ten we will comment afterwards that really he does much better when he concentrates his talent on the novel. We have lost the ability to think in terms of an equation saying that novel *plus* play equals achievement. Present to us a man of Priestley's extraordinary range, show us the breadth of his craft and the depth of his vision, and we cannot even see him. We see only one work at a time, or at the most only one genre of work at a time; so that most readers or critics uttering an opinion of J. B. Priestley would find, if they were to look carefully into their minds, that they were thinking primarily in terms only of one Priestley: probably the novelist, perhaps the dramatist, with a vague awareness of the essayist or the social critic lurking behind. And any man who judges in this way is doing his subject less than justice, for there is no one Priestley. No specialist of that name exists; only a man of letters, whose work, if it is to be judged at all, must be judged entire.

After all, he has never confined himself even to his own branch of the arts. If he is a more perceptive observer and owner of paintings than many writers, it is because he is also a painter himself, who on a good day can capture in some swift bright gouache a mood or detail almost as vivid as those in his own best prose. In *Lost Empires* you can hear his own relish when the narrator Richard Herncastle, purring over a fat new pad of cartridge paper, writes of the painter's pleasure in his materials.

And music, as anyone familiar with Priestley's work knows, has as permanent a place in his life and delight as that pipe. The piano in his study, and the autumn chamber music festivals which he used to organize at his home in the Isle of Wight, are tokens of his devotion to the only other art in which he has been as much involved as in his own. He listens to music endlessly, though nowadays more in recording than in concert-hall. 'For a long time now,' he wrote in *Trumpets Over The Sea*, 'I have believed that the symphony orchestra is one of the greatest achievements of Western Man. Perhaps it is his noblest achievement.' And of course from the beginning music has echoed everywhere in his work. It is celebrated in many of the essays, subtly employed in many of the plays; and among all his novels there is scarcely one in which music does not sooner or later matter a great deal— whether it supports the whole structure, as in *Bright Day*, or provides a magical interlude like the well-known passage from *Angel Pavement* in which a concert sends little Mr. Smeeth floating be- witched through the wet dark streets of Stoke Newington with the great theme from the last movement of Brahms' First Sym- phony glorious in his ears. Priestley's heroes, from the pianist Inigo Jollifant to the clarinet-playing Cosmo Saltana, are often as much involved in music as their author—who is after all, as a 'man of letters', very much the literary equivalent of a composer. (Perhaps he would have done well to have described himself as such all along, taking shelter beneath the saner musical tradition which still feels it quite natural that a man who writes a symphony should also choose to write an opera or a string quartet, a concerto or a sonata.) Throughout his writing, particularly at its most reflective, you find everywhere the small signs of the genuine musician—as in the marvellous little image at the end of his cheerful essay, 'An Apology for Bad Pianists', where in one sentence the delight of the performer and of the listener are rolled into one.

> I believe that at the very end, when the depths of our folly and ignorance are fully revealed, when all our false notes have been cast up into one awful total by the recording angel of music, it will be found that we, the bad pianists, have been misjudged among men, that we, too, have loved and laboured for the divine art. When we file into Elysium, forlorn, scared, a shabby little band, and come within sight of Beethoven, whom we have murdered so many times, I believe that a smile will break through the thunder-cloud of his face. '*Ach!* Come you in, children,' he will roar, 'bad players, eh? . . . I have heard. . . . Very bad players. . . . But there have been worse among you . . . The spirit was in you, and you have listened well. Come in . . . I have composed one hundred and fifty more symphonies and sonatas, and you shall hear them all.'[1]

Response to a writer as complicated as this is inevitably itself complex and diffuse. There are readers enough who can claim to have read the whole of Priestley's vast *œuvre*, but few who have ever done so over anything less than a couple of decades. The writers of those tributes were not really being defensive; they were being impatient—forgetting that when a man has done as much work as this, spread over so many years, nothing is ever properly likely to shake it down into its final pattern except Time. They perhaps did have an idea of that eventual pattern; and

[1] 'An Apology for Bad Pianists', in *Essays of Five Decades*, p. 11.

had found it astonishing, in the way that one is astonished by contemplating the range and quality of the work of Shakespeare or Beethoven or Dickens or Proust. Do not mistake me; I am making no great mad claim that would put J. B. Priestley up there on the shiniest tower with the immortals. He is no genius; his work is at no point even brushed by genius; he was not born with that strange and magically luminous kind of imagination. But he belongs to the family of the giants all the same: he inhabits that same castle, if not its topmost turret. He is larger than the rest of us. He has taught and entertained us, drawn pictures of us, laughed at us, always with an honesty and compassion that have seemed in this century to grow rarer every day.

> You do look, my son, in a mov'd sort,
> As if you were dismay'd; be cheerful, sir. . . .[1]

Priestley quoted his old master, the greatest Englishman of them all, at his seventy-fifth birthday dinner; the man of letters speaking with the craft of the man of the theatre as he leaned forward, looking out at the rows of his friends' faces, and let his voice drop to a husking whisper, each small weighted word audible in every corner of the room: 'Be . . . cheerful . . . sir. . . .' He was talking of an intuitive philosophy, as he had done in *Literature and Western Man*, but he might as well have been talking of his own achievement. We have, all of us, been often dismayed; we live in a world that is now more dismaying than it has ever been. It takes humour and optimism, but also a great deal more than either, to make us cheerful in the contemplation of such a world; only the giants among enchanters can do it, the true initiates of one or another of the arts, and in the art of literature most of those giants are dead. It doesn't of course matter that they are dead, since the power is there in their work, but all the same there is an extra brightness to the world in the knowledge that one of them is alive and working (*'I love it . . . still, in my seventies, I love pouring it out . . .'*). It's a comfort, to have a benevolent giant about the place. And we should make the most of the

---

[1] *The Tempest*, IV. i. 146.

one we have, for while Priestley will certainly not seem by the end of this century to have been the last of the English giants—the power of that great tradition will always draw another somehow out of the land—it is not easy to identify his successor yet. That even rarer creature, the genius, blazes with a light that is fairly easy to spot, if it doesn't dazzle you entirely; but giants, like the oaks, take a long time to grow.

In a genial echo of vanishing traditions, Heinemann had arranged that birthday dinner to celebrate the seventy-fifth year of the man who had for nearly fifty of those years been a major name on their list. If it was a formal occasion, it was formal only in appearance; and if it was a gathering of a formidable amount of talent and fame from all branches of the arts, it was so only by accident. Essentially, it was a gathering of Priestley's friends. They converged on the Savoy from all parts of Britain, from the Continent, from the United States; the only absentees were those held at a distance by illness or work. One way of describing Priestley is to point out that he is the kind of man who has friends of this kind. And perhaps the magic came from the friendship; the fact that some 150 men and women had been drawn together by their affection and respect for one man. Magic is a word that has crept quite often into this book, and I offer neither apology nor justification; it is a word for the indefinable, the force that emerges from the imagination of some men and draws an answering force from the imaginations of others, and that seems to exist on its own, either in a Jungian world-mind or in something else. We should leave it at that; it is wise, as Priestley observes, to leave loose edges in our universe. At all events there the friends were, with a representative few speaking for them; Sir Kenneth Clark, Robert Robinson, Iris Murdoch and Norman Collins. It was like a gigantic family party, and on all hands people who had never met before in their lives found themselves, with no astonishment, talking energetically away to one another with the casual assurance of those who have been close friends for years. Through Priestley, they all spoke a common language; he, and his writing, had played a part in all their lives.

'He brings us together,' said Robert Robinson, and he was speaking not only of that gathering but of the millions beyond it 'not, like the image-men, in order to sell us something, not in order coldly to exploit our weaknesses rather than warmly to gratify our desires—but at the level where men and women are truly joined, the level where the dreams are dreamt, Priestley broaches the reader's own dream, by broaching his own. And he gives us what only the rare ones give us—a sense that we are collaborating, rather than simply paying to go in. He admits us to the country of ourselves.' He glanced across at the stocky figure with its plum-coloured velvet jacket and mask of melancholy resignation; and then out at the faces. 'I remember going out to dinner with Priestley,' he said. 'The waiter asked him: have you a reservation? And I remember thinking in a moment, as the mundaneness of the situation seemed just for a second to be transcended, that—No, he has no reservation. But in the roll-call of Time he will turn out to have something rather better: he will turn out to have been among the founders of the feast.'

One picture began this book, another ends it. On the evening before the publishers' dinner, a programme compiled to celebrate Priestley's seventy-fifth birthday was shown on BBC Television. He and his wife watched it with two of their closest friends, Diana and John Collins, in the Collins' house next to St. Paul's— beneath the looming shadow of that cathedral whose dome, silhouetted against the red sky of a burning city, Priestley had made into a symbol of the survival of England, reason and Christian ethics, in his broadcasts during the Blitz. The television programme, truth to tell, was not very good; a number of Priestley's friends offered memories and portraits, and their affectionate sincerity only barely triumphed over their discomfiture at finding themselves talking at the little red light on a camera while standing riveted to chalk-marks on a studio floor. They, and some readings from Priestley books, were followed by a condensed version of the last act of *Johnson Over Jordan*; and again there was an awkwardness, for this more than any of his plays translates badly to the medium of television, needing the

depths of a craftily-lit stage to suggest the immensities of space-
less time in which it takes place.

But then, like the moment Priestley once celebrated 'when
suddenly and softly the orchestra creeps in to accompany the
piano', the magic that one had been hoping for all along suddenly
came filtering through this television programme; for the part of
Robert Johnson was being played here by the man for whom it
had been written some thirty years before, Ralph Richardson,
and Richardson and Priestley between them, actor and dramatist,
magicians both, wrought a spell that produced, despite all handi-
caps, the real thing. Time had made one of those curious spiralling
turns, for Richardson had grown older to meet the play, and
fitted easily now into the role for which he had once had to draw
in an extra couple of decades on his face; he played it without a
false move or a marred inflection, and by the time he turned to
walk into infinity, Everyman in a bowler hat, leaving one dimension for another unknown, I had forgotten the deficiencies of the
small screen and could indeed hardly perceive its outlines at all.
I had never seen *Johnson Over Jordan* in the theatre, but it
had always moved me even as a written play, and I had never
expected to have the chance of seeing Richardson act the part
which had been so subtly tailored to his talent and voice. Now,
however inferior his surroundings, I had. I blew my nose rather
hard, and glanced across at Priestley.

I don't know what I expected him to offer us: a non-committal
snort, perhaps; a rumble of technical criticism; at the most, a bit
of knowledgeable praise for Richardson. But Priestley sat silent
for a moment, gazing into space, looking unusually small in a
very large armchair; and then he rubbed his eyes. 'I shed tears,' he
said, rather gruff and low, 'not for what I have seen, but for what
I have been remembering.' Then he hoisted himself up, and was
his proper height again.

For a moment, he had been caught by a spell himself; caught
by Time, by his own magic, and by that of his friend, and trans-
ported on to that other dimension where still there is playing the
first production and every production of *Johnson Over Jordan*—and

of *As You Like It* and *The Cherry Orchard* and *Arms and the Man* and all the rest—and where a younger Richardson is turning to walk not into the shadow of a cramped television studio but into the glitter of stars and the blue-dark cosmic depths that Basil Dean had created on a great stage, while Benjamin Britten's triumphant finale sounded out over the audience. Priestley wasn't really remembering, not really looking back; he was looking outward, into the level of Time where there is no forward or backward, no youth or age, no beginning or end. Like all the great enchanters, he has always seen it plainer than the rest of us yet can.

WORKS OF J. B. PRIESTLEY (b. 1894)

This bibliography is not comprehensive, but is limited to the books and plays mentioned in the text. Thus it omits a number of minor works like *The Chapman of Rhymes*, which was Priestley's first book: a slim volume of verse published when he was twenty-one. By now, no doubt, it omits his latest book as well. Titles of plays are printed in italics.

1922 Brief Diversions: Papers from Lilliput
1923 I for One
1924 Figures of Modern Literature
1925 English Comic Characters
1926 George Meredith; Talking
1927 Adam in Moonshine; Open House; Thomas Love Peacock; Benighted; The English Novel
1928 Apes and Angels; English Humour
1929 Farthing Hall (with Hugh Walpole); The Balconinny; The Good Companions; The Town Major of Miraucourt
1931 Angel Pavement
1931 *The Good Companions* (dramatized with Edward Knoblock)
1932 Self-Selected Essays; *Dangerous Corner*; Faraway
1933 Wonder Hero; *The Roundabout*; *Laburnum Grove*
1934 English Journey; *Eden End*
1935 *Duet in Floodlight; Cornelius*
1936 *Bees on the Boat Deck*; They Walk in the City
1937 Midnight on the Desert; *Time and the Conways*; *I Have Been Here Before*; *People at Sea*
1938 The Doomsday Men; *When We Are Married*; *Music at Night*
1939 *Johnson Over Jordan*; Rain upon Godshill; Let the People Sing
1940 *The Long Mirror*; Postscripts (broadcasts)

1941 Out of the People
1942 *Goodnight, Children*; Black-out in Gretley
1943 *They Came to a City*; Daylight on Saturday; The Man-Power Story; British Women go to War; *Desert Highway*
1944 *How Are They at Home?*
1945 Three Men in New Suits
1946 *An Inspector Calls*; *Ever Since Paradise*; The Secret Dream; Bright Day
1947 The Arts under Socialism; Theatre Outlook; Jenny Villiers; *The Linden Tree*
1948 Home is Tomorrow
1949 *Summer Day's Dream*; Delight; *The Olympians* (libretto for opera by Arthur Bliss)
1950 Last Holiday (film)
1951 Festival at Farbridge
1952 *Dragon's Mouth* (with Jacquetta Hawkes)
1953 The Other Place
1954 The Magicians; Low Notes on a High Level
1955 *Mr. Kettle and Mrs. Moon*; Journey Down a Rainbow (with Jacquetta Hawkes)
1957 *The Glass Cage*; Thoughts in the Wilderness; The Art of the Dramatist
1958 Topside, or The Future of England
1960 Literature and Western Man
1961 Saturn over the Water; The Thirty-First of June; Charles Dickens
1962 The Shapes of Sleep; Margin Released
1963 *A Severed Head* (a dramatization, with Iris Murdoch, of her novel)
1964 Sir Michael and Sir George; Man and Time
1965 Lost Empires
1966 The Moments, and Other Pieces; Salt is Leaving
1967 It's an Old Country
1968 Out of Town (Volume I of The Image Men)
1969 London End (Volume II of The Image Men); Essays of Five Decades; The Prince of Pleasure

About the Author

Susan Cooper was born in Buckinghamshire in 1935, and read English at Oxford. For several years thereafter she was a staff writer for the *Sunday Times;* she then married an American scientist and moved to the United States, where she now lives. She has two children and three stepchildren.

Her books include *Behind the Golden Curtain,* a study of the U.S.A., *Mandrake,* a novel, and two novels for children.

In 1968 she edited the collection of J. B. Priestley's essays, *Essays of Five Decades.*